What people are sayin

Portalism

Jeffrey Laird has achieved a rare accomplishment with his theory of *Portalism*. In Western philosophy, since Thales of Miletus, metaphysics has been the field of investigation into the relationship between subjective experience and the cosmos. Laird's theory could well be the beginning of a breakthrough in the human understanding of reality. With the hypothesis of Portalism holding Consciousness as a fundamental force of nature, we may now have a foothold for a scientific study of consciousness. Supremely recommended for those interested in the philosophy of mind and the nature of consciousness, Mr. Laird's concise and enjoyable style, his cogent explanations, depth of field and impressive defense, make for a potentially revolutionary philosophy with significant implications across the field.

Jack Bolton, Engineer and Philosophy Enthusiast

Portalism

An Externalist Theory of Consciousness

Portalism

An Externalist Theory of Consciousness

Jeffrey Laird

IFF
BOOKS

Winchester, UK
Washington, USA

JOHN HUNT PUBLISHING

First published by iff Books, 2022
iff Books is an imprint of John Hunt Publishing Ltd., No. 3 East Street, Alresford,
Hampshire SO24 9EE, UK
office@jhpbooks.com
www.johnhuntpublishing.com
www.iff-books.com

For distributor details and how to order please visit the 'Ordering' section on our website.

ISBN: 978 1 80341 038 8
978 1 80341 039 5 (ebook)
Library of Congress Control Number: 2021916489

A CIP catalogue record for this book is available from the British Library.

Design: Stuart Davies

UK: Printed and bound by CPI Group (UK) Ltd, Croydon, CR0 4YY
Printed in North America by CPI GPS partners

We operate a distinctive and ethical publishing philosophy in
all areas of our business, from our global network of authors to
production and worldwide distribution.

Contents

– after all, it may be a requirement for a theory of consciousness that it contains at least one crazy idea.
David Chalmers

This book is dedicated to the memory of Professor Robert C. Solomon, PhD, whose lectures on Existentialism changed my life.

It is with great appreciation that I acknowledge my wife Leslie and my friend Jack Bolton for their infinite patience with me, and for their diligent efforts in helping to make this book a reality.

Introduction

About two years ago, I was browsing the Internet looking for information regarding supervenience theories of consciousness, with the idea of composing an argument around the premise that they were not so much physicalist theories as they were forms of property dualism. In the process I stumbled over a 2014 TED Talk titled *How Do You Explain Consciousness?* The speaker was Dr. David Chalmers, the Australian dualist and cognitive scientist whose work I was already very familiar with. I was charmed by his easy manner of communicating profoundly complex concepts, as he discussed the hard problem of consciousness, a dilemma well known to every student of metaphysics, and went on to propose that "radical ideas may be needed" in the search for a solution. I understood this to be a call for fresh new approaches that lie outside of the strict doctrine of reductive materialism. I agree with this idea, myself having rejected monist materialism some time ago for its lack of explanatory power. He then said something that intrigued me greatly. He proposed that 'perhaps' consciousness, as a *datum*, could be a fundamental force of nature, not unlike James Clerk Maxwell's electromagnetism.

Philosophy is my second university degree, my first being in geography, followed by a thirty-five year career as a mapping scientist and GIS programmer-analyst. So when Chalmers mentioned the word 'datum', the cartographer in me perked up, as we are unable to correctly map anything without first establishing a coordinate system and map projection which must then be tied down to a datum, the most common, at least for terrestrial mapping, being a mean value of sea level observed over a period of years. My thought then, was that if mapped features on the earth can be projected onto a statistical datum in order to establish their horizontal and vertical accuracy,

1

couldn't it be analogous if sensory input was 'projected' upon a fundamental datum of Consciousness, resulting in subjective phenomenal experience manifesting as a localized state of consciousness – in other words, *a mind*.

The more I mulled this idea over, the more fascinated I became with it. Having entered the philosophy curricula at the University of New Orleans as a self-professed contemporary monist idealist and rejecting the idea that any physical reality exists beyond our perception of it, I like to think that I am well disposed towards being receptive to counterintuitive thinking. Eventually I became disenchanted with idealism and began looking for a metaphysical position that embraced the same explanatory power while acknowledging the existence of a physical universe. After giving it much thought, I became convinced that the idea of Consciousness as a ubiquitous force of nature might indeed meet my needs, so I began to search for more detailed information on the concept. I found none. The closest I could get were the externalist theories of W. Teed Rockwell, Ted Honderich, and Riccardo Manzotti – close, but not quite where I was headed. Still, by reading their work, I realized that the enactivist philosopher from Berkeley, Dr. Alva Noë, was spot on with his lucid observation that the physicalists, neurophilosophers, and neuroscientists were all looking for consciousness where it isn't, and that we needed to start looking for it where it is.[1] I then embraced the philosophy of phenomenal externalism and set about fleshing out my own theory, which I have named Portalism, predicated upon the idea that consciousness lies outside of the corporeal body – Descartes' *res extensa* – and that the brain is not the mind.

My intention in this work is to present a metaphysical theory that draws a distinction between Consciousness (note the upper case 'C' which I will explain later) and mind. Essentially, Portalism holds that Consciousness is irreducible and a fifth fundamental force of nature, along with the strong and weak nuclear forces, electromagnetism, and gravity. As previously stated, outside of the claim that Consciousness *could* be a fundamental force, I was unable to locate any details or concrete information regarding this hypothesis, or any descriptions or proposals related to the mechanics necessary to make such an idea feasible. Neither have I found any defense of the concept as any sort of established metaphysical position. The more I considered Portalism in relation to the mind-body problem, the explanatory gap, the substance debate, and other metaphysical issues involving consciousness and being, the more I began to realize that its potential for explanatory power made it a position that warranted further exploration.

One does not need to be a philosopher to grasp the contents of this book, but I am assuming that my audience has at least a rudimentary comprehension of philosophical terminology as well as an awareness of the metaphysical problems associated with monism, dualism, consciousness, and the philosophy of mind in general. For the sake of readability I have elected not to use footnotes or book and page references in the text. In their place I give notations in superscript and cite references to the authors in the *Notes and Citations* section of this book. I believe that philosophers will be all too familiar with the context of the citations, while the nonphilosopher need not be distracted by constant footnotes and subtext.

I consider my philosophy to be in the continental tradition as opposed to the analytic. Analytic philosophers tend to have an aversion to what has been termed 'the mysteriocity of language' used by the German Idealists and continental philosophers like Husserl, Heidegger, and Sartre. I have no problem with it, and in fact I revel in it. To be clear, I harbor no animosity toward the analytic tradition, although I fear that their dismissive attitude toward metaphysics and the ferocity of their commitment to science does not bode well in terms of the ability of the discipline of philosophy to remain relevant in the long term. For over one hundred years the analytic movement, now dominant in contemporary philosophy, has contributed a great deal. With its intense focus on language, much progress and improvement have been made in the branches of epistemology, the philosophy of language, and in symbolic logic. Still, an argument can be made that the analytic movement is equally responsible for a significant amount of detrimental impact in terms of the totality of the discipline.

How can one make such a claim? I have observed that over time the position of monist materialism has ossified into rigid dogma, exhibiting a tendency to evaluate new metaphysical proposals using physicalism as the comparative metric. As one might expect, the ranks of monist materialism have been diminishing as new iterations of physicalist theory undergo even more creative and convoluted philosophical acrobatics in an effort to explain the identity theory of consciousness – that the mind is the brain. The reality is that subjective experience cannot be explained using the objective tools and empirical methodologies of science, regardless of how cleverly nuanced a new reductive or supervenience theory might be. The fact remains that no materialist theory has ever explained qualia, intentionality, aesthetics, or the *something-that-there-is-to-be-ness* of experience. So as physicalists circle their wagons, the opposing positions of contemporary monist idealism, variable aspect theories, and even dualism are enjoying renewed attention and reconsideration, perhaps due to their embrace of creative new thinking.

Yet just when reductive materialist theories of mind-brain identity appeared to have run their course, new life has been breathed into them via the fantastic technological advances in neuroscience and brain imaging. In the process a new class of philosophers has taken the analytic spotlight – the neurophilosophers – convinced beyond doubt, and in error I believe, that consciousness somehow is the brain, that mental states are reducible to physical states, and as such have become resistant toward looking beyond the intuitive non-solutions of internalism and cranialism. Brain images, detailed and sophisticated as they may be, illustrate only neural activity, not cognitive processes. In some cases they are perhaps correlative to subjective experience, but the images and brain activity they capture are not the experience itself, because the brain is not the mind; it does not 'think' and it cannot 'understand'. This is not to say that advances in imaging, cognitive science, and neuroscience are not valuable – they certainly are and should be continued – but they will never find consciousness. Dissect the brain and nervous system down to the atomic level, and you will never find a thought, a preference, or an idea. Consciousness and subjective experience lie outside of the body. In truth, to an externalist it is unthinkable that subjective experience could ever be intuitively imagined as an *internal* phenomenon, when the act of 'experiencing' is external by definition.

In terms of who I am, there are in this world philosophers and philosophy enthusiasts, and among these, I am principally in the camp of the latter. Although the theory of Portalism as described in this work falls within the sphere of radical phenomenal externalism, I will not be surprised if other externalists, or even philosophers in general, find my work coarse and unsophisticated. Having recently retired and no longer operating within the familiar confines of geographic information systems technology, I am now a stranger to this world of profound thinkers. I do not philosophize from ivory towers, or university lecterns, or any other academic platform, and at this point in life it is too late for me to aspire to such lofty heights, although I do sit in honest admiration of those that have attained them. Instead, I can be found among the people that philosophy has forgotten – and therefore among those who need it most – at the sidewalk cafés, the pubs (especially the pubs), and the local bookstores. I am the one discussing Spinoza's pantheism with friends over a pint of ale, or perspectives on the temporality of McTaggart and Augustine, or working through Kamm's Principle of Permissible Harm with lawyers and politicians holding ethical opinions very different from my own. Together we dialog; that lost art enjoyed by the Greeks as they lounged in the baths or took their seats at Epicurus' table – an art now cast into disuse by the isolation of social media and the decline of liberal arts education. I believe that philosophy belongs to all those that ask *the question* – that seek the truth – and not, as William Barrett says, only among academicians sequestered in university cloisters whose "disputes have become disputes among themselves".[2]

I feel that I may have something to contribute, or at least something to say, and so it is my intention here to articulate my idea of Portalism and to argue its plausibility. In describing Portalism, I focus primarily on the *nature* of consciousness as opposed to its cognitive workings, and by 'nature' I mean its character, as described by David Chalmers as the 'easy' problems of conscious.[3] I happily leave cognitive mechanics to the epistemologists, the neuroscientists, and neuropsychologists. My ultimate purpose in this work is to present a cogent argument from abduction that will demonstrate a strong probability that Portalism is a viable dualist theory of consciousness, and that as a consequence reductive physicalism is false. In the process I will illustrate how many of the major problems surrounding consciousness and phenomenal experience can be answered by Portalism. If I am successful in this pursuit, perhaps better thinkers can take up the theoretical framework I describe, improve upon it, and advance the truth of phenomenal externalism.

I have intentionally designed the layout of this book to be as friendly to the nonphilosopher as reasonably possible, while at the same time adhering to the professional standards that any presentation of a metaphysical theory mandates. It is a juggling act to be sure, as I would not wish the casual reader to lose interest by becoming enmeshed in cryptic philosophical terminology, neither would I risk losing the attention of the philosopher by endlessly explaining terms and concepts familiar within the discipline. As such, crusty veterans of the search for truth can skip chapter 1, which is essentially a review of the substance debate intended to provide background for the introduction of non-traditional theories of mind. That said, some may find the section on *Materialism's Troubled Path Toward Dogma* interesting as it contains my critique of the analytic tradition both pro and con. Chapter 2 is an introduction to the different concepts of what consciousness might be, including a brief account of my dalliance with monist idealism and how it served to predispose me toward radical externalism, as well as a short explanation of the uniqueness of Portalism. Chapter 3 introduces the theoretical framework of Portalism, while chapters 4 through 7 discuss in detail the fundamental elements of the theory and their relational interdependence, these being the world, the portal, the brain, and the mind. Chapter 8 is the defense of Portalism, tying these elements into a coherent phenomenal externalist theory and presenting cogent explanations illustrating how Portalism answers the arguments against dualism as well as several additional philosophical challenges that must be addressed by all reasonable theories of consciousness. The final chapter is a comparison and contrast between Portalism and three other relatively recent externalist theories, as well as my thoughts on the future of philosophy.

So in the spirit of the Pre-Socratics, Descartes, and Bishop Berkeley, all of whom conceived radical ideas about the nature of reality and being, I invite readers to open their minds and give thoughtful consideration to new explanations that lie outside the boundaries of traditional metaphysics. It is in just such a spirit that I offer my own theory, Portalism, as a plausible solution to the problems found in the philosophy of mind.

Invoking the epoché of Edmund Husserl, I urge the reader to bracket off what they think they already know about materialist concepts of consciousness and consider what *could* be. In the end, whatever judgement they may render upon my ideas will be gratefully accepted.

Chapter 1

Overview of the Substance Debate

In disclosing an alternative theory of consciousness it is conventional practice to first offer a brief discussion of the topic in the interests of providing the reader with background, notwithstanding that consciousness has continued to defy definition for over three thousand years. We might compare consciousness to gravity in the sense that no one really knows what it 'is', only how it appears to behave. Although it is my belief that consciousness is self-evident, many philosophers, in particular those within the analytic tradition, do not agree with this view. Eliminative materialists like Paul and Patricia Churchland, Daniel Dennett, and Frank Jackson hold that what many of us consider to be consciousness, meaning a non-physical subjective state, is either nonexistent, an example of folk psychology, or a form of illusionism that exists when one confuses mental states with neural processes. Other thinkers like the emergentist and neuroscientist Sam Harris disagree, observing that simply having *the thought* that consciousness does not exist is evidence that consciousness exists. He correctly states in his book *Waking Up* that, "Consciousness is the one thing in this universe that cannot be an illusion."[1]

The idea of a conscious mind being a subjective state distinct from physical matter goes back to Pre-Socratic thinkers like Pythagoras and Heraclitus, who among others roughly equated it to the 'soul'. This non-physical concept could survive death, walking as a shade through the underworld until – as Plato proposed – it is reincarnated within another life form. The source of the contemporary debate over consciousness begins with Rene Descartes and the *cogito*, found in Part 4 of the *Discourse on Method* wherein he initiates the dawn of modern philosophy with his famous observation cogito, ergo sum, which we commonly paraphrase as: "I think, therefore I am."[2]

Following Descartes' idea are four hundred years of metaphysical concepts, doubts, proposals, opinions, and hypotheses, extending into the current contemporary period and all of them failing to yield any irreproachably definitive position regarding the *nature* of consciousness. Philosophers of mind commit themselves to the task of explaining consciousness, and also to how the relationship, if any, between subjective experience and the physical universe operates. Traditionally these thinkers break into two fundamental schools of thought – Monism and Dualism – with dualism holding that mind and body are ontologically separate, while monism holds that the universe of objects is composed of only a single substance. Taken together these two perspectives form the historical premise of the substance debate. However, recent appearances of theories involving supervenience, externalism, and enactivism, have effectively blurred the traditional lines of this dispute to the point that thinking about the problem of explaining the mind in terms of 'substance' has become dated, even irrelevant. But before jumping into an idea as nontraditional as phenomenal externalism, it is important to first achieve some understanding of the common positions held by philosophers of mind, and how they came to reason themselves to those conclusions. So to that end I have provided summaries of these ideas in the following sections.

Cartesian Dualism

Substance dualism, also known as Cartesianism, holds that physical states and mental states consist of two separate 'substances' or 'stuff'. The thinking substance, or *res cogitans*, operates *internally* within the corporeal body – the *res extensa* – and continues on *externally* after the body dies. The author of this idea, Rene Descartes (1596-1650), considered human beings to be a single unity of the mental and physical substance, with the relational mechanism bonding the two residing in the pineal gland. Cartesian philosophy is heavily predicated on the existence of God, to the point where he equates the *res cogitans* with the 'soul', but we must remember that he was writing in the 17th century when advancing a theory not accommodating of God was inadvisable, perhaps even dangerous. Cartesian ontology was largely rejected because of its inability to empirically account for how the two substances causally communicate, specifically how a mental event could cause a physical event. Yet recently, some new ideas about consciousness have surfaced that could be argued to be at least diagrammatically Cartesian. Portalism, in its assertion that mind is external to the body, in strict terms could meet that definition.

The theory of Cartesian dualism being what it is, the philosophical importance of Descartes' thinking, the elegance of his *Discourse on Method* (1637) and the impact of the *Meditations on First Philosophy* (1641) on Enlightenment thinking cannot be overstated. Regardless of who you are and which metaphysical theory you may favor, Rene Descartes has influenced your life. *Cogito, ergo sum* lifted all of us out of the darkness of the Middle Ages and into the light of reason, striking off the chains of dogma placed upon us by institutions that would have kept us obediently ignorant. Many say the fundamentals of modern and contemporary philosophy can be traced back to Kant, and that is probably true, but even Kant was influenced by Descartes.

Property Dualism

There are several dualist theories that fall under the label of property dualism, and these in turn break down into reductive and non-reductive ontologies. All of them agree that consciousness derives from a physical substance, but that once manifested becomes irreducible to physical states. Consciousness therefore becomes a *property* of physical substance, not unlike the idea

11

that extension, mass, form, number and motion are primary properties of all physical objects. Property dualists disagree over how this mental derivation from the physical substance actually occurs, as well as on the precise nature of mental states and even over the precise definition of the term 'irreducible'.

Emergentism, also known as emergent materialism, is perhaps the most intuitive form of property dualism, holding that consciousness 'emerges' whenever matter is arranged in some specific fashion. Once emerged from this physical substrate, consciousness becomes ontologically independent and cannot be reduced to physical states or explained in physical terms. Like many property dualist theories, emergentism seeks compatibility with physicalism, holding that although the mind is not a physical entity it is nonetheless derivative of physical sources. Regardless of the popularity of emergentism, the exact manner in which matter can be arranged so that a mind can emerge remains unknown.

Epiphenomalism is a theory predicated on causality. It concedes that mental events exist, but holds that they are absolutely dependent on physical functions. Mental states have no physical existence and so cannot cause physical events. Because these mental states are not causally reducible to physical states, they become causal dead ends, reducing the mind to no more than a dangler on the brain. For epiphenomenalists, the causal highway goes one way only, this being from the brain and nervous system upwards to consciousness, rejecting any idea of downward causality. Epiphenomenalism is an attempt to reconcile the causally closed universe of the physicist with the self-evidence of phenomenal experience by conceding the existence of the non-physical while at the same time dismissing it as causally irrelevant. Yes the mind exists – so what? Epiphenomenalism has been explored by thinkers like David Chalmers and Frank Jackson, possibly as an answer to closing the explanatory gap, but has been found to be lacking in its inability to account for qualia and intentionality.

Anomalous Monism is a theory with an interesting empirical perspective on consciousness proposed in a paper by Donald Davidson (1970). This token-identity theory of mind rejects epiphenomenalism and holds that mental events are identical to physical events (A=A). More importantly, he claims that reasons can be causes, implying that causal traffic flows both ways between mental and physical events, a position critical to dualist and externalist theories as it instantiates the concept of downward causation. According to anomalous monism, although mental and physical processes are ontologically identical, they are not translationally identical in that mental events remain irreducibly different in *character* to their physical counterparts. Although the relationship of identity permits mental and physical events to be connected, mental events remain 'anomalous' (failing to fall under a law), meaning that the relationship of mental events to physical events cannot be described by strict physical laws. Davidson's third principle, which he calls 'the Anomalism of the Mental', states that "there are no strict deterministic laws on the basis of which mental events can be predicted and explained."[3] As Davidson reminds us, such an explanation will require 'psycho-physical laws' which have yet to be discovered. There is a lot going on in this theory, and the idea that physical and mental events are identical ontologically but different in character can be difficult to embrace, yet it is that same distinction that makes Davidson's theory a candidate for both non-reductive physicalism and predicate dualism, causing it to fall under the label of property dualism. Davidson has revised his theory periodically as it has come under criticism, but such is precisely how philosophy is supposed to work.

The last property dualist theory that I will discuss is panpsychism. Although most analytic philosophers wish that panpsychism would quietly go away it refuses to die, and has recently been enjoying both new adherents and blistering criticisms within the philosophical community. Panpsychism traces its origins back to Thales and the Pre-Socratics. It underwent refinement and gained notoriety in *The Monadology* of Gottfried Leibniz (1714), appears in the thinking of luminaries like Alfred North Whitehead, Bertrand Russell, and Carl Jung, and is conceptually considered in more recent works by both Thomas Nagel and David Chalmers. Panpsychism also appeals to those outside dualism with its idea of the possibility of widespread consciousness, even influencing neuroscientific theories like the integrated information technology theory of consciousness (IIT) proposed by Giulio Tononi (2004). Whereas monist idealism holds that everything in the universe exists in mind, panpsychism holds that everything in the universe *has* a mind – every physical object, including electrons. In his 1979 book *Mortal Questions*, Thomas Nagel provides a proof for the truth of panpsychism, while David Chalmers offers a similar argument in dialectical format in his 2015 paper *Panpsychism and Panprotopsychism*.

Panpsychism has several variants, one of these being a recent version known as Cosmopsychism. Where Leibniz's panpsychism envisions consciousness as a property of every particle, Baruch Spinoza envisioned a pantheistic universal consciousness manifested as the mind of God. Cosmopsychism is essentially Spinoza's concept without God, as particular consciousness simply derives from an overarching and ubiquitous cosmic consciousness.

I mention panpsychism and cosmopsychism because together both are sufficiently counterintuitive that to even consider their possibility requires one to open the mind to the enigmatic. This is important because to embrace either of them is not unlike embracing idealism, as one must bracket off one's own intuitive beliefs about the world before one can sincerely consider that which appears to be impossible.

Monism

Monism is an 18th century term coined by German philosopher Christian von Wolff. Where dualism claims that there are two 'substances' in the universe – those being the mental and the physical – monism holds that the universe contains only a single substance, the categories within monism disagreeing as to its precise nature. Monist theories include contemporary monist idealism, neutral monism, and materialism, this latter also referred to in contemporary terms as physicalism, the original term requiring an update to include advancements in particle physics and quantum mechanics. Let us begin with idealism.

Monist Idealism

Monist idealism first appeared as the radical subjective idealism proposed in 1713 by George Berkeley, the Anglican Bishop of Cloyne. Essentially an argument against the empiricism of John Locke, Berkeley held that nothing exists outside of the mind, stating that "to be is to be perceived", and that no physical reality exists beyond our perception of it. It is an alarmingly counterintuitive position, but its explanatory power far outpaces that of materialism. If only mental states exist, then everything we perceive, feel, think, and do, is merely a 'state' of mind. Within subjective idealism, most of the hard problems of consciousness – the mind-body problem, the explanatory gap, the problem of other minds – become uninteresting, as these complications are predicated on the reconciliation of the mental to the physical, and if there is no physical, then there is no problem. In his work *Three Dialogues Between Hylas and Philonous*, Berkeley patiently walks the skeptical Hylas through his line of logic, answering the obvious problem concerning object permanence by claiming that although we might turn our attention away from an object, that object persists in the mind of God, and so when we turn our attention back to it, it will still be there.

Contemporary monist idealists, notably Bernardo Kastrup, have replaced the universal mind of God with the notion of a ubiquitous universal consciousness somewhat akin to the collective unconscious of the psychologist Carl Jung by its overarching accessibility, similar also to the 'folded cloth' metaphor of Merleau-Ponty in which each individual mind is but a 'wrinkle' in a bedsheet that will eventually be 'smoothed out'.[4] In his book *Why Materialism Is Baloney*, Kastrup uses the metaphor of the whirlpool to explain how individual minds are only localizations of consciousness in the same way that whirlpools are localizations of water in a stream, stating that "there is nothing to the whirlpool but water itself."[5] By extension, he proposes that "to say that the brain generates mind is as absurd as to say that a whirlpool generates water."[6] If one can accept that only mental states exist, and subsequently abandon thinking of idealism in realist terms, the possibility of idealism becomes apparent, especially when one is reminded that from a logical standpoint, neither Berkeley's nor Kastrup's position can be proved wrong.

In the interests of full disclosure, I began my metaphysical journey as a contemporary monist idealist. I have more to say on that later in the book regarding what I found attractive about the theory, how I eventually became disenchanted with it, and how it ultimately led me to Portalism.

Neutral Monism

Neutral monist theories hold that the universe consists of neutral elements, neither mental nor physical, yet capable of producing mental and physical properties through their interactions.[7] This neutral 'stuff' takes on different arrangements according to the interrelationships of its parts. The character of this relationship between groups of elements determines whether it is mental, physical, both, or neither. Neutral monists deny the existence of any mental/physical chasm needing to be breached. Within this category also lie the aspect theories, which have of late garnered considerable attention, particularly with double-aspect theory and information-based philosophies such as that of Kenneth Sayre, Bob Doyle's conceptual model of the mind as an 'experience recorder and reducer' (ERR), and Giulio Tononi's integrated information theory of consciousness (IIT). Double-aspect theories reject traditional thought holding that what we consider to be mental and physical are in truth only two perspectives (aspects) on a single substance, with some theories proposing even a third underlying substance. An extreme example of this is the case of computationalism, a theory devised by machine functionalists wherein the irreducible underlying 'substance' consists only of bits with values of 1 or 0. The wide variance of neutral monist theories requires an open mind, and these days a working knowledge of neuroscience can be quite helpful.

Materialism

This brings us finally to monist materialism, a term interchangeable with physicalism. Materialist metaphysics dates back to the atomism of Democritus, and came into prominence through the Enlightenment thinking of the empiricists Thomas Hobbes, John Locke and David Hume. Materialism holds that only the physical substance exists, and, more importantly, that nothing non-physical can exist. This position is in direct contradiction with monist idealism, while both positions reject the Cartesian perspective that both physical and non-physical substances exist. In holding that only the physical exists, it falls upon materialism to account for mental states, including intentionality (feelings, beliefs, emotions, desires) and qualia, which is best defined as the *something-like-there-is-to-be* experiencing of an object or states of affairs in the world. Materialism has the gift of intuitiveness, unlike that of monist idealism which is decidedly counterintuitive. To many philosophers, it just makes common sense that if mind exists at all, it must somehow be either a physical part, or a functional process, of the brain. Thus there is no need to complicate matters by assuming that something non-physical exists – something that has no mass, extension, form, number, charge, or spin. Materialists justify this reasoning through the proposition that the existence of anything non-physical would defy the laws of physics, and to do that would be unscientific.

Early materialist theories were reductionist, meaning that they meant to account for mental states by reducing them to physical processes. The most current physicalist theories are non-reductionist, positing different, sometimes quite creative solutions for mental states that supervene upon the brain. Other theories have found ways around the reductive/non-reductive issue entirely. Eliminative materialism is in this group, which divides itself further into hard and soft factions, with soft eliminative materialists holding that what we consider to be qualia is actually only folk psychology and thus we are mistaken in elevating such feelings to the status of mental states, whereas hard eliminative materialists reject the problem by denying that mental states exist at all.

Type identity theories posit a one-to-one relationship between brain states and mental events, this position being popular among the neuroscientists. For example, certain neural firings in the brain must equate, or correlate, to certain types of subjective experience, such as pain or emotion. Such theories suffer from many weaknesses, not the least of which is the lack of empirical evidence explaining the strict causal relationships between brain activity and experience. In addition, this strict form of identity theory is unable to overcome two significant problems; the first being neural chauvinism, wherein a presupposition is made that only human brains – or even brains in general – can be the mechanisms of consciousness; and the second being multiple realizability, which acknowledges that there can be many different mechanisms in which a function, in this case phenomenal experience, can be realized.

Eventually interest began to shift toward non-reductive materialist theories. Token identity is one of these, while another was discussed earlier under anomalous monism. Like type identity, token identity theories claim that mental states and physical states are identical, but instead of a strict one-to-one identity they envision a 'token' in its place. For example, instead of finding a neural correlate for the experience of a 1974 blue Chevy four-door, a correlative token for 'automobiles' in general will suffice – the set of 'automobiles' serving as a token for any and all cars. Such philosophical acrobatics are not uncommon in materialism, and this one serves to bring basic identity theory in line with multiple realizability.

Functionalism is neutral in the substance debate, taking an entirely different perspective on consciousness by characterizing the existence of mental states in terms of their function, wherein a mental state's function is based upon sensory input that yields a particular behavioral output. Mental states are conceptualized as functional states forming causal connections to other functional states. Machine functionalism is the extreme form and holds that the mind is no more than a Turing machine with the brain acting as hardware and the mind as software. In 1980 John Searle introduced his theory of biological naturalism, wherein mental states are not ontologically reducible to physical states, yet are causally reducible. For Searle, the brain is a biological machine necessary for consciousness, yet this does not imply that consciousness cannot be created by things other than brains. Such theories are attractive in their compatibility with multiple realizability and their ability to escape charges of neural chauvinism. Most importantly, they allow for things other than brains, namely computers, to be a theoretical source for consciousness, although Searle vigorously disputes that computers could ever achieve consciousness. Nevertheless, functionalism is very popular among those scientists and philosophers engaged in artificial intelligence and robotics.

Physicalist theories of supervenience stray perilously close to dualism in their clever explanations of subjective experience while seeking to find plausible reasons for consciousness and free will. Supervenience theories hold that mental states exist and are *dependent* upon the brain while not being *determined* by the brain. This concept enables these theories to avoid, at least to some degree, the limitations imposed by a causally closed universe and its implications of hard determinism. Many of these positions can also be argued to be nuanced forms of property dualism as, at least by some definition, they admit the existence of mental states. In doing so they would seem to remove the pivotal distinction between monist materialism and property dualism.

The one common attribute that all materialist theories share is that none has ever been able to account for intentionality or qualia, or to explain the nature of subjective experience. This is because the tools and methods used to explain our physical world in empirically verified scientific terms are useless for explaining non-physical phenomena. For example, one cannot explain a thought in physical terms. That said, materialism, qua physicalism, remains by far the most prominent metaphysical position in philosophy, largely due to the success of the analytic tradition.

Materialism's Troubled Path Toward Dogma

Most contemporary materialist theories can trace their lineage back to logical positivism and the beginning of the analytic movement in philosophy towards the end of the 19th century. The analytic tradition was founded by materialist philosophers with strong scientific backgrounds, particularly in mathematics and language, as in the persons of Gottlob Frege, Bertrand Russell, Ernst Mach, and Ludwig Wittgenstein. Rejecting the mystical language and obscurity of continental German Idealism, their embrace of logical positivism as imposed by the Vienna Circle cemented the movement's dismissal of metaphysics as neither empirically true nor false, thus ultimately having no meaning. To the analytic philosopher, the world we know consists of independent facts, verifiable and concrete, and as such there is no time or energy to spare for subjects like phenomenology, ontology, ethics, or aesthetics. The Vienna Circle, being the body of intellectuals involved in establishing the empirical scientific framework for 20th century materialism, held that only synthetic statements *a posteriori* (statements from experience), and analytical statements *a priori* (logic and mathematics) – meaning those statements that can either be reduced to experience or are tautological by nature – are the only semantically meaningful propositional forms. This rigid epistemological criterion, framed as verificationism, was to be the standard to which all scientific claims would be held. In their view, Kantian synthetic *a priori* statements – those propositions being determined by reason alone – are meaningless, if indeed they can exist at all. According to Kant, all metaphysical statements are synthetic *a priori* propositions and as such are unverifiable by experience. For the Vienna Circle, Kant's claim was sufficient to render metaphysics scientifically useless, thus consigning an entire philosophical field of inquiry to oblivion.

To be fair, many within the Vienna Circle, being scientists as well as philosophers, and justly committed to Enlightenment values, considered metaphysics to be the last refuge of magic, the supernatural, and God. Being scientists committed to the eradication of mysticism, one can see the purpose if not the logic in their actions. Nevertheless, they threw the baby out with the bath water, metaphysics being the baby. From the standpoint of externalism, in their zeal to embrace empiricism they committed a composition error by assuming that anything non-physical must, by definition, be unnatural, or worse, supernatural. In doing so, they removed the subjective from the purview of science, an action that would have a detrimental effect upon any materialist theory that attempted to account for subjective experience. Rejecting the possibility of the existence of a realm of non-physical experience was the materialist equivalent of painting oneself into a corner.

Cracks in the armor of logical positivism began to appear as World War II caused many members of the Circle to flee Europe. Subsequent problems arose with the verificationism principle in light of William James' concept of fallibilism, which states that no idea can be absolutely verified as true when our knowledge base is ever changing. The death knell for logical positivism came when science embraced the falsifiability criteria (critical rationalism) of Karl Popper (1959), allowing for the capacity of a claim to be contradicted by new evidence as a more efficient metric for the evaluation of scientific theories. In time Popper, a mind-body dualist, would boldly claim that he had 'killed positivism'.

Science is now firmly established in contemporary analytic philosophy, and that's not necessarily a bad thing, provided that the analytic movement and its emphasis on language and science do not lead us to the gates of scientism. This melding of science and philosophy so characteristic of the analytic tradition has resulted in valuable contributions to the philosophy of language, particularly semantic logic, resulting in a plethora of reductive, non-reductive, and supervenient physicalist theories that continue to the present day.

It is important to understand how contemporary physicalism has come to be where it is. No one can deny that the scientific method, with its empiricism, deductive reasoning, and criterion of falsifiability, has comprised a toolset proven to be invaluable in explaining the physical world we live in, but consciousness being subjective, is not physical. Nevertheless, materialists insist upon attempting to explain consciousness in physical terms, struggling to employ this same proven toolset to the exploration of subjective experience, a methodology which, as one would expect, has yielded consistently disappointing results. Still, consciousness as the medium of subjective experience must be accounted for both scientifically and philosophically in any credible theory of mind. It is not good science to dogmatically hold on to a concept that defies proof, no matter how intuitive it may seem. If we did so, then the earth would be flat and the sun would revolve around it – both examples of observations leading to intuitive and obvious conclusions. For many materialists it is equally obvious that the mind must be the brain in spite of the fact that this assumption has never been proven to be the reality, and it is here that materialism begins to fall apart.

Mercifully, I have neither the time nor the inclination to hold the reader's hand as we tiptoe through the wreckage of one rejected materialist theory after another. The road from logical positivism to non-reductive supervenience physicalism is a long one, with multiple theories and perspectives proposed by many truly gifted thinkers over the last one hundred and forty-odd years. Yet no matter how cleverly packaged, creatively nuanced, or ingeniously modified these explanations have been, to date no materialist theory can account for the *something-like-there-is-to-be-ness* of phenomenal experience. In the end, physicalism was ultimately faced with a choice between three non-solutions, these being eliminative materialism/illusionism which holds that we are mistaken in our beliefs about the existence of qualia and intentionality; or new mysterianism which holds that the mind of man will never have the capacity to comprehend consciousness; or simply taking shelter in the belief that an evolving science must one day show us the way – a desperate last stand that is not really science at all, amounting only to faith.

Current Day

Just as the last shovelful of earth was being thrown onto the grave of reductive materialism, it has been resurrected by a relative newcomer to the analytic movement – the neurophilosopher. These are men and women with strong backgrounds in philosophy and neuroscience, many of them quite gifted thinkers. They dwell in the fantastic world of neuro-imagery, searching for the 'correlates of consciousness' using cutting-edge imaging technologies like positron emission tomography (PET), electroencephalography (EEG), and functional magnetic resonance imaging (fMRI).

Many of these philosopher-scientists are physicalists, convinced that the mind is the brain, being internal, cranial, and epiphenomenally causal, presupposing a neural counterpart for every conscious event. It is valuable, exciting work and the images of brain activity can be intriguing. But that's all that they are – intriguing images of brain activity. As Alva Noë states in his book *Out of Our Heads*, "Brain scans are not pictures of *cognitive* processes of the brain in action."[8] Brain waves are not thoughts, and although the images of brain activity may be correlative to a thought, they do not *cause* the thought, neither are they *the* thought. Correlation is not causality. The problem surfaces when neuroscientists attempt to imagine "that two quite different things are the same thing: the thought itself, and its supposed neural basis."[9]

Neuroscience has also given functionalism new avenues of exploration. If the biology of neural states can be mapped to individual subjective experiences, then it is plausible that such a relationship could then be coded into a program that could enable a machine to become consciously aware. John Searle believes that computers will never be truly aware, and illustrates why in his famous thought experiment of The Chinese Room. For what it's worth I am firmly with him on this one, and going further I believe also that artificial intelligence will ultimately prove to be a dead end due to its insurmountable limitations and its overreliance on language. At this writing the neurophilosophers are the new stars of metaphysics and the last hope of physicalism, and yet: "... though we give the materialists their external bodies, they by their own confession are never the nearer knowing how our ideas are produced; since they own themselves unable to comprehend in what manner body can act upon spirit, or how it is possible it should imprint any idea in the mind."[10]

Theoretical Outliers

As David Chalmers has proposed, it may be time to stop thinking in historical terms of substance altogether. The term 'substance' attempts to characterize *what* a thing is – mental or physical – *res cogitans* or *res extensa*. For many theorists it is more meaningful to describe *where and how* a thing is. Such theories of mind go outside the boundaries of the traditional substance debate, some holding "that phenomenal properties are ontologically wholly distinct from physical properties, that microphysics is causally closed, but that phenomenal properties nevertheless play a causal role with respect to the physical". Chalmers categorizes these types of non-reductionist theories as "type-O dualism" based upon causal overdetermination, wherein simple A to B causal traffic is extended into a 'nexus' that includes a route through the mind.[11] Such theories include those within the categories of enactivism and phenomenal externalism, where the term 'nexus' is used in reference to an expansion of the definition of consciousness that includes relationships between brain, body, mind, and world.

Enactivism

According to Evan Thompson, enactivism "emphasizes the interactions between mind, body and the environment, seeing them all as inseparably intertwined in mental processes."[12]

Enactivism is more closely associated to research in cognitive psychology and artificial intelligence than it is to theories of consciousness, but its embrace of the idea that mind emerges as the result of interactions between the body and the world is a recurring theme in externalist theories of mind as many concepts involve a nexus of physical and subjective processes taking one form or another. Some enactivists take a non-analytic approach to their philosophy by advocating phenomenological techniques and thus invoking continental thinkers like Husserl, Merleau-Ponty, and Heidegger. Evan Thompson sees phenomenology as necessary, enhancing science so that "science itself is properly situated in relation to the rest of human life and is thereby secured on a sounder footing."[13] As Portalism is an idea disposed more toward the continental tradition, I firmly support this emphasis on the value of phenomenology as a tool for exploring the subjective.

The two perspectives of enactivism and externalism have different goals yet they overlap in several areas. Although Portalism focuses on the nature of consciousness and mind as opposed to its content as described by cognitive science and epistemology, those of us researching ideas in phenomenal externalism inevitably blunder into enactivist territory and rightfully so. As such it deserves mention and clarification here. Readers with an interest in these areas of alternative cognitive research are encouraged to read the works of Evan Thompson, Eleanor Rosch, Francisco Varela, and Mark Rowlands.

Phenomenal Externalism

Not to be confused with the semantic externalism of Hilary Putnam (1975), theories of phenomenal externalism have at least one assumption in common – that the conscious mind is a result of neural/nervous system processes in concert with phenomena existing or occurring *outside* of the body. Externalists hold that mind is not just the brain, if the brain at all, but that there are external factors necessary to consciousness. As a position, it rejects cranialism which holds that the locus of consciousness is inside the head. Externalist positions tend to focus on either cognitive or phenomenal aspects of mind. Portalism falls into the latter category in an attempt to concentrate on the nature of consciousness while leaving exploration of cognitive mechanics to the neuropsychologists. Several contemporary theories of mind focusing on phenomenal aspects agree that consciousness arises, or at least to some degree operates, inside the head, while others posit that although consciousness supervenes upon the brain, the phenomenon of perception may actually be dependent on other processes within the body in addition to neural processes. These theories embrace an idea known as embodied cognition. Enactivists like Maurice Merleau-Ponty and Alva Noë imagine that the composition of mind extends beyond neural processes to include a holistic ecological connection to the world. Some radical externalists like philosopher Ted Honderich, who coined the term, identify consciousness with existence. He argues this concept of a subjective physical world in his theory of Actualism,[14] while W. Teed Rockwell submits the idea of mind supervening upon a brain-body-world nexus,[15] both theories appealing to the common externalist concept of 'world' being a necessary condition for mind.

Riccardo Manzotti embraces this necessary world concept in his theory of spread mind, binding mind and world through the identity property.[16] Within the identity of the spread mind, the physical apple we experience *is* the experience – the ontology of the two is the same – there is no difference between the knower and the known as together they comprise a singularity. Although the theory is externalist because of its subjective/objective identity, it is also physicalist because, as he argues, if the experience of the apple is identical to the physical apple, then only the physical exists. This convenience allows Manzotti to present spread mind consciousness using purely empirical reasoning, with no appeal to metaphysical mysticism or any additional requirement for a subjective realm. This is a feature of considerable importance to him, being a prominent scientist in the field of robotics.

Portalism is a phenomenal externalist theory of consciousness. Like some of the theories described above, it might be difficult for the nonphilosopher to get their arms around, but that's part of the fun. Here at the end of our substance debate tour, the reader should at least carry away the notion that within externalism, enactivism, computationalism, functionalism, and neurophilosophy, these philosophers of mind are all thinking beyond the traditional limitations of monism and dualism.

Summary

To the nonphilosopher, this tracing of the arc of modern and contemporary metaphysical theory might seem comprehensive, but let me assure you that I have barely scratched the surface in terms of their number, variance, and impact on philosophical thought. In actual practice, many of these theories raise as many questions as they answer regarding locus, causality, neural chauvinism, multiple realizability, solipsism, and skepticism.

Excepting idealism and phenomenal externalism, the theories discussed above assume that consciousness is embodied within the *res extensa*, with many claiming that the mind is no more than a clever interpretation of physical brain states. This position is referred to as cranialism, and it is false. Consciousness does not arise, emerge, derive, or emanate from the brain. The brain is a biological machine, and as such it cannot create consciousness any more than a radio can create music, and it has no more cognitive ability than a thermometer can know whether something is hot or cold. Consciousness – mind – does not originate from matter, whether that matter is a brain in higher animals, or a biochemical reaction in lower animals and bacteria, or fungal clusters on a plant's root tips. As I will show, it is unnecessary for consciousness to emerge from the brain because it already exists as a ubiquitous force in the universe, and all that is required is a portal through which we can enter into it and actualize a mind.

Chapter 2

Whither Consciousness?

The descriptions of dualist and physicalist philosophies of mind presented in the last chapter illustrate a wide variance in perspectives upon what and where consciousness is. Many insist upon a type or token identity between mind and brain. Some attempt to redefine what we consider to be 'brain' as the entire nervous system, or even the entire body, but these specialized approaches create specialized problems regarding the definitions of 'thinking things'. If consciousness is the brain, then the brain thinks. If we extend that definition, does this mean that other parts of the body, say the stomach, is 'thinking' when it 'considers' which contents to digest? Are immune system lymphocytes 'thinking' when they chemically signal problems or decide to attack viruses? One could almost argue as neuroscience continues to discover more wonderful things about the central nervous system, that the goal of reconciling mind to brain resembles a search for clever speculations able to shoehorn these new facts into existing theories, as opposed to boldly following where the science wants to lead us. The goals of neuroscience would seem to be at odds with those of philosophy, in that its emphasis on the scientific 'how' tends to overshadow the 'what' and 'where' interests of the philosophers. As the pragmatist Teed Rockwell keenly observes: "... the neuroscientists are more interested in gathering data than in pondering its implications."[1]

Some philosophers within the analytic tradition appear to have no interest in exploring the character of consciousness, while others have simply given up. Among these are the eliminative materialists, the functionalists, and the new mysterians. Eliminative materialists claim that it is a mistake to consider qualia and intentionality to be proof of a non-physical subjective realm, as these phenomena amount to no more than folk psychology or some other form of illusionism, thus dismissing certain classes of mental states including emotions, desires, feelings, and beliefs as nonexistent. But in order to become an eliminative materialist, one must believe that this is true. If one believes that this is true, then beliefs exist and eliminative materialism is false. Such is the argument from self-refutation, which to be fair has been disputed (P.S. Churchland 1986, Ramsey 1991), mainly on semantic grounds. In addition to eliminative materialists, functionalists decline to address the character of mental states at all, redefining consciousness in terms of sensory inputs and behavioral outputs – function over process, while the followers of New Mysterianism, like Colin McGinn, hold that the mind "is a mystery that will never be unraveled."[2]

Neuroscience has set for itself the goal of determining how consciousness emerges from the brain. In doing so they are presupposing that consciousness does indeed 'emerge' albeit there is no empirical evidence to support this. It is true that sophisticated brain imaging technology has established that there is some correlation between subjective experience and neural activity, and specific areas of the brain that respond to specific stimuli have been mapped. Yet the locations of these brain activities can vary from brain to brain, and the bottom line is that there remains no proof that these images of brain activity are in fact evidence of cognition or consciousness. As Alva Noë reminds us, "Brain scans are not pictures of cognitive processes in the brain in action."[3] I will reiterate that I believe neuroscience is a worthwhile pursuit that is expanding scientific knowledge, although I am convinced that it will never reach the goal of explaining consciousness in terms of brain activity, because consciousness is not an emergent property of the nervous system. Further, its locus is not cranial. For the mind to be identical to the brain the mind would have to be physical, but it is subjective and as such not a physical part of the world of objects. Chalmers is succinctly correct when he observes that "if we cannot explain consciousness in terms of physical processes, then consciousness cannot be a physical process."[4]

So where does this leave us? The first step would be to determine whether or not consciousness exists, and if the answer to that is 'yes', where does it reside if not in the brain? In the previous chapter I presented a number of dualist and physicalist positions. They differ in terms of how they perceive consciousness, but they make the same fundamental assumption of embodiment, a word not to be confused with the enactivist term as defined by Mark Rowlands. Throughout this book I will use Teed Rockwell's definition wherein embodiment refers to the locus of the mind inside the body, as opposed to existing outside the body, qua being-in-the-world. In all of the dualist and physicalist positions that I have previously described, the mental locus is consistently assumed to be embodied within the *res extensa*, regardless of whether consciousness exists as a separate substance, an emergent property, or a monadic component. This assumption is false, and all theories based upon this assumption are equally false. As I will show in later pages, the mind is not the brain, and consciousness always already is, in the world.

Beyond dualism and physicalism I also discussed neutral monism and the aspect theories, including Donald Davidson's intriguing anomalous monism. These kinds of creative theories do not tie themselves down to a strict physical embodiment, although they may propose a kind of hybrid mental-physical solution that may depend on many different factors, such as relationships. But the ultimate rejection of embodiment belongs to monist idealism, denying that a physical world outside of our perception exists at all. Contemporary monist idealism, painfully counterintuitive as it may be, easily exceeds physicalism in terms of explanatory power, but it is not technically an externalist position since nothing exists to be external to. I was once an idealist, and the reasons I am no longer one are worth considering.

A Sojourn in the Sphere of Idealism

Before pursuing a formal degree in philosophy I had already spent over a decade reading, researching, and discussing a considerable number of positions focusing on the fields of ethics and metaphysics. Eventually I became, and remain, an existentialist and a true son of Sartre, Kierkegaard, Schopenhauer, Nietzsche, and Heidegger. But existentialists are neutral on the substance debate and I found that unsatisfactory, so I went in search of an explanation of reality, and found the freedom of monist idealism almost existential in itself.

Monist idealism is intriguing on several levels. The contemporary idealist, Bernardo Kastrup, envisions mind as a localization of a collectively shared mind in the same way that the whirlpool is a localization of water in a stream, this whirlpool image being his famous analogy.[5] This concept seemed to fit well within Heidegger's ontology of Being, casting Dasein in the role of the localization. Idealism also answered many of the problems in the philosophy of mind by simply removing their premises. If there is no body there can be no explanatory gap, and no need to explain the causal mechanisms that govern mind-body communications. If one is open-minded enough to embrace a non-physical universe, then as a theory it can be elegant in its simplicity while many of Kastrup's arguments in his books and YouTube offerings can be quite compelling.

I eventually fell out of love with idealism over two ideas that I was unable to reconcile to my own satisfaction, the first of these being death and the body left behind. Specifically, if there is no physical world then why do corpses have to lie around decomposing? As Kastrup observes: "If the body is an image

33

of a process of conscious localization, then when that process stops the image should also disappear, just like the whirlpool. But a corpse stays in empirical reality for a while after death..."[6] He then seems to borrow a concept from Alan Watts wherein the reason the corpse lingers is due to an 'echo' of a process no longer in existence. I grasped the reasoning, but I personally found this explanation to be trivial and thin. I asked myself why the body wouldn't just suddenly disappear in a cloud of dust, not unlike the 'daemons' of characters in the novels of Philip Pullman that turn to 'dust' when their human counterparts perish.

My other problem with idealism reduced to Occam's razor. If everything is mind, then why are the mechanics of the world so complex? Even a simple walk in the backyard reveals level upon level of interdependent causes and effects in the form of food chains, illnesses, defects, codependencies, weather, climatic zones, species differentiation, and communication. This is the same question I present my non-atheist friends with – 'Why did God create such an intricately labyrinthine and interdependent universe?' Idealistically speaking, if all is mental, what could be wrong with a more simplistic world to exist in? Perhaps even an 'Edenic' world, as David Chalmers envisions in his book *The Character of Consciousness*. Why establish Polar Regions and arid deserts where little can live? Why isn't the whole world like Hawaii, or Amsterdam? Why do we need food, and why do we get sick? Why are there birth defects? If the physical does not exist, then why have defects at all? In fact, why die at all? If idealism is true, then the universe and everything in it, every mechanical and evolutionary process, is a localization of a wider consciousness – essentially only a thought. Why can't these thoughts just be simpler? To this day, I am still unable to convince myself why such evolutionary complexity should be necessary in an idealist universe.

Nevertheless, I grew philosophically as a result of my

dalliance with monist idealism, and took away several important lessons. Without this experience it would have been difficult to navigate the path that would eventually lead me to phenomenal externalism and from there to Portalism. For example, in order to embrace monist idealism one must first reject physicalism, particularly mind-brain identity theories, that which Rockwell has so elegantly and derisively named 'Cartesian materialism'.[7] Doing so can free one's thinking from the confines of materialist dogma. More importantly, it can extend one's conceptual boundaries and promote the serious consideration of non-traditional, counterintuitive, and radical alternative theories within the philosophy of mind.

I also came to the conclusion that the existence of a physical world persisting beyond our perception of it made realistic common sense, and fit better within existentialist concepts like universal indifference, reflective and unreflective consciousness, and the ready or unready-to-handiness of equipment in the world. Embracing a physical world also seemed to be the first logical step toward accounting for the apparent uniformity of nature, an explanation that I find lacking in monist idealism. Essentially, if only mental states exist, and the world is exactly as it appears, then why does it appear in this uniformly particular way? Idealism made me think more about ontology, as idealism holds that only the mental exists, its ontology is straightforward – consciousness is ontologically irreducible because consciousness simply *is*. I began to draw conceptual metaphysical parallels between the idea of the collectively shared mind and the ontologies of being as described by Heidegger and Hegel, as illustrated in Kastrup's observation that, "The medium of mind remains the sole ontological primitive of all existence."[8]

I also began to understand the concept of the 'world' differently. Idealism holds that everything we perceive as being an object in the world is in fact only 'in mind', as no physical reality exists. By extension, the idealist's individual localization of consciousness – the mind – *is the world*. In idealism, the mind is necessary and sufficient to the actualization of the world, the content of the world being vibrations resonating through one's individual psyche (in the interests of brevity I am vastly simplifying Dr. Kastrup's explanation to make my point).

To the non-idealist, this might sound pretty far out, but what one needs to take from this idea is not the plausibility of an explanation of how the world manifests itself, but the idea that the world *is absolutely inseparable from the mind*, and that consequently any questions regarding the physical substrate of the world become irrelevant. The mind is not in the brain – the mind is in the world – and in terms of perception and subjective experience, the mind *becomes the world*, causing the lines between subjective and objective to dissolve as the knower and the known synthesize into a single unity.

The reason I have spent significant time with this discussion of contemporary monist idealism is to illustrate that without committing to this philosophy I would likely have never been exposed to the premises and concepts that spawned the characteristics of Portalism and nurtured its development. My open attitude toward the serious consideration of divergent theories lying outside of traditional philosophical thought, beginning with the possibility of monist idealism and extending into phenomenal externalism, has proved to be fundamental and crucial in moving forward with the development of a theory of consciousness that I find entirely satisfactory.

A Possibility of Plausibility?

All we are is mind. It is only through mind that we, as human beings, are able to experience the world of objects, as well as personal phenomena including feelings, beliefs, emotions, and as Thomas Nagel has famously characterized, the *'something-like-there-is-to-be-ness'* of experience. But consciousness extends beyond this simple being-in-the-world, compelling us to self-examine by turning our perception inwards, becoming reflexively aware, being-for-itself as Sartre says, and questioning who we are and why.

What exactly is *consciousness*? Perhaps the functionalists are onto something when they place the focus not so much on what consciousness is, but on what it does. We all know what we are referring to when we talk about consciousness, and we know how it *'feels'* to be conscious, we also understand that consciousness is necessary in terms of what we can do with it and that we can do nothing without it, but what *is it* exactly? As we have seen, many great thinkers are convinced that consciousness arises from the brain, and that its locus is inside the skull. But such beliefs are no more than that – beliefs – as we have yet to see any empirical evidence that such is the case.

If the mind is the brain, then where exactly in the brain is it located? If subjective experience correlates to brain activity, what precisely is this relationship? Is it causally epiphenomenal or can causation flow both ways from the physical to the mental and back again? Does this relationship extend beyond neural responses to stimulus to include reflexive experiences such as thoughts, and if so how? If brain scan images are held to be pictures of thoughts and feelings then why does the evidence not support this? And why are these images of brain activity inconsistent from brain to brain?

Not all questions deal with neuroscience. For example, are only human beings conscious or is such a belief only an example of anthropocentric presupposition? Don't animals have minds? Do trees? Is having a 'brain' even necessary for subjective experience, or does such thinking amount to no more than neural chauvinism? If a brain is not necessary, does this mean that a machine could theoretically become self-aware? Is everything in the universe conscious to some degree as the panpsychists hold, or is the entire universe of creation just one consistent plane of consciousness from which every mind is derived, as the cosmopsychists believe? I could go on, but I think that by now the reader is sympathetic to the idea that when one attempts to account for subjective experience the resulting explanations only engender more questions, while consciousness continues to defy definition. Nevertheless, any plausible theory of mind must address them, seriously and successfully, as numerous as they might be.

In the next chapter I describe the metaphysical framework of the theory that I have named Portalism. Readers acquainted with the works of Davidson (1980), Rockwell (2005), Noë (2010), Manzotti (2017), and Honderich (2017), will notice several conceptual similarities between Portalism and the distinctive theories of these impressive thinkers. One commonality that will immediately stand out is the fundamental role that the environment, or 'world', plays in the holistic approaches of the latter four philosophers. Although these four thinkers are to some degree radical externalists, I have also included the non-reductive physicalist Donald Davidson in this group for two reasons: his rejection of epiphenomenalism in favor of his principle of causal interaction validates the concept of downward causality which is necessary to Portalism, and his agreement that mental events are anomalous by failing to fall under a law at least *implies* a subjective realm, even though he insists upon a mind-brain token identity.

Commonalities between theoretical concepts are not unusual. Progress in science as well as philosophy is accomplished by either criticizing or expanding upon the work of one's predecessors and peers. I firmly believe that the thinkers I mention above, as well as others including Hume, Merleau-Ponty, Leibniz and particularly Martin Heidegger, have all discovered pieces to the puzzle – important ideas that can be collected into an alternative approach that best explains the nature of consciousness. I claim no originality for the theory of Portalism beyond the name itself. I am merely building on, extracting from, reassembling, extending, and acknowledging the heavy lifting done by others before me – fleshing out a unique combinative concept, as it were. Portalism is a theory of phenomenal externalism because it holds that mind is absolutely and entirely extracranial and that all subjective experience takes place external to the body. This is not to say that brains don't have a role to play; only that their role is purely physical, essentially homeostatic and hormonal, that they cannot think, and as such are not equipped to assign meaning or context to conscious experience. As a phenomenal externalist theory, Portalism is one of the most radical due to its crucial foundational principle – that Consciousness is a fundamental force of nature.

Portalism maintains another significant contrast to most other theories of consciousness in that it rejects neural chauvinism by extending consciousness to all living organisms. Portalism unconditionally holds that all biological systems have at least some degree of consciousness. The following chapters will describe how these integral elements of Portalism are possible, and how they combine to make the theory plausible. Finally, because my theory embraces both physical and subjective realms, it is therefore a type of nontraditional dualism, that is, it is not Cartesian nor is it a property dualism. In 1949 Gilbert Ryle published his famous attack upon dualism, whereupon he envisioned the possibility of two substances as a category mistake, further arguing that if mental and physical stuff were embodied together then the relationship between the two would be the equivalent of having a 'ghost in the machine'. But I argue that the brain *is* physical and the mind *is* subjective, and although Portalism is a dualism, there is no ghost in Ryle's machine; the ghost is in the world, and the ghost is biocentric.

Chapter 3

The Concept of Portalism

Metaphysics will never put forth its full powers so long as it is
expected to accommodate itself to dogma.
Arthur Schopenhauer

In this chapter I will describe the concept of Portalism, a theory of
radical phenomenal externalism that lies outside contemporary
metaphysical norms. Basically put, there are three critical
components to the theory: these being the universal horizon
of Consciousness; the 'portal', which I define as a biologically
embodied mechanism through which access into Consciousness
is achieved; and mind – a synthesis of portal and Consciousness
whose locus is entirely external to the *res extensa*. What follows
are the detailed descriptions of Portalism, its assumptions, and
its perspective on the nature of consciousness.

Portalism is Continental Philosophy
Before jumping into the theory itself I should declare to the
reader that Portalism as a theory is not in the analytic tradition,
being closer in resemblance to continental philosophy, or at least
so I shall claim. Analytic philosophy tends to view philosophical
questions as discrete abstractions placing emphasis on knowledge
supported with empirical evidence; its focus being upon the
logical analysis of a particular phenomenon. Continental
philosophy favors rigorous descriptions of phenomena and the
manner in which they conform within the whole of existence.
The continental tradition is thematically holistic as opposed to
being analytically particular, but it is important to mention that
both disciplines embrace clarity and precision, and both have
valuable contributions to make. Continental philosophers use

phenomenology and hermeneutics as their exploratory tools, while analytic philosophy applies the scientific method. Both can be effective approaches, but while I freely recognize that the scientific method has lifted us out of mysticism by consistently proving to be unsurpassed in its ability to explain the physical world we live in, I question whether it has license to operate within the realm of metaphysics. The empirical tools and methods that analytic philosophy uses so deftly in the physical world do not appear to be serviceable when the scene shifts to the realm of subjective experience.

To argue the plausibility of Portalism I cannot use empirical tools. Portalism was conceived 'on my sofa', as the classroom definition of Rationalist *a priori* reasoning would maintain. I cannot argue the theory deductively, as I have no experimental results or empirical evidence to offer. For the same reasons that idealism cannot be explained using realist terms, subjective experience cannot be explained in empirical terms. No viable theory of mind can perceive consciousness as a series of discrete physical processes when mind is clearly a comprehensively holistic phenomenon involving a synthesis of both objective universe and subjective agent. Given this, I must claim a continental tradition and proceed with the reasoning that this totality of phenomenal experience and physical reality is bound by conditions best understood through abductive reasoning and Rationalist reflection, as opposed to scientific explanations that struggle to conform to preconceived physicalist dogma.

Since we do not yet have a subjective science to furnish us with the tools and language necessary to compose an empirical explanation of Consciousness, the best I can do is undertake to formulate a theory that provides the most *plausible* answers to problems that face philosophers of mind. I will endeavor to present and defend a cogent theory, wherein my burden is not to prove that Portalism is true, but only that it is plausible. Since I have no choice but to work within the linguistic limits of objective morphology, the arguments in defense of Portalism will not be deductive and empirical, but inductive and synthetic *a priori*, which according to Kant, is the only form that metaphysical arguments can take. Thus I proceed along the lines of the continental tradition as I understand it.

The Six Assumptions of Portalism

Portalism is a theory of consciousness premised on the principles of radical phenomenal externalism, and like all theories it makes certain critical assumptions. The following are the six assumptions of Portalism:

1. A nonphysical subjective realm exists, as does a physical realm independent of our perception of it.

2. The mind is not the brain. The locus of the mind is entirely external to, but causally connected to, the *res extensa*.

3. The horizon of Consciousness is a fundamental force of nature and is ubiquitous throughout the universe. It is ontologically irreducible and precedes the distinction between subject and object. Consciousness is the all-encompassing structure that enables the possibility of subjective experience. The horizon of Consciousness is devoid of content, it being the subjective ground and not the subject.

4. All living organisms harbor an innate and intrinsic bio-mechanism capable of facilitating an individual connection, forthwith known as a 'portal', into the horizon of Consciousness.

5. A portal/Consciousness connection is necessary and sufficient to manifest the localized, individual state of consciousness actualized as mind. Such a connection is the necessary condition before any mind can be.

6. Only Mind has content.

Portalism is predicated on the assumption that Consciousness is a fundamental force of nature, taking its place among the weak and strong nuclear forces, electromagnetism, and gravity. As such it is ubiquitous throughout the universe and an irreducible all-encompassing horizon that is and always already was. Consciousness is the gateway to mind and the medium wherein subjective experience becomes possible.

Portalism draws a distinction between portal, Consciousness, and mind. The portal, discussed in detail in a later chapter, is an embodied biological/biochemical mechanism that facilitates access into the horizon of Consciousness. Each living thing, every biological system, possesses one. When the portal connects to Consciousness, the result is a localized actualization of that fundamental force. This resulting consciousness (small 'c') is localized to the individual by virtue of its portal connection and is actualized as 'mind'. Only minds have the potential to realize experiential content, as Consciousness, being the ontological ground, is in and of itself devoid of content. Different minds will experience different levels of awareness based on the sophistication of their portal mechanism. The quality of an agent's subjective experience is dependent upon the sophistication of its portal mechanism, while the ubiquitous horizon of Consciousness simpliciter remains eternally constant. The potential for experiential content is in turn dependent upon the dynamic potential of the portal connection. This connection creates a localization of Consciousness manifested as an individual consciousness. This consciousness exists as the medium of subjective experience and there is nothing that exists beyond it that we can be conscious of.

Big 'C' and Little 'c' Consciousness

The reader will have already noticed that I have elected to spell Consciousness with a capital 'C' when referring to it as a fundamental force of nature, while using the small case 'c' when describing consciousness in the case of a localized medium of subjectivity. I have borrowed this Heideggerian nomenclature to make the distinction between the ubiquitous horizon of Consciousness and an individual localized state of consciousness – a mind – that each living thing enjoys. For those readers who have not read Heidegger's *Being and Time*, he draws a distinction between the ontological ground of *Being*, denoted by the capital 'B', and the ontic *being*, that is each of us as the agent of care, what he refers to as 'Dasein'. In Heidegger's terminology, 'Being' is the condition necessary before any being can be. Congruently, in Portalism, a connection to Consciousness is necessary to the manifestation of the localized realm of individual subjective experience. Such a connection is the necessary condition before any mind can be.

The portal enables access to Consciousness, resulting in an individual localized state of consciousness, otherwise known as *mind*. In Portalism, the concept of Consciousness as an irreducible ontological ground is analogous to Heidegger's 'Being', and going forward in this book I will consider the terms 'mind', 'subjective experience', and 'consciousness' (small 'c') to be synonymous.

What Price Ubiquity?

As we have seen, Portalism assumes Consciousness to be a fundamental force of nature, a ubiquitous horizon that enables the possibility of subjective experience. So what is the criterion that must be met before one can consider something to be a fundamental force? According to Chalmers: "It might further be suggested that physical theory allows any number of basic *forces* (four as they stand, but there is always room for more) and that an extra force associated with a mental field would be a reasonable extension of existing physical theory. These suggestions would invoke significant revisions to physical theory, so are not to be made lightly, but one could argue that nothing rules them out."[1]

Thus one might think that as fundamental forces go, acceptance of yet another force of nature within this exclusive group might be a complicated affair, but surprisingly it comes down to only two essential constituents. The first is that the phenomenon be irreducible. The second is simply our agreement that it is so.

The four fundamental forces of nature are defined as the weak and strong nuclear forces, electromagnetism, and gravity. The strong force governs the attraction between protons and neutrons that keep atomic nuclei together, while the weak force mediates the radioactive decay of unstable subatomic particles. These two nuclear forces, outside of their irreducibility, are of little interest philosophically, so having defined them, albeit simplistically, they can be dispensed with. The remaining two forces are of high relevance in terms of making an argument for the inclusion of Consciousness as a fundamental force.

Electromagnetism governs the attraction between electrically charged particles. It is responsible for chemical bonding, electromagnetic waves, and visible light. Its range is infinite and it is the strongest of the four known forces. Although many scientists have made significant contributions to the study of electromagnetism, arguably the foremost would be James Clerk Maxwell, who proved that electric and magnetic forces are the same thing; that magnetism, electricity, and light are manifestations of the same phenomenon. His subsequent equations paved the way for the theory of relativity and quantum mechanics. What is important about electromagnetism is that it didn't become a fundamental force overnight, as science spent decades trying to explain it in terms of classical mechanics. The mechanistic incompatibilities of this force were eventually solved by Albert Einstein through special relativity, but most importantly it is agreed that electromagnetism is irreducible to any other interrelationships.

Gravity is a fundamental force of particular interest, because like consciousness, no one knows what it is in any fundamental way. Although gravity is the weakest of the four forces, like electromagnetism its range is infinite. Scientists may not know what gravity is, but they know a great deal about how it *behaves* as a force of attraction between any two masses – from particles to planets to galaxies. Unlike the other three forces, gravity does not affect nuclear particles (in any relevant way) and does not affect physics. Gravity is unique among the fundamental forces in that the other three have 'force carriers', these being messenger particles that deliver or give rise to forces between other particles, but gravity has none. The weak and strong forces have bosons and gluons as carriers respectively, while electromagnetism uses photons. Gravity does not fit well into the Standard Model of particle physics. For gravity not to have a carrier would seem to be unacceptable, as gravity is clearly a force, defined in general relativity as a 'spacetime curvature' powerful enough to bend light and slow down time in spacetime models, therefore there must be a carrier particle that delivers that force.

Enter the graviton, a hypothetical force carrier that is theoretical, unobservable, and massless. Being massless is not a problem, as photons are also massless. Being unobservable is another issue entirely, meaning that in any models or calculations that describe an exchange of gravitons, as in quantum field theory, graviton activity must be characterized as 'virtual'. In short, not possessing a force carrier makes gravity problematic for certain theoretical models, *so science made one up* – they invented the graviton so that science could move on. As a result gravity conforms better within the world of physics, thereby enabling science to continue progressing in its mission to describe the workings of our universe.

I confess that the scientific descriptions above are highly generalized, but my intent is not to pull the reader into the arcane universe of particle physics, when I only seek to illustrate similarities relevant to the argument for the inclusion of Consciousness as a fifth fundamental force of nature. These similarities are:

1. Electromagnetism was not considered to be a fundamental force until decades of efforts to explain it through classical mechanics had failed. Similarly, consciousness has endured decades of failed attempts to explain it through reductive materialism.

2. Magnetism, electricity, and light were objectively proven to be manifestations of the same phenomenon – electromagnetism. There currently being no subjective scientific method to draw upon, "we can appeal to nonempirical constraints"[2] to fundamentally show that mind is the localized manifestation of portal, Consciousness, and world.

3. Fundamentally, no one knows what gravity is. Fundamentally, no one knows what consciousness is.

4. Consciousness, like electromagnetism, is irreducible to any other interrelationships. Like gravity, consciousness does not affect nuclear particles, nor does it affect physics, and it has no force carriers.

5. Under classical mechanics, gravity didn't fit well into physics, but then a new theory, relativity, came along that better accommodated it. Consciousness doesn't fit well into mind-brain identity theories, property dualism, or supervenience physicalism – all forms of cranialism – but new phenomenal externalist theories better accommodate it.

6. Electromagnetism and gravity are considered to be irreducible. "Conscious experience... is a phenomenon to be explained in its own right. And if it turns out that it cannot be explained in terms of more basic entities, then it must be taken as irreducible."[3] Since consciousness cannot be explained in physical terms, consciousness

cannot be physical – if not physical, then it is subjective – and if subjective, then consciousness is irreducible, as consciousness and subjectivity are synonymous terms.

If Consciousness, being the ontological ground of all consciousnesses, is irreducible, then all that remains for it to be considered as a fundamental force in nature is our agreement that it is so.

Though the above is clearly an argument from analogy, I believe that the variety of examples presented along with their relevance is strong; however, the degree of relevance between the similarities that I draw is certainly open to scrutiny. For Consciousness to be added to the list of fundamental forces would be self-justifying if, as in the case of electromagnetism, it was discovered that once accepted, Consciousness then becomes an enabling force toward the furthering of scientific inquiry. Such an expansion within the philosophy of mind could be manifested in broader new avenues for thought and theory, and even perhaps toward the establishment of a framework for a subjective science. After all, the scientific method does not begin with a hypothesis; it begins with an observation and an idea, both of which dwell in the subjective realm.

Neither Panpsychism Nor Pantheism

I wish to remove any ambiguity concerning the term 'ubiquitous'. Its definition is "existing or being everywhere at the same time" (Merriam-Webster), which is appropriately descriptive of the horizon of Consciousness which, like gravity, is everywhere in the universe, omnipresent at all times, its range infinite. As it is ontologically irreducible, it cannot be a quality or property of any being in the world. I mention this because the word ubiquitous is often used in descriptions of panpsychism. Panpsychism holds that consciousness is an innate property of all matter, right down to electrons, wherein "the basic components of the material world also involve very basic forms of consciousness, from which the more complex conscious experience of humans and other animals derive."[4] In the panpsychist view, consciousness is 'ubiquitous' among the *components* of the material world, while Portalism holds that Consciousness, as the horizon wherein subjective experience becomes possible, is ubiquitous not within the components of the world, but *throughout the world itself*.

Panpsychism has been around since Thales and Anaximenes, but its more modern rendition begins with Gottfried Leibniz in the 17th century, and his concept of the monad as the elemental component of existence. In paragraph 3 of *The Monadology* he boldly asserts the existence of monads as atoms of nature "and in fact, the Elements of things."[5] Each of these contain thinking 'souls' and by aggregation create more complex things, eventually even people. Simply put, each monad is different with regard to its qualities, and these unique monads combine to form a hierarchy of complex things that he calls *entelechies*. Leibniz assigns consciousness to monads in paragraph 14 with: "The passing condition which involves and represents a multiplicity in the unity, or in the simple substance, is nothing else than what is called Perception."[6]

Regrettably, panpsychism is often too easily dismissed. Like monist idealism, it can present an elegant and attractive description of the universe for the free thinker. It can solve the hard problem and the problem of other minds, and it constitutes one of the earliest attacks on Cartesian dualism. Philip Goff has improved upon Leibniz's concept by connecting it "with a form of neutral monism associated with Bertrand Russell" wherein "objective observation does not give us the real nature of material events."[7] Panpsychism can be attacked in a number of ways, primarily because it suffers from the problem of aggregation. Leibniz, one of the premier Rationalist thinkers along with Descartes and Spinoza, is long on his descriptions of monadic qualities, but short on exactly how they go about bonding together to form larger compositions of things. The mechanism for aggregation is not explained, and this is what Goff has attempted to solve through the lens of neutral monism. Leibniz defends his reasoning in paragraph 32 with the famous Principle of Sufficient Reason, followed by an appeal to God in that, "Most frequently, moreover, these reasons cannot be known by us."[8] Goff's panpsychism operates without the limitations of having to include a role for a supernatural deity to play, a feature that was incumbent upon Leibniz and the other Rationalists of his period. His success with this concept, as with any metaphysical theory, is up to the reader to decide, but what is most important to take away from this particular discussion of panpsychism is that the idea itself, particularly in Leibniz's time, and including Goff's enhancement, represents exemplary out-of-the-box thinking regarding the character of consciousness.

Similar to panpsychism is pantheism, another concept that dates back to the Pre-Socratics and whose modern interpretation is attributed to Baruch Spinoza, a Rationalist thinker also from the 17th century. Pantheism takes a different perspective from panpsychism holding that the material world and God are a single unity – everything is God, and as an identity exists between spirit and nature, everything therefore follows *from* God. Spinoza's ideas caused a stir among Enlightenment thinkers looking for an alternative to atheism and deism, and it particularly upset the established Church. The Church objected on two basic grounds; the first being Spinoza's idea that 'neither intellect nor will pertain to the nature of God', meaning that God, being everything, was a God that not only did not intervene in the affairs of men, but was a God incapable of loving us back. The second objection was much scarier, because if Spinoza was right then there was no heaven or hell, so when one dies their soul simply merges with God again. If this is the case, then what do we need the Church for? Needless to say, the Church took Spinoza to be an existential threat and acted accordingly by excommunicating him.

Modern pantheism takes the form of Cosmopsychism, which rejects the idea that the most elemental particles combine to form more sophisticated compositions, instead holding that the entirety of reality is a single consciousness. In cosmopsychism, this universal panconsciousness replaces Spinoza's God, yet all things are still derivative of it. Where panpsychism is exposed to attack on the basis of aggregation, cosmopsychism faces attack from the opposite direction on the basis of disaggregation, and for failing among other things to explain how some disaggregated conscious entities are capable of broader fields of subjective experience. For example, if clams and cats are cut from the same universal cloth, then why do cats enjoy an obviously wider reality? Cosmopsychism can also be criticized on its own basic premise of universal consciousness, as Raymond Tallis argues: "A consciousness as a whole universe would presumably be a consciousness of everything, which is impossible to imagine. Less obviously, it might be a consciousness of *nothing* – since there would be nothing outside of its consciousness for it to be conscious *of.*"[9]

If it is true that many philosophers have discovered pieces to the puzzle of consciousness, then G.W. Leibniz and Baruch Spinoza certainly rank among them, but Portalism is not panpsychism, nor is it pantheism. What makes Portalism distinct is its claim that *only living things* are capable of subjective experience, where panpsychism holds that *all* things, including electrons, are conscious thinking things, and where pantheism implies that all things being derivative of a master panconsciousness are therefore inherently conscious. Portalism rejects the idea that non-biological entities can be conscious.

For example, the Los Angeles Dodgers coffee cup in my hand is admittedly a wonderful thing, but it is not capable of subjective experience. There is *nothing-like-there-is-to-be* a coffee cup, or a paperweight, or a rock. Inorganic matter does not have the ability to form portals and so cannot connect into Consciousness. Rocks exist within the objective realm, have primary qualities and possess only instrumental value. The ability to experience phenomena in the world would in no way improve the rock. There is no sufficient reason in assigning consciousness to inanimate matter because there is no teleology, no design or purpose, in doing so. As Consciousness always already exists as a fundamental force of nature, Portalism can reject both panpsychism and cosmopsychism on the grounds that they are unnecessary.

Chapter 4

The World

As Maurice Merleau-Ponty tells us in the *Phenomenology of Perception*, "All consciousness is consciousness of something."[1] Without the world there would be nothing to be conscious of other than one's own consciousness, which, as many philosophers of mind have rightly noted, leads to circularity and skepticism. Therefore the world is a necessary condition for consciousness. We can't be phenomenally conscious unless we are in the world, for the same reason that we "can't swim where there is no water."[2] Portalism is compatible with this position, holding that the horizon of Consciousness is a fundamental force of nature, nature being the world. As Sam Harris observes, "What are we conscious of? We are conscious of the world; we are conscious of our bodies in the world; and we also imagine that we are conscious of ourselves within our bodies."[3]

Sam Harris has used a metaphor likening the individual's mistaken perception of the world to the viewpoint of a little man sitting in a chair behind our eyes, guiding our bodies through the world of objects by means of some embodied control panel.[4] As common as this illusion might be, it is nonetheless vulgar. We are not like a fish in a tank looking out from behind the glass at some external reality. As Noë frequently reminds us in *Out of Our Heads*, "We are in the world and of it."[5] Therefore I, as mind, am surrounded by a world that always already was, and as mind, I am *in* it. Mind and world, subjective and objective, mental and physical, although ontologically distinct nevertheless operate together as a singular totality within a relationship of *de facto* identity. Even the biological naturalist John Searle, an unmovable mind-brain internalist, recognizes this singularity as he states that: "Some people still think that the ontological irreducibility of consciousness makes consciousness not a part of the physical world. They are mistaken."[6]

My consciousness is not an object in the world but my body is, as the existentialist Merleau-Ponty describes, "The body is the vehicle of being in the world, and having a body is, for a living creature, to be intervolved in a definite environment, to identify oneself with certain projects and be continually committed to them."[7] My body is a platform housing the sensory modalities through which I am able to encounter things in the world. Merleau-Ponty understood this body-platform concept "not as a collection of adjacent organs, but a synergic system, all of the functions of which are exercised and linked together in the general action of being in the world, in so far as it is the congealed face of existence."[8] This concept is important, as by extension I am able to project this same definition onto all living things, including other human beings that I might encounter and that might encounter me, each existing objectively as things in the world.

The importance of the world is a recurring theme in most, if not all, works of radical phenomenal externalism. In the book *Mind: Your Consciousness is What and Where?*, Ted Honderich's theory of Actualism collapses the common perspective of distinct subjective and objective worlds into a unified *subjective physical world*, unique to each individual, while still maintaining the importance of world stating that "subjective physical worlds are dependent on several things, one being the objective physical world."[9] Riccardo Manzotti's theory of spread mind takes a different position by establishing identity between an object in the world and the object in itself, and in so doing establishes world as necessary to consciousness. "Objects are just physical entities and experience is identical with them. *We are the world and the world is us – everything is physical.*"[10] And again, as he states in his preface for the book *The Spread Mind: Why Consciousness and the World Are One,* "experience, since it is real, is a part of nature. I am real. My conscious experience is real, thus consciousness must fit in nature as everything else. Nature is not a club that does not want me as a member. Nature is the totality of the physical world. Whatever exists partakes of it."[11] His point being that nature encompasses experience. Finally, the externalist Teed Rockwell, positing a nexus of mind-brain-world in his book *Neither Brain Nor Ghost*, also reinforces the necessity of world. "When we inquire into the world, we discover the system whose natural parts are the body, the brain, and the world. But we have no reason to assume that the brain can produce experience without the other two, any more than the lung can perform its proper function without oxygen."[12] I discuss in greater detail these innovative externalist theories and how they compare and contrast with Portalism in the final chapter of this book.

All of the thinkers cited above attest to the philosophical necessity of world to consciousness, but it is my opinion that no philosopher frames the concept of world better than Martin Heidegger. Although his prose can be daunting at times, his explanation of the unity of self and world sets the gold standard for any explanation of the interactions between subjective agent and physical universe. In this claim I am including phenomenal as well as reflexive consciousness, as Heidegger addresses both in how we, as mind, move back and forth between everydayness and authenticity through *Dasein*, Heidegger's famous phenomenological mechanism of accessibility. To simplify for the nonphilosopher, *we* are Dasein, manifested as an individual mind, and we always already are in-the-world.

When encountering things or equipment (objects in the world that have utility), we are in the mode of *everydayness*, akin to what Ned Block (1998) refers to as *phenomenal* consciousness. When we turn our consciousness reflexively inward, as in introspective thought, memory recall, or in the instance of self-awareness, we are in *reflexive* consciousness, where in Heideggerian terminology, we become *authentic* in the awareness of ourselves. The default mode of Dasein is everydayness, blithely navigating the world of objects, taking care, and managing equipment. "We do not first need to put ourselves in the place of this way of being in dealing-with and taking-care. Everyday Dasein always already *is* in this way; for example, in opening the door, I use the doorknob."[13]

Heidegger describes the world as an encompassing structure, or horizon, where the encountering of beings, things and equipment, the sphere of nature, and Dasein itself become manifest. It is the medium of subjective experience wherein objects and states of affairs become known. The world is necessary to Dasein, for without it Dasein cannot achieve the thinghood of ontic being. To paraphrase, if all we are is consciousness and the world is necessary to consciousness, then without the world we cannot exist. The world is essentially necessary to Dasein as the projection of its possibilities and as the structure in which it comports itself to all beings. As Heidegger explains, Dasein *is* being-in-the-world, it did not exist before Dasein and it belongs to Dasein, who casts it forth as an all-encompassing net within which all things can be made accessible, manifest, and encounterable. In other words the question regarding whether or not a world of physical objects exists is irrelevant if we are not *in it*, because with no world to *be-in*, there is nothing to experience.

For those unfamiliar with the lexicon and style of Martin Heidegger, the concept of *being-in* or the mode of *being-in-the-world* is not to be confused with spatial location. It is not like being *in* Paris, or being *in* my room. When consciousness, as mind, is being-in-the-world, it should be interpreted as being *of* the world, or even more graphic, being *absorbed* into world. And once absorbed, mind and world achieve a relationship of *de facto* identity wherein distinctions between object and subject collapse, where knower and known synthesize into a single unity. Through this relationship of identity, mind essentially *becomes* world, experiencing world *as world*. As Heidegger frames it, "The perception of what is known does not take place as a return with one's booty to the 'cabinet' of consciousness after one has gone out and grasped it."[14]

As such, Dasein is not an object in world – Dasein does not walk through world observing that which is not-Dasein, rather Dasein *is* world through its *being-in*. "Being-in is not a property... It is not the case that human being 'is', and then on top of that has a relation of being-in-the-world."[15] We are surrounded by a world which, like Dasein, always already was, constituting a unity with Dasein while ontologically preceding the distinction between subject and object. By virtue of my experience in and of world, I *am* world, and Manzotti (2017) is correct when he observes that, "Experience lies not inside the body, but rather *is* the world we experience."[16]

Dasein has the ability of experiencing things that it encounters in the world, and it perceives by observation, through the sense modalities, what is objectively present. Heidegger refers to this as *'dealings in the world'* with innerworldly beings, namely things and equipment. Some of these encounterable things are valuable; valuable things are useful because of their utility, and to be useful is to be relevant. To be relevant implies letting something *be-together-with-something-else*, for example letting the nail be together with the hammer, thereby enabling the *possibility* of construction. In Heidegger's view, it is not the things at hand that are relevant in themselves; rather it is the *relationship* between useful things *that makes them relevant*.

Twenty-five years after *Being and Time* was written, the concept of the relationship between things-in-the-world would become one of the essential underpinnings of the philosophy known as Structuralism, which abandons the atomistic perception of the universe in favor of an organic view. For structuralists everything is a system, so a *thing* in the world is defined not by what it is or does but by its relationships with other things. Everything in world is related to everything else. This becomes important when we consider that the limited part of the world that we can encounter within our field of perception, otherwise known as our environment, is actually much more than just a random collection of discrete objects. This organic concept of world harkens back to my earlier discussion of the manner in which the analytic and the continental traditions prefer to consider phenomena, this being a strong example of the continental perception. It is the observable field within the all-encompassing horizon of world in which we are always already *being-in* and *being-of*. As minds in the world, we are ontically constituted by our being-in-the-world.

Heidegger's thought can be challenging not only as we wrestle with his prose, but also with his perspectives. Regarding the subject of world, what is most important to come away with here is the idea that the physical reality surrounding us, our perception of this reality in mind, and the relationship between the two, is a single totality. This is a rationalist concept, but Rationalism is very appropriate when describing this mind/world identity, as Donald Palmer defines it: "Rationalism is the metaphysical view that everything in reality is consistent with everything else in reality, and the view that this logical consistency can be grasped by the human mind because the human mind reflects the logical nature of reality."[17]

The realm of the subjective, meaning our subjective experience – our mind, our consciousness – together with all physical things in the objective realm, comprises a single universal totality. The world is necessary for minds to experience reality, and minds are necessary for reality to be experienced. Phenomenologically, one cannot exist without the other, and this synergy is all that there is. There is nothing beyond it, and nothing without it.

Realms

In the philosophy of mind, the terms 'subjective' and 'objective' are used frequently and can take the form of just about any part of speech. To be sure, anything subjective is in reference to mental phenomena, while the objective characterizes the physical. Some philosophers, such as the logical positivists, hold that the subjective simply doesn't exist, and that only the physical world is real. Physicalists conflate the two mediums in varying forms of mind-brain identity, holding that what we consider to be qualia is only an illusion that will one day be explained by an evolving science. Cartesians are firm in their belief that the two mediums are ontologically irreducible and distinctly separate, while property dualists attempt to account for the problems created by orthodox dualism in positing several hypotheses, wherein the mental emerges or derives from some unknown arrangement of physical matter.

Descartes used the word 'substance' to characterize the subjective and objective mediums, while more contemporary thinkers have referred to them as 'fields', or 'worlds', or else have seen no reason to create the idea of a container at all, simply calling them 'the subjective' and 'the objective'. And finally we have the functionalists, who envision the objective as computer hardware while subjective references take the virtual form of addressable memory – information residing on storage devices or obtained from sensory equipment that must be loaded into virtual memory before it can be operated upon.

The nuances of characterization being what they are, the issue nevertheless reduces to the same age-old question: Are the mental and the physical two distinct properties or only one? If this is how the question is framed, then Portalism belongs to the dualist camp, and I prefer to use the term describing these mediums of reality as 'realms'. There exists a mental subjective realm, as well as a physical objective realm, the main difference between Portalism and Cartesianism being that the locus of subjective realm, as consciousness, is not embodied inside the *res extensa*. In the chapter defending this theory I provide explanations regarding how the two interact causally, and am here only defining the basic nature of each realm.

The Objective Realm

By far the easier of the two distinctions to conceptualize, the objective realm is the physical world, the ontologically irreducible universe of objects and a deterministic physical reality independent of our perception of it, where everything physical that can be encountered, accessed, and experienced exists. Everything in the objective realm is natural by its *being-in* nature, and therefore subject to the laws of physics, extended, and bound to space and time.

Within this realm are five irreducible forces of nature: the strong and weak nuclear forces, electromagnetism, gravity, and Consciousness. The strong and weak forces govern nuclear interactions; electromagnetism acts upon electrically charged particles including chemical bonding; gravity acts on all particles having mass, always attracting and never repelling; Consciousness is the horizon for subjective experience, ubiquitous and universal.

It might seem odd to include the horizon of Consciousness within the physical realm, yet that is where it operates as a fundamental force. Consider that although gravity affects all particles having mass, as a ubiquitous force its range encompasses all areas of space including those devoid of particles. As such it is always already available and accessible. Consciousness is no different, being always already available and accessible to any organism possessed of a functioning portal mechanism. When mass occurs, wherever and however it occurs, gravity manifests. When a portal mechanism physically occurs, wherever and however it occurs, access to Consciousness manifests, this phenomena being immediate, involuntary, autogenic, and invariable, creating an individualized localization of consciousness actualized as mind, residing in the world.

The Subjective Realm

The subjective realm is the universe of experience. Like the objective realm it is ontologically irreducible, but unlike the objective realm it is unbound by space and time; it is indeterministic, unextended, and not subject to the laws of physics.

Based on the description given in the last section, one could argue that the subjective realm is derived from, and even supervenient on, the objective realm, and in a way it is, with the horizon of Consciousness being ubiquitous within the objective universe, always already there, waiting. But this horizon of Consciousness has no content. Only mind can have content, and when that mind is permanently extinguished, its content is lost. The horizon of Consciousness is necessary to the localization of consciousness, and this individualized localization of consciousness, called mind, is the medium of subjective experience – the subjective realm.

I discuss mind in more detail in another chapter, so let it suffice to say that the subjective realm is where both phenomenal and reflexive consciousness are to be found. Phenomenal consciousness is defined as being the awareness of being-in-the-world and of the beings, things, and states of affairs encountered there, while reflexive consciousness is the being aware of being aware, otherwise known as self-awareness. These two consciousnesses together comprise the mind, which is the realm of subjectivity.

The realm of the subjective is also the location where abstracts can be found. Mathematics and symbolic logic (although Bertrand Russell claims that they are the same thing)[18] are purely subjective experiences. Though it is true that the brain holds the memories of how these abstractions can be manipulated, they are not in themselves things in the physical world. They can be actualized only in mind and within the realm of subjective experience.

Direct Realism vs. Representational Realism

One of the oldest debates in modern and contemporary philosophy is that between direct, or naïve, realism and representative realism, and it is inappropriate to offer an explanation of mind without addressing it. The essence of the dispute concerns the visual modality, thus to a blind person whatever conclusion is arrived at would be a moot point. The issue is one of perception. Specifically, when we observe an object in the world, what are we *actually* seeing? Is it the object-*in-itself* or is it the object-*as-itself*? For example, if I perceive a grapefruit, am I seeing the actual grapefruit or am I only seeing a representation of the grapefruit, that is, am I only able to perceive how the grapefruit represents itself to my particular visual modality?

This metaphysical debate, like so many others, bleeds into epistemology, as the question includes *how* we know that this is how a grapefruit really appears. This question of appearance extends to all objects in the world that we encounter. Because of the way that our eyes work, we never really see the grapefruit-in-itself, we only receive wavelengths of light reflected off of the grapefruit's surface, and without light we don't see the grapefruit at all. Nagel's bat 'sees' through sound imaging, thus the grapefruit appears entirely different to the bat from the way a human sees it. So it is with the compound eyes of an insect, or the stalks of a crab that can see in 8,000 directions at once.

Nearly every great thinker has chimed in on this 'Argument from Illusion'. For idealists like Berkeley and Kastrup, who recognize that only mental states exist, the world is exactly as it appears. The common sense realist Thomas Reid would have agreed with them, however, Reid's nemesis David Hume disagreed, holding that all we can ever see are 'impressions' of a thing, and never the thing-in-itself. Descartes and Locke call these impressions 'ideas', while Bertrand Russell named them 'sense data', but as is so often the case, the last word on the subject is often attributed to Immanuel Kant. As per Kant's Transcendental Idealism, we can never see the object-in-itself, what he refers to as the 'noumenal' world, or the world how it *really is*. Through our sensory modalities we are only ever able to perceive a phenomenal world, a picture in our mind that only represents the world as it *appears*. This epistemological dilemma is eloquently framed by John Searle in his book *Seeing Things as They Are*:

> The basic argument in many different forms was the foundation of modern epistemology, where 'modern' means from the seventeenth century on. I have claimed rather briskly that it had disastrous consequences. Why? Notice that the only reality that is accessible to us on this account is the subjective reality of our own private experiences. This makes it impossible to solve the skeptical problem: How, on the basis of perception, can we ever know facts about the world? The problem is insoluble because our only perceptual access is to private subjective experiences, and there is no way to get from the ontologically subjective experiences to the ontologically objective real world.

Searle goes on to offer proof that the Argument From Illusion is based on a fallacy of ambiguity, and holds, if I understand it correctly, that any encounterable object in the physical world intrinsically possesses the causal capacity of causing the experience of that object in the mind of the perceiver. "First, for something to be red in the ontologically objective world is for it to be capable of causing ontologically subjective visual experiences like this. There is an internal relation between the fact of being red and the fact of causing this sort of experience."[19]

At the outset of this book I made it clear that my intent was to address the character of consciousness and not the cognitive or epistemic issues surrounding the content of consciousness. So why do precisely the latter in discussing direct vs. representative realism and the mechanics of perception? Because it is necessary to show that Searle's assertions in his theory of perception are compatible with the concepts of a brain/mind/world totality of consciousness advanced by many phenomenal externalists. Although it seems to support direct realism, Portalism as a theory of consciousness is neutral in the debate because it is entirely compatible with either option. Portalism is not dependent on *how* an object is perceived, only *that* the object is perceived. I, as mind, am the world, and if the *something-that-there-is-to-be-experiencing* of an object happens to be caused by that object's causal capacity to engender the subjective experience of it, then Searle's theory of perception will mesh with Portalism quite elegantly. Thus it would seem that for man, bat, spider or crab, the world is exactly as it objectively presents itself.

Chapter 5

The Portal

Before mind can be actualized, a 'portal' into consciousness is necessary. In discussions of mind as an absolute externality others have described this mechanism of accessibility as a 'link', or 'hook', into Consciousness. I prefer to use 'portal' as it connotes a more flexible entity in terms of the interpretive potential of its hypothetical composition, while the other two terms impart a restrictive simplicity. In short, the word 'portal' just works best for me in terms of visualization.

As I explained in the previous chapter, Consciousness is a fundamental force of nature. The theory of Portalism holds that access to this all-encompassing horizon of Consciousness is realized through a connection, or 'portal', which all living things possess in some form. Once this portal passage is established, an individualized localization of Consciousness is autogenically manifested wherein mind becomes actualized.

Portal connections can be additionally conceptualized as throughways, avenues, bridges, tunnels, paths, or routes – indeed any transportation related term that implies two-way traffic. The importance of this semantic requirement will become apparent later in the section on causality. The portal establishes the connectivity of the *res extensa* into the horizon of Consciousness, creating an external locus of consciousness to which the world is disclosed and made available.

The character of any consciousness in terms of its depth of experience and the width of its reality is determined by the sophistication of its portal. Portals are biological, and being biological they grow and develop. A human baby's consciousness is limited by its underdeveloped portal. Its depth of experience is confined to that which is in its field of perception at the moment, and not yet having an understanding of object permanence, when an object leaves that field it no longer exists. Babies are essentially Berkeleyian idealists in this respect. Whatever they touch goes into their mouths, whatever they hear beyond their mother's voice remains a mystery, and the capacity of their mind for language processing is still in its earliest stages of development. Depth of subjective experience expands commensurate to the development of the portal mechanism.

As an adult, in most cases, the portal is as fully developed as it is going to be, yet it can still be directly enhanced or retarded by drugs, hallucinogens, alcohol, injury, or disease, even to the point of shutting down and closing out consciousness completely, as in the case of being knocked out due to severe trauma, coma, or total anesthesia. Finally, in old age, neurological disorders or disease can degrade portal throughput to the point where the depth of conscious experience is once again no greater than the infant's.

The all-encompassing field of Consciousness, as a ubiquitous force of nature, is constant at all times but devoid of content. Localizations of this field actualized as individual minds have content subjective to the individual agent. The bridging principle between the body and the mind is the portal, thus when the portal becomes impaired or damaged, what is diminished is not Consciousness but the content of consciousness. "Consciousness is consciousness through and through, it can only be limited by itself."[1]

If the locus of mind is outside of the body, if it is not the brain, then a problem concerning how subjective experience arises from or correlates to neural processes goes away. Simply put, the hard problem of consciousness is the problem of explaining how and why physical processes give rise to consciousness. The answer from phenomenal externalism is that they don't, thus as stated there is no problem. That said, it does not mean that externalist explanations do not bring forth problems of their own, but such is the way with philosophy, and it falls to me to present solutions to them. Many of the problems associated with consciousness presuppose that the mind is the brain. Phenomenal externalism overcomes many of those problems by denying their fundamental premise. This does not mean that the brain and nervous system, at least in humans and higher animals, is not an important and necessary element in Portalism, as it absolutely is, only not in the way that physicalism holds that it must be. I will come back to these issues later in the chapters on mind and in the defense of my theory, as for now I will limit myself to a discussion of portal mechanisms in and of themselves.

Portalism is Biocentric

The majority of discussions about consciousness focus primarily on human consciousness. This would seem natural since consciousness, being subjective, can only be discussed by the subject, while the term 'discuss' implies language which is something that only human beings appear to have. Consciously, one can only know one's own mind and never anyone else's. Since I have a body and a mind and I can perceive that other humans have bodies similar to mine, I then have a reasonable expectation in the belief that other bodies also have minds. As Merleau-Ponty observes, "If my consciousness has a body, why should other bodies not 'have' consciousnesses?"[2] I will discuss the problem of other minds in a later chapter, so let us dispense for now with skepticism and solipsism and assume that other minds do indeed exist.

First person experience is an individual phenomenon – only I have actual knowledge of how 'I' feel, and this actuality extends no further than me. Yet third person descriptions of the experiences of others are all too often like my own, so it is upon this environment of similarity that we are able to participate in discussions on human consciousness from firsthand expertise. In the broadest view, each of us understands the *something-like-there-is-to-be* a human as it applies to each of us, and once this is established, that understanding can be projected onto the rest of the species giving us all a reasonable idea of what it is for others to be human by virtue of being human ourselves.

But this claim falls down when we begin to talk about the consciousness of non-humans. Although we might have a good idea of what it is to be like a human being, as Thomas Nagel famously reminds us, we have no idea what it is like to be a bat. Pondering the consciousness of other living things is to speculate based on comparisons to the only minds we are familiar with, these being our own. We can only visualize being a bat by imagining ourselves in a furry bat suit flying about, hanging upside down, and snatching up moths in mid-flight. These are bat behaviors that we have observed, but this is far from *being* a bat. It actually amounts to no more than visualizing ourselves as what we imagine *something-like-there-is-to-be* a bat might be like. We can do no more, and what we are able to do is insufficient to our purposes. This state of affairs is partly the reason that some philosophers and scientists refuse to believe that any non-human life can be conscious, that all of the actions that animals take are somehow essential, innate behaviors. Others grudgingly accept that the higher primates, and perhaps dolphins and whales, might have *some degree* of consciousness, but certainly not extending to self-awareness. Very few would argue that turtles, insects, mollusks, or pine trees have consciousness. I believe that to assume so is not only anthropocentric arrogance, but also unscientific in the sense that the nature of non-human consciousness, or even consciousness simpliciter, cannot be evaluated using human consciousness as the metric. Again, a subjective science is required before any consciousness, including human consciousness, can be explored beyond the level of the hypothetical.

Why does a human experience a wider reality than a snail, or a spider, or a cat? It is certainly not because our perception of reality is superior to the other occupants of our taxonomic tree. Human modalities include sight, sound, smell, taste, and touch. There could be more – blindsight for example – but these five are the ones traditionally attributed to us. Yet in comparison to the general animal kingdom, they are woefully inadequate. For example, a shark can detect blood at one part per million of seawater at a distance of half a kilometer. Cats can discern the tread of a mouse through the pads on their feet. Squirrels can remember the exact locations of over a thousand buried nuts. Dung beetles navigate by the stars. Bats see sound, snakes and lizards can determine the direction of smells through their tongues (tropotaxis), and fish can sense minute changes in water pressure and the magnetic field that indicate the presence of a large body nearby. The list is a long one, but these innate sensory modalities do not in themselves qualify as consciousness. Their function is to provide critical environmental information for evaluation and decision making. It is this process of evaluation – the assignment of meaning and context to data – in combination with the formulation of a decision and the choice of an action taken or not taken, that can only occur in mind.

Considering the higher mammals and birds, if you own a cat or dog, if you raise livestock, or if you are a hunter, it should be readily apparent to you that animals are demonstrably conscious of themselves, other animals, and of their immediate environment. Animals are certainly aware, so what is the difference between their consciousness and ours? With the possible exception of certain species of higher primates, non-human animal consciousness is not reflexive, meaning that they are not aware that they are aware. In addition, they cannot reason abstractly and are unable to determine what is *not* the case. Nevertheless, they are conscious of their surroundings and of their presence in, and their relationship to, those surroundings.

They lead social and emotional lives, they grieve, and they remember. True, non-human animals do not have the language sophistication necessary to communicate subjective experience to one another, but they do reason. Just place a can of tuna on a high shelf and watch the cat work the problem. Or hang a bird feeder from a chain with a rat catcher on it and watch the squirrel strategize, formulate, execute, fail, reformulate, and learn. All of these are examples of intelligence, as they include problem solving, reasoning, planning, and learning. They are also examples of memory. The next time the squirrel sees a fully loaded bird feeder it will attack it using the previous winning strategy first. If this fails due to some modification in the feeder suspension, the squirrel will begin the process of improving its strategy.

Even in lower animals memory is apparent. When I enter my office in the morning and turn on the light, the fish in my aquarium become agitated and rise to the top, expecting to be fed. Admittedly it is only a Pavlovian response, nevertheless they remember and this is observable in their behavior. A spider will construct its web near an outdoor floodlight. If I destroy the web, it will have replaced it within hours in the same location, remembering that the light attracts juicy flying insects at night. With only 100,000 neurons in the average spider's brain, it still remembers. Pets remember their owners, even after lengthy absences, and silverback gorillas recognize other silverback gorillas that they have not seen in years.

All animals have some procedural memory; how to bury nuts, how to swim, how to spin a web. But these examples are also indicative of explicit memory, particularly episodic memory. The squirrel remembers where the nuts are; the spider remembers that the light comes on at night; the cat understands that to get to the tuna first requires a jump onto the counter, followed by a leap to the top of the refrigerator. Memory is the retention of information over time for the purpose of influencing future action. In human beings, memory is stored in neurons at different locations in the brain. The neurons that fired when I first saw the Eiffel Tower (immediate episodic memory) are the same neurons that fire when I recall that event (mediate memory/reflexive consciousness). The brain captures and maintains a memory, assigning it a chronological time stamp, for example, when I first saw the Eiffel Tower in person it was *after* Reagan was president but *before* I bought my 2006 Mustang. Within this same process the brain establishes ties to other related memories, as when I was at the Eiffel Tower I was with my wife; it was a sunny April day, and I held her hand as we walked together down the Champs de Mars.

Although the brain is responsible for information storage, memory retrieval is initiated from within mind, and the experience of any recalled mediate memory occurs entirely in consciousness. The brain serves as the database and storage unit, while the actualization of the retrieved memory is a mental state external to the brain. Consciousness is a necessary condition for memory cognition. If we accept the previous definition that memory is the retention of information over time for the purpose of influencing future action, then memory presupposes consciousness. Granted, these memory processes will have differing levels of dynamics and capacities dependent upon the sophistication of the brain and its portal mechanism, but this is not sufficient reason for rejecting consciousness in non-human life.

Having addressed memory in animals I turn now to communication, another property that affirms consciousness. Humans have language and communicate through speech and signing; however, communication is not language, as language implies infinite combinations of syntax and semantics that simple communication does not possess. But what is *functionally* important is that information gets exchanged. If a squirrel sees a cat it will bark a warning unmistakably interpreted by other squirrels and even other forest animals as the presence of a threat. Dolphins and whales are highly communicative, with some research even pointing to rudimentary language constructs. Birdsong can be highly communicative, as can dog barks and the attitude of a cat's tail. The fact is that the methodological process of interpretation, decoding, and the ultimate assignment of meaning to audiovisual input data occurs *in mind* – the brain can't do it. Through its sensory modalities the brain certainly gathers the audiovisual data of communication, but it is not capable of rising to the level of cognition. Language and communication presuppose consciousness.

Finally, consider the lower animals on the taxonomic scale. How can consciousness possibly be attributed to them? Remember that the key lies in the abandonment of preconceived anthropocentric assumptions about what constitutes mind. For example, the inchworm crawling up my arm is a miracle of biology and chemistry – millions of specialized cells working harmoniously in their inchwormness. If I bar its way with my finger it will rise upon its little back feet and begin looking for an alternate path. It will try one, then another, perhaps eventually climbing onto the finger itself. This is indicative of problem solving, and the inchworm is certainly conscious, for if it were not there would be no way in which it could navigate its reality as without consciousness it would have no reality to navigate. Reality can only be experienced subjectively, and to experience the world requires consciousness. That which is unconscious experiences nothing. The reality of the inchworm is certainly limited in comparison to higher life forms, yet even that limited reality is nevertheless subjectively experienced. The inchworm concerns itself with little more in life than finding food and avoiding death at the hands of its predators long enough to transform itself into a moth and lay its eggs. For this it depends upon its sensory modalities and the processing of sensory input. That which passes for the inchworm's brain collects the data through its sense modalities, but the subsequent processing of that data into that which stands for inchworm information requires a mind, primitive though it may be by human standards. How conscious is the inchworm? The inchworm is as conscious as inchworms need to be.

It is not difficult to extend these same characterizations of animal consciousness onto paramecium, hydra, or single celled life such as amoebas and bacteria. Even with only a single cell, these animals are possessed with *microbial intelligence*, and the presence of intelligence presupposes consciousness. The conclusion is that even single celled animals must therefore be conscious to at least some degree. To be sure, the content of an amoeba's subjective reality may consist of no more than a binary proposition determining that a contact is [food] or [not-food]; together with a biochemical flag that indicates when it is time to split in two. Having abandoned using human experiential parameters as the metric, it becomes reasonable to accept that the character of consciousness can come to us in many forms. As summarized by Chalmers, "Where there is simple information processing, there is simple experience, and where there is complex information processing, there is complex experience."[3]

Another Green World

Portalism holds that portal mechanisms inhere in all living organisms and that therefore all living organisms have consciousness. Having addressed the animal kingdom in the last section, I now make the same argument for the consciousness of plants. It is over this distinction that even the most radical thinkers often draw the line by rejecting any idea that plant consciousness can exist, even though recent advances in plant neurobiology tell a different story. When we examine arguments denying that plant consciousness is possible, we often uncover the appeal to anthropocentric speciesism. But just as it is within the animal hierarchy, the case for plant consciousness is dependent upon one's definition, and when we formulate this definition we must take care not to fall into the trap of using human consciousness as the comparative metric. The concept of plant consciousness is certainly not new. Writings from as far back as Empedocles and Pythagoras discuss plants having 'souls', and we are certainly free to interpret this concept in the Cartesian sense wherein 'soul' and 'consciousness' become synonymous terms. In this section I will make the argument that plant consciousness is certainly within the realm of plausibility.

In 2015 the Italian botanist Stefano Mancuso gave an interesting TED Talk entitled *Are Plants Conscious?* He describes how humans can be prone to 'plant blindness' when surveying their immediate environment.[4] Due to human evolutionary adaptations that assign a greater threat status to animals over plants, it is other animals that we tend to focus on and in the process plants become background – meaning that we "do not see the green stuff" – yet plants comprise 99.7% of all biomass on the planet. The fact that we generally do not consider the question of plant consciousness is not hard to understand, as plants are comprehensively different than animals, being sessile and having no organs, causing them to often be dismissed as objects of the merest instrumental value; fuel to burn, wood to build with, or fruit to eat. I believe that to consider them so amounts to ignorance on our part. Especially since, as Prof. Mancuso illustrates, plants can see without eyes, hear without ears, touch without hands, smell without noses, and communicate without speech.

In elegant fashion, Mancuso makes a compelling case for plant consciousness, predicated on an argument similar to one that I used previously in making the case for the lower animals, which is that intelligence presupposes consciousness. Mancuso defines intelligence as the ability to solve problems, and submits several experiments that demonstrate how plants go about doing just that. To begin, plants are indisputably aware of their environment. This awareness extends to air and soil temperature, air pressure, humidity, the direction in which gravity points, soil chemistry (salt content in particular), electrical and magnetic fields, and the proximity of other plants. They are sensitive to light and put leaves and pine cones in motion in response to it. What is the human ability to see if not a sensitivity to this same light? Based upon the angle on the sun, plants can calculate the time of year. To do this requires some form of memory. Plants are sensitive to vibrations, and experiments with seedling roots show that they alter their downward path of growth toward the source of the vibration. What is human hearing if not the interpretation of vibrations, such as that of a guitar string being plucked?

In a particularly compelling experiment Mancuso places a pole equidistant between two bean plants in an otherwise empty room. Using time lapse photography, we see the plants begin to grow 'feelers' called tendrils that begin moving in sweeping arcs as they search for a contact to latch on to, but the plant on the left sends its tendril to the right, while the plant on the right sends its tendril to the left. How do they know where the pole is? This is the equivalent of human blindsight, wherein a blind person will reach in the correct direction for an apple that they cannot possibly see. Yet they 'sense' that it is there. This is likely because although the blind person and the plant are both deprived of eyesight, they are nevertheless still connected to the world. When the plant on the left finally makes contact with the pole it secures it. What is compelling about this experiment is that when the plant on the right eventually locates the pole, it somehow understands that there is already another plant secured to it and sends its tendril off to search for an unclaimed pole – in essence, feeling without hands.

Plants are also social. They are capable of 'kin recognition' – the awareness of plants nearby that are their own progeny as well as plants that may not be relations but are of the same species. Subsequently their behavior manifests as cooperation versus competition, which is exactly the same behavior we note in animals competing for the same limited resources. The ecologist Ariel Novoplansky of Ben-Gurion University expands on this in a 2012 TED Talk entitled *Learning Plant Learning* wherein he describes the ability of plants to warn each other of impending danger or experiences.[5] When attacked by disease or insects many plants begin to manufacture chemical deterrents. In order to alert other plants in the vicinity of the impending danger, they pass information via gas exchange through their stomata. Once another plant receives this gas warning it begins to generate defense enzymes in anticipation of the attack. If we frame this in human terms, the delightful aroma of my mother's apple pie and the repellant odor of gasoline amount to no more than this same inhalation of gas, using olfactory nerves in place of plant stomata – smelling without noses. These are clearly examples of problem solving, and "if we consider intelligence as the ability to solve and overcome problems, we have to recognize that plants possess it, and it is intelligence that allows plants to develop and respond to most of the problems that they encounter throughout their ontogenesis."[6]

In referencing the research of these scientists I have accounted for how plants see, hear, touch, and smell, but how they communicate can be even more impressive. When we walk through a field and observe a stand of cottonwood trees we might think that we are seeing five or six individual trees, but the reality is that we are actually looking at one big 'tree'. This is because we see only the surficial representation of the trees and not the massively extensive network of roots that lies underneath, and it is below the surface that a plant's neural equivalent of animal brains and nervous systems can be found. Peter Wohlleben, the German forester and ecologist, also argues that trees are capable of subjective experience. In his book *The Hidden Life of Trees*, he explains how tree societies are facilitated through their roots, capable of nutrient exchanges, communication, and kin recognition. These root systems extend more than double the spread of a tree's crown, intersecting with and growing into the roots of their neighbors. The roots penetrate into dense communities of fungal colonies called hyphae, which form vegetative networks collectively known as mycelium. Wohlleben describes it best:

> These fungi operate like fiber-optic Internet cables. Their thin filaments penetrate the ground, weaving through it in almost unbelievable density. One teaspoon of forest soil can contain many miles of these hyphae. Over centuries, a single fungus can cover many square miles and network an entire forest. The fungal connections transmit signals from one tree to the next, helping the trees exchange news about insects, drought, and other dangers.[7]

It is difficult to overlook the functional similarity between the plant/mycelium system and the synaptic/neural network of the animal nervous system. For example, envisioning a teaspoon of soil containing many miles of hyphae is not unlike imagining the 100 billion neurons in the human brain, or understanding the explanation of information transmission across this fungal network as being comparable to a biologically realistic connectionist model of a neural network. Some might argue that an equivalence between the mechanics of the fungal/root symbiosis, otherwise known as a mycorrhizal association, and the synaptic/neural networks of animals is inappropriate, as a neural network can transmit information from the little toe to the brain in about 120 milliseconds at roughly 275 mph, while information passing from roots to branches, or to other trees, can take hours, even days. This would be a fair objection if I was claiming identity, or that one system is in some manner more efficient or powerful than the other, but my claim is only that they are *functionally* similar.

Although I discuss temporality at greater length later on, in regard to the significant difference in transmission rate between neural and fungal networks, I would submit that is not unreasonable to consider that plants experience time quite differently from animals. All objects in the physical world are bound in space and time, but if we are considering time by the Newtonian definition, its linear 'flow' will be at a very different rate for plants than for animals. At some point in evolution certain cell communities decided that motility was unnecessary for propagation and nutrition, and these organisms became sessile. Although both animal and plant kingdoms are intricately codependent, their very natures are radically different in nearly every way, perhaps the most obvious being that one breathes oxygen and expels carbon dioxide while the other does precisely the opposite. All objects in space have relative positions and directions, but with plants being sessile their spatial experience is nothing like that of the motile animals (not all animals are motile – corals for example) and are certainly nothing like the experience of human beings. Since the spatial experience of plants is so radically different from that of most animals, wouldn't it be reasonable to assume that a similar inequality applies to their concept of time?

The Case for Consciousness throughout the Zone of Life

The term 'intelligence' is critical to the claim that at least some degree of consciousness inheres in all living things. In the interests of clarity I will define the term 'intelligence' as the capacity for logic, understanding, learning, reasoning, planning, and problem solving; and the term 'mind' as the medium of subjective experience. The capacities of intelligence can only be actualized in mind, and there is nothing unconscious that is intelligent. The degree of intelligence enjoyed by any organism is correlative to its capacity for subjective experience, which in turn is dependent upon the level of sophistication of its portal into Consciousness. The more sophisticated the portal mechanism of an organism, the higher the capacity for mental content, and the greater the possibilities for intelligence.

In the previous sections I provided examples that indicated the capacity for problem solving, planning, and communication throughout the animal and plant kingdoms, while learning and reason, by human definitions, are apparently limited to the higher animals. These traits all substantiate intelligence. But how does this constitute consciousness?

In answering, I would submit that the grounds for assigning consciousness to all living things, from human beings to algae, must depend upon one's definition. If to be conscious is to be self-aware, to have language, to think abstractly, or to create art, then the answer would be no, as these are no more than rigid anthropocentric properties. Portalism holds that consciousness, as the ability to experience reality, is inherent in all living things. To be living is the condition that distinguishes organisms from inorganic objects and dead organisms; living being manifested by growth through metabolism, reproduction, and the power of adaptation to environment through changes originating internally. In all forms of life metabolism and reproduction require, at a minimum, the intelligent capabilities of problem solving. To solve problems a thing must first experience its reality, as it is that reality that furnishes the problems to be overcome, and there can be no experience outside of consciousness. No matter how primitive or sophisticated an organism's reality might be, that organism must be conscious in order to navigate that reality. Therefore all living things are conscious by definition.

In reference to the examples and arguments presented in the previous sections:

P1. All living things are capable of problem solving.
P2. Problem solving presupposes intelligence.
P3. Intelligence presupposes consciousness.
C1. All living things are conscious.

Aside from how advanced or primitive a plant or animal might be, by virtue of its portal mechanism consciousness inheres in all living things and is the necessary condition for subjective experience. The depth of an organism's phenomenal experience is dependent upon the sophistication of its portal mechanism, which is sufficient to each organism's ability to navigate its reality. In light of this wide diversity of a given organism's capacity for subjective experience, all living things are as conscious as they need to be.

Portal Differentiation – Neural Chauvinism Rejected

Portalism claims that all living things possess a portal into consciousness. This portal ability is an innate property of all living organisms, and as such this portal mechanism can take many different biological and/or biochemical forms. Plant portal structures will be radically different than those of animals, and animal portal structures will vary widely depending on the sophistication of the species.

The purpose of the portal is to enable the organism to access Consciousness, the fundamental force of nature, thereby creating a localization of consciousness exclusive to that organism which is actualized as mind. As previously stated, the portal is the bridging principle that ties the *res extensa*, being the physical body, to mind. Neuroscientific research, together with common sense, would seem to point to the locus of the portal being within the brain, at least in the higher animals, more specifically as some element or composition of elements within the central nervous system. But where within the nervous system does the portal actually reside? Descartes suggested that it might be the pineal gland, which he mistakenly determined was the seat of the soul, where its actual function is to receive information about light/dark cycles from the environment and subsequently pass information on for melatonin secretion. It is much more likely that the portal is not some hidden organ as we might be prone to visualize, rather that it is a composition of biological structures and sympathetic chemical processes that cause the body to become sensitive to Consciousness. As a force of nature, Consciousness acts upon all bodies, the same as gravity and electromagnetism do, and as with those forces if a body is in a position to be receptive to Consciousness, meaning that its portal is functional and not traumatized or diseased, then a localization of consciousness is autogenically manifested, and the possibilities of subjective experience become available to that body. Nothing more than that need take place. If a body jumps off the roof it will fall downwards toward the gravitational center of the earth because it is in the range of gravity. By the same principle, if a body has an operative portal mechanism, it will be conscious, as it is in the range of Consciousness. A body's responsiveness to Consciousness is no more unusual than its responsiveness to gravity, there is no choice in the matter, it being a persistent aspect of nature and an omnipresent dynamic in the world.

Most animals have brains, even insects (250,000 neurons in an ant), and arachnids (100,000 neurons in a spider). Some social animals, like ants or bees, can also attain a collective intelligence. Collective intelligence is a shared intelligence that emerges from the collaboration of many individual minds and appears in consensus decision making. Some collective ant intelligences can even approach the number of neurons as large as the brains of many mammals. A bird's brain comprises 1.3 percent of its total body weight and even earthworms have a bi-lobed brain ganglion with 302 neurons. But even in the light of neurological evidence it would be a mistake to claim that all portals are elements of brains, as although most animals have brains, some do not. For example, jellyfish and sponges are animals without brains – sponges have no nervous system at all while jellyfish have a rudimentary 'ring' of neurons which govern their ability to swim. Like plants most sponges are sessile. They are built to pump water and do very little else, but they can develop toxins that discourage predators, which is a form of problem solving. Nevertheless, a sponge's reality is likely on a par with that of protozoa which could make it a candidate for microbial intelligence. Having no nervous system, the sponge's portal would likely be a purely biochemical construct, facilitating a subjectivity capable of realizing no more content than the binary reality of the amoeba.

In the previous discussion of the plant root/fungi symbiosis I drew a functional equivalence between these networks and synaptic/neural networks, and I should point out that these mycorrhizal associations extend to submerged plants as well. If these fungal networks *function* in roughly the same manner as animal neural networks in terms of information exchange and mediate memory retrieval, then it would not be unreasonable to posit that they can also function as plant portals into Consciousness. Again, what is important regarding portal mechanisms is not their anatomical structure, but their bridging functionality.

Having abductively speculated on the possibilities of portal locations in plants and animals, I turn now to the protist kingdom. Regarding taxonomic kingdoms, there is disagreement among biologists as to their number and content, with candidates ranging from Aristotle's two kingdoms all the way up to eight kingdoms or more. The point of contention appears to center upon different kinds of microscopic chromista, bacteria, and protozoa, as well as a disagreement on fungi being a part of the plant kingdom at all. As the focus of this book is metaphysics and not the nuances of taxonomy, for the purposes of expediency I will proceed by embracing the three kingdom concept as established by Ernst Haeckel in 1866, which does consider fungi within the plant kingdom. Haeckel also combines chromista, protozoa, and bacteria into the 'protist' kingdom, which better suits my purposes, as the subjective reality of these non-animal/non-plant living things has in essence already been speculated upon in the previous discussion of the amoeba. Accordingly, I render apologies to any taxonomists who might hold themselves aggrieved by this decision.

The living organisms in the protist kingdom are possessed of microbial intelligence, defined by John Rennie as the concept encompassing complex adaptive behavior shown by single cells, and altruistic or cooperative behavior in populations of like or unlike cells mediated by chemical signaling that induces physiological or behavioral changes in cells and influences colony structures. As Dr. Rennie observes:

There is no reason to think that bacteria, slime molds, and similar single-cell forms of life have awareness, understanding or other capacities implicit in real intellect. But particularly when these cells commune in great numbers, their startling collective talents for solving problems and controlling their environment emerge. Those behaviors may be genetically encoded into these cells by billions of years of evolution, but in that sense the cells are not so different from robots programmed to response in sophisticated ways to their environment. If we can speak of artificial intelligence for the latter, perhaps it's not too outrageous to refer to the underappreciated cellular intelligence of the former.

The slime mold Physarum polycephalum sometimes barely qualifies as a microorganism at all: When it oozes across the leaf litter of a forest floor during the active, amoeboid stage of its life cycle, Physarum is a huge single cell, with tens of thousands of nuclei floating in an uninterrupted mass of cytoplasm. In this form, Physarum is a superbly efficient hunter. When sensors on its cell membrane detect good sources of nutrients, contractile networks of proteins start pumping streams of cytoplasm in that direction, advancing the slime mold toward what it needs.

But Physarum is not just reflexively surging toward food. As it moves in one direction, signals transmitted throughout the cell discourage it from pushing counterproductively along less promising routes. Moreover, slime molds have evolved a system for essentially mapping their terrain and memorizing where not to go: As they move, they leave a translucent chemical trail behind that tells them which areas are not worth revisiting.[8]

Keep in mind that, at a minimum, what we are looking for is intelligence, as intelligence is the single common denominator that through logical presupposition leads us to consciousness in all living things. The example given above describes problem solving capabilities in even the simplest forms of life. So what form would a portal take for these dwellers of the microscopic world? Like the lowly sponge, it would likely consist of a biochemical composition, and like the lowly sponge, the subsequent possibilities for subjective experience and mental content would manifest at the most primitive levels.

The examples above describe hypothetical possibilities for the many diverse forms that the biological/biochemical construct of a portal mechanism could take, and it is this same diversity that confirms Portalism as a theory that rejects neural chauvinism. As all living things are conscious so all living things have portals, and it is the *function* of the portal that is relevant, more so than a description of its mechanics. As to this latter I would simply note that as portals exist within the physical realm, the discovery of their exact characterization is a challenge I gladly lay at the feet of science.

Portalism is Compatible with Functionalism

I have previously claimed that inorganic matter is unable to form the portals necessary for the connection to Consciousness and ultimately for the actualization of mind. To a functionalist, being concerned with process over composition, this statement could raise interesting possibilities. For the higher animals, certainly for human beings, neurophysical evidence overwhelmingly points to the brain and/or the nervous system as the most probable locus for a portal into Consciousness, but it does not have to be so, as one could argue that portal theory does not necessarily presuppose a biological origin. Theoretically a portal is necessary for any living thing to access Consciousness, but any mechanism that accomplishes this function should be admissible, be it biological, chemical, electrical, mechanical, or even perhaps ethereal. In the view of the functionalist, it is access to the horizon of Consciousness that is of interest, and not the integral workings of the mechanism itself.

From the standpoint of theory, Portalism is completely compatible with functionalism. It is also free from neural chauvinism and compatible with multiple realizability, as there could hypothetically be any number of functional portal constructs. I have stated that all living things are to some degree conscious as only living things can develop the biological portal into Consciousness, this connection being necessary and sufficient for mind to be actualized. A machine functionalist could argue that if neuroscience were to isolate the portal mechanism and map its operational mechanics, then it would be reasonable to believe that its function could be synthesized. If portal functionality can be synthesized, then it should follow that this synthesized portal could be placed within a computer, a robot, or any other non-living system and that in doing so that system could obtain access to Consciousness.

As any new theory of mind requires a good thought experiment, let us pursue this one. If we have a robot computer brain with a synthetic portal that successfully accesses the horizon of Consciousness, does this actualize mind? To explore this one needs to examine one's definition of 'mind', as it might be a rush to judgement to hold that although the robot portal into Consciousness should be sufficient to autogenically manifest a localized consciousness, is this enough to also *actualize* mind? Is the case of mechanical consciousness equivalent to the case of biological consciousness? In other words, functionally speaking, is the portal sufficient for actualizing mind, or is some other element required? Even if we agree that robot consciousness is present, is this sufficient for the realization of subjective experience, of intentionality, beliefs and feelings?

My answer would be that although the robot is conscious, it possesses only the *possibility* for subjective experience, as being lifeless it remains unable to connect with the world around it, and so would always have a conscious possibility but without content. Phenomenal experience requires a dynamic relationship to the world, a *being-in-the-world*, which all living things always already are. Thus the robot may exist in an ontic physical sense, but never in a phenomenal one. Noë states that experience encompasses "thinking, feeling, and the fact that a world 'shows up' for us in perception."[9] Never being-in-the-world, the world never 'shows up' to the robot 'mind'. A connection to Consciousness merely makes subjective experience a theoretical possibility, but mental content requires more. As living things, "we are not merely recipients of external influences, but are creatures built to receive influences that we ourselves enact; we are dynamically coupled with the world, not separate from it."[10] Through a portal, the possibilities of experience become available, but the robot cannot manifest subjective experience because it has no means to transcend its own objectivity. It can walk through the world identifying and evaluating things that are not-robot, but its sensory modalities are only processing an external reality that it cannot experience or cognate without *being-in*. To use an example from Chalmers in reference to partial zombies, "when it sees a flower it might gain certain abilities to recognize and discriminate, although even these will be severely constrained since they cannot involve experience."[11] Such it is to sense without experiencing. The motion detector on my garage detects my approach and turns the light on, but it cannot experience my presence, and it cannot associate any meaning, contextual or otherwise, to its own action. The robot therefore amounts to no more than equipment ready-to-hand, a Chalmersian zombie, with its mental possibilities present yet eternally empty and devoid of content.

As far as this philosophical topic goes, I am in agreement with John Searle's position that a machine will never be capable of subjective experience, and I further believe that the best result one could hope for would be one of David Chalmers' philosophical zombies. Still, if Portalism is true and a functional portal could be mapped and synthesized, strictly speaking a robot or computer could hypothetically achieve a *potential* mind. Although I am no functionalist, I can nevertheless accept this possibility on the basis that it would be conscious beings creating these synthetic portals. After all, Consciousness, as a force of nature, is always already available to anyone or anything capable of accessing it. But I would still reject that a portal could ever manifest itself naturally within inorganic material – a rock for instance – for if it could, then we would have essentially returned full circle to panpsychism.

Summary

In this section I have made the claim that all living things are conscious. I have argued, largely through analogy, that at some level all organisms demonstrate problem solving and therefore meet the criteria for intelligence. The major premise in my argument is that intelligence presupposes consciousness, and my conclusion is that all things, being intelligent to some degree, are therefore conscious. I believe that this argument is cogent if not sound, and I will offer a more comprehensive defense of this theory in a later chapter.

I have also claimed that to be living is to be navigating one's reality, as, "All consciousness is consciousness of something."[12] Everything that lives is *in* the world and experiences the world through its *being-in*. Whether human or inchworm, all living things experience reality, and to experience reality one must be conscious. Therefore living things, as organic systems, are conscious by definition.

Also in this section I have offered numerous examples of plants, animals, and even microorganisms carrying out actions that meet the criteria defining intelligence. On the premise that intelligence presupposes consciousness, and as per the theory of Portalism, these organisms must then have biological and/ or biochemical portal mechanisms as such mechanisms are necessary to consciousness. It may appear that I have committed a composition error in holding that what is the case for some is the same case for all, but I think not, as the examples I provide cover both advanced and primitive species and thereby should apply equally to the universal.

The mind-body problem and the hard problem of consciousness demand theories that are within the realm of possibility and that provide significant explanatory power based on defensible plausibility. I believe that phenomenal externalist theories give philosophers of mind the greatest amount of blue sky to work with toward the development of theories capable of meeting those challenges, and I think that Portalism is one of them. Consciousness lies outside waiting, and the portal is our bridge to the mind.

Chapter 6

The Brain

The beauty of thinking about the brain and human experience is that it enables us to appreciate why the brain is vitally necessary for human experience without treating the brain as if it possessed magical powers.
Alva Noë[1]

As Teed Rockwell correctly observes, "There is no question that brains are an essential part of the puzzle, but there is also no reason to assume that they are the entire puzzle."[2] If consciousness is not the brain, then how is the brain important to Portalism and what role does it play? In the interests of expediency when I refer to 'brain' in this section I am including the entire central nervous system. As advances in neuroscience and neurotechnology offer reasonable indications that the locus of the portal mechanism in humans is most likely in the brain, this chapter will confine its scope to the set of higher animals. For a discussion of the possibilities of alternative portal constructs in lower animals and the plant and protist kingdoms, please refer to the previous chapter.

Although the brain can be a fascinating subject, I will not be leading the reader through fathomless pages of neuroscientific data and research. I make this decision for two reasons: mainly that not being a neuroscientist myself I am decidedly unqualified to do so, and secondly because it appears that the vast majority of scientists consumed by neuroscience, neurotechnology, neurophilosophy, and neurobiology tend to initiate their search for the neural correlates of consciousness from the presupposition that the mind is the brain. As a result they are frequently disappointed when their results are inconsistent or fail to provide the evidence that they are convinced must be there. So there is little purpose in presenting detailed examples of neuroscientific research, if its results are not reliable due to its bedrock assumption being in error. To be sure, any attempt to map subjective experience to neural correlates is certain to be a daunting task, as Raymond Tallis observes in his example of perceiving a red tomato: "There is nothing red or even red-like about neural discharges in the pathways associated with vision in the cerebral cortex, so how could they be identical with the experience?"[3]

An argument could be made that starting experimentation with any hypothesis based upon the assumption of mind-brain identity is not good science to begin with, as it is akin to making facts fit within a preconceived theory as opposed to formulating a theory based upon facts. An example of this is the research being done on Readiness Potential (RP). In one experiment a student was asked to move a hand in one direction or another. Presented as a measurable electrical change in the brain that precedes an act we choose to make, RP was held to be a marker that conscious decisions are actually determined unconsciously beforehand. But there were problems found in both the experimental premise as well as the conduct of the experiments that raised legitimate questions regarding conclusions not being supported by the results. And in any case, "the RP demonstrates that the expected brain activity always occurs before a decision but does not reveal the result of the decision."[4] It is not fair to condemn an entire field of scientific inquiry on the basis of a few questionable experiments, but when it comes to empirical science making claims about consciousness, and particularly when those claims exhibit a bias toward mind-brain identity, it is critical that the science behind those claims be examined with rigor.

This is not to say that physicalism is false, as the externalist theories of Manzotti (2017) and Honderich (2017) present plausible explanations of consciousness that require no departure from physicalism, but it does indicate that physicalist theories based on mind-brain identity are not the case. Cutting edge imaging technologies have often been interpreted as demonstrable proof that consciousness is a function of the brain, but this is misleading. As the enactivist and cognitive neuroscientist at Berkeley, Alva Noë, frames it, "The pictures we see in the science magazines are not snapshots of a particular person's brain in action. It is important to be clear that there is no sense in which PET or fMRI pictures deliver direct information about consciousness or cognition. They do not even deliver direct representations of neural activity."[5]

If readers still wish to immerse themselves in a discussion regarding developments in neuroscience and their relation to externalist philosophy, I recommend Alva Noë's book *Out of Our Heads* for a very readable account. For now I shall return to my description of the role of the brain in the theory of Portalism.

What the Brain Does

While the brain may be necessary but not sufficient for consciousness, it remains absolutely essential to Portalism for many reasons, the most important one being that it keeps the body alive. When the body dies, the brain dies, and when the brain dies the portal closes and the localization of individual consciousness is thereby dissolved with the result that the mind vanishes. It is here that Portalism rejects Cartesian dualism, which holds that the mind, the *res cogitans* or 'soul', exists within the body but continues on after corporeal death. In Portalism, the locus of the mind is external to, yet existentially dependent upon, the brain. Even if the brain is eventually found *not* to house the portal mechanism, whatever biological and/ or biochemical constructs *do* compose the portal must remain dependent upon the body, as they will continue to be embodied physical objects.

The homeostatic responsibilities of the brain are therefore essential, as they keep the body alive and the portal intact. These include temperature regulation, body fluid composition, blood sugar levels, gas concentrations, blood pressure and many more. As mind exists external to the brain, it can have an effect upon the conditions of the body via downward causality, for example in seeing a scorpion that might raise the blood pressure and heart rate, yet mind cannot directly interfere with the brain's causal regulatory response to that physical stimulus. In fact, although the brain has no determinative power over mind, its determinative power over the body is absolute, and in an existential crisis its actions will ultimately take precedence over mind.

For example, if I am mountain climbing at high altitudes and my extremities begin to freeze, the brain will shut off blood flow to my hands and feet, redirecting it in the interests of self-preservation to itself and the major organs. As mind, I may *will* the brain not to do this, but it does no good; the brain's priority for self-preservation overrides the will in all cases. Even when I eventually fall unconscious and collapse into the snow, the brain will continue to execute its homeostatic responsibilities until it finally freezes to death. The mind has no direct influence over the homeostatic responses of the brain, although willing oneself to breathe slowly and deeply can affect blood oxygen and heart rate, which might be causes of the homeostatic regulation that the brain is responding to. These regulatory responses have evolved through time, the brain relentlessly monitoring the body and continually making adjustments regardless of whether or not the mind is even operational. In extreme cases involving great pain or trauma, the brain can shut the portal down completely, incurring unconsciousness, while still continuing on with its homeostatic mission until injury overwhelms it or it runs out of fuel.

Aside from regulating the body, the brain is responsible for the operation and maintenance of the senses. Whether these are the human modalities of sight, hearing, touch, smell, and taste, the radar of Nagel's bat, or the forked tongue of the lizard, the brain maintains these sense organs but is incapable of formulating any understanding of that which is sensed. The assignment of meaning and context to sensory input occurs in mind. For example, the ears detect the sounds emitted from another human being. The operational mechanics of the tympanic membrane, the stapes, and the cochlear nerve send impulses to the brain, but the cognition of language – the decoding and interpretation of sounds – occurs in mind. The brain only receives the auditory impulses; it does not have any ability to assign meaning to them. The recognition of certain sounds as speech and its interpretation according to syntactic and semantic rules stored in procedural memory, the subsequent understanding of the sounds as words and the formulation of any response as per that understanding, occur entirely in mind.

Imagine that you are playing baseball and are up to bat. You observe the incoming ball and must decide to swing or not to swing. The split second you consciously decide to swing, the brain orders the release of the acetylcholine necessary to contract the muscles that enable you to swing the bat at the ball. The mind does not consciously initiate and regulate the process of acetylcholine release, or any of the other internal processes incessantly occurring as per the regulatory mission of the brain. By the same token the brain has no idea when to swing the bat, neither is it cognizant of why the bat needs to be swung at all, because it cannot think.

The brain stores, catalogs, and links memories, retrieving and passing them to mind for experiencing, either on demand or as a response to a stimulus in the world. The neurons that fire the first time the immediate memory is created and stored are the same neurons that fire when it is mediately retrieved.

But the subjective experience of a memory, and the cognition of its context and meaning, is a function of mind; the brain can't do it. Using the computer metaphor favored by machine functionalists, the memory, as stored data, is time-stamped and resides on a disk or an SSD. When requested, it must be retrieved and loaded into addressable memory before anything creative can be done with it.

Consider what happens during unconsciousness, as when the portal closes in the case of total anesthesia. Although there has been some promising research of late, scientists remain uncertain as to exactly how general anesthesia works. The prevailing school of thought is that it weakens or otherwise impairs the transmission of electrical signals between synapses. From the standpoint of Portalism, what is important is not the mechanics of general anesthesia but the fact that it effectively causes the portal to shut down completely. There is no subjective experience at all, not even dreaming, because if the portal is down, then there is no localization of Consciousness and therefore no mind. If there is no mind then there is no experience, and without experiencing there can be no ascertainable change, so effectively even time stops. Yet the senses still operate, as does the rest of the body although the brain itself functions in a state of diminished neural activity. So even as the surgeon's scalpel may cut deep, and the nociceptor neurons that respond to noxious high-intensity stimuli are properly firing in response, no sensory information is being causally transmitted to the mind, whether as pain or anything else. The portal is closed, thus the mind is unavailable. If during anesthesia the operating room should grow cold enough to drop the body's internal temperature, the brain may still respond homeostatically, but 'you' – as mind – will never 'know' that you are cold. In terms of the subjective 'self' under total anesthesia, you – as mind – are essentially, if only temporarily, dead.

The Relationship of Brain and Portal

Throughout this work I sometimes use the terms 'pass' or 'passing' when describing the movement of processed sensory data from the brain to the mind, and conversely mental acts of agency that originate in the mind subsequently moving to the brain. Although 'passing' might create the mental picture of a causal flow of information or willful agency between the physical and subjective entities, I want to be crystal clear in stating that although this image may be *functionally* correct, nothing is actually being passed 'through' the portal. The portal is a biological mechanism, not a tunnel with one end in the New York brain and the other in the New Jersey mind. Although such a tunnel, or any other transportation metaphor, accurately describes Portalism's bidirectional causal pathways, it is no more than that – a metaphor. The portal is the bio-mechanism through which sensory data, after being filtered and processed by the brain, becomes disclosed to mind. At the same time, it is the same bio-mechanism through which mental agency in the form of decisions and intentions (swinging the bat) are disclosed by the mind to the brain. These events of disclosure are instantaneous; there is no time lag waiting for these data to be 'passed' along some pipeline-like structure – and to suppose that such a construct actually exists, despite how one may choose to envision it, would be incorrect.

As I will describe in greater detail in the chapter on mind, merely having a functional portal autogenically manifests mind – there are no other preconditions. The locus of mind is external to the body; therefore it is in the world. Through its *being-in*, mind discloses the world to the sensory modalities of the brain, through which objects and states of affairs within the world are made encounterable to mind. Any conceptualization that would involve information exchanged from eye to brain, then physically 'passing through' a portal tunnel into the mind would be absolutely false. The truth, although perhaps more difficult for some to envision, is that mind becomes actualized by the portal's access into the horizon of Consciousness, and at that moment any distinctions existing between mind, brain, and world effectively dissolve into a singularity, becoming the subjective totality we understand as the 'I'.

If we accept the plausibility of the brain being the locus of the portal into consciousness, we are then in a position to examine the effects upon the mind that may be caused by events impacting the brain. If the mind is the brain, as mind-brain identity theory holds, then that which impacts the brain must also impact the mind, but this is not necessarily the case with externalist theories. As Portalism holds, Consciousness is a fundamental force of nature and as such it cannot be damaged or enhanced. In its irreducible ontological state, it simply *is*. Individualized localizations of consciousness inherit this same ontology, however, as minds they have two important differences; they have content by virtue of their being-in-the-world, and as localizations of the horizon of Consciousness, they become existentially dependent on the portal mechanism. So situated, the mind cannot be directly impacted, but the portal can, and in fact often is, the effect of these impacts being manifested not in the nature of consciousness, but in its content. Consciousness simpliciter is constant and unchanging, wherein the content of consciousness is altered, either augmented or diminished, correlative to the condition of the portal. The list of events wherein the portal might be impacted to a degree where an alteration in the content of consciousness becomes apparent to a first and/or third person observer is probably endless, but to make the point I will confine my descriptions to the more obvious ones. These will include age, trauma, nootropic drugs, mental illness, ASD, and savant syndrome.

Age and Intellectual Potential
Age is perhaps the most obvious causal agent to consider, as

it arguably has the greatest effect upon the portal mechanisms of higher mammals. Some animals, sharks for instance, are entirely capable of navigating their realities and fending for themselves at birth. It can be a lot different for the rest of us. One of the starkest examples would have to be the human infant, born helpless into a severely limited reality. Assuming normal development, a child's capacity for subjective experience demonstrably changes, slowly at first but rapidly increasing as they age from infancy to childhood. Immediately responsive to tactile stimuli, after about a year and a half they begin to demonstrate self-awareness, while curiosity about their environment approaches the unbounded. As brain capacity continues to develop, so does the portal, accompanied by a correlatively expanding consciousness. By the age of twenty-five the portal has reached the end of its development and the mind, with whatever intellectual capacity it might be endowed with, becomes mature.

As each person is genetically different, so will their portals be. Without delving too deeply into neuroanatomy, suffice it to say that each hemisphere of the human brain has frontal, temporal, parietal, and occipital lobes, Broca's area and the cerebral cortex, and that, working in tandem, these determine sensory and motor capabilities as well as the limits of intellectual capacity. People that have suffered damage to certain areas of the brain from trauma or tumors demonstrate impairment in the intellectual and/or motor functions that those areas are associated with. The limits of intellectual capacity will differ from person to person, due to a variety of factors that include but are not limited to DNA, nutrition, and external environmental factors. Not all of us can speak six languages, comprehend astrophysics, hit a baseball out of Yankee Stadium, or write *Faust*. People like Blaise Pascal, Stephen Hawking, or Albert Einstein will be able to understand abstractions that are beyond the comprehension of others. Some will create enduring art and music, or write profound poetry, while others may only be vaguely talented, or be outright inept in the sciences and arts, yet be possessed of great capacities for love, empathy, and compassion. Certainly the sources of differences between people extend further than the biochemical mechanics of their portals, embracing traditional, cultural, economic and environmental factors. But all outside influences being equal, the sophistication of the portal will govern the possibilities of mental content for the mind that it facilitates, which in turn will be governed by the intellectual limits of the individual brain. Most people, for whatever reason, will likely live out their lives in everydayness, never conscious of or caring about their own limitations, mental or physical, and many will nevertheless find happiness in doing so. Yet there is a reason that Nietzsche exhorts us to live dangerously, and that is to test those very limits.

In some cases genius becomes quickly apparent. Child prodigies like Mozart, Chopin, and Pascal would have had exceptionally well developed brains and portals, resulting in extreme mental capabilities. The power of the intellect is one observable characteristic of the dynamic synergy of brain, mind, and world. The more extensive the intellectual capacity of the brain is, then the greater will be the depth of subjective experience from the richness of an expanded reality.

Eventually, the aging of the body must affect the mind in terms of content and cognitive ability. In a few cases people may see no deterioration of cognition due to age, but most will at least to some degree, while some will become severely disabled. As consciousness remains constant, it is the portal mechanism that physically deteriorates. This might be due to a loss of elasticity, the development of sclerotic tissue, a change in body chemistry – all or none of the above. For whatever reason, portal quality diminishes with age, and just as intellectual power was observably indicative of portal robustness, mental debilitation is indicative of portal decline. For diseased brains afflicted with what medicine determines as 'cognitive' disorders, it is not consciousness that is altered, but the content of that consciousness. This deterioration of the content of consciousness is what makes conditions of mental decline observable to third parties. Consciousness, as the ontological ground of subjective experience, remains unaffected, but because the portal is diminished, the possibilities for subjective experience within the individualized mind become aggressively reduced.

Mental Illness and ASD

Mental illness has long been assumed to be associated with disease of the brain, yet there is no biological evidence to support this. By 'mental illness' I am referring to bipolar disorder (formerly manic depression), depression, and schizophrenia. For over a century psychiatry has struggled with two perspectives on mental illness, one being the analytical Freudians who rely on psychoanalysis and psychotherapy, and the biologicals (biological psychiatrists) that advocate drugs, electric shock, lobotomies, and other physio-chemical solutions. This long and tortuous conflict is very readably documented in Anne Harrington's book *Mind Fixers: Psychiatry's Troubled Search for the Biology of Mental Illness*. What doctors and psychiatrists desperately sought was "a coherent causal explanation for disease that led logically to a strategy for treatment."[6] The result was the science of psychiatry being split into two camps, each battling for supremacy within the discipline. For example, in the case of treatment for schizophrenia, the neo-Freudians saw their methods of psychotherapy as effective and humane, viewing the drugs and shock treatments of the biologicals as barbaric and dehumanizing, while the biologicals viewed psychoanalysis as archaic, unscientific, and useless. In the end both were right.

Harrington (2019) submits that one of the most unfortunate events plaguing the concept of mental illness was in fact manifested by the huge success of curing syphilis. Some patients with syphilis present a form of dementia referred to as neurosyphilis (paresis of the insane, also called GPI) that includes erratic behavior and hallucinations and that was originally thought to be a form of madness. When penicillin was found to cure syphilis, mitigating the associated madness in the process, many biological psychiatrists took this to be evidence that all mental illness was therefore biological in origin, and embarked upon similar treatments for depression, bipolar disorder, and especially schizophrenia based on that success. But they misled themselves by misinterpreting the evidence. "The conclusion seemed clear: GPI was a form of syphilis in which the bacteria colonized the brain. It was an *infectious* disease. For the first time, psychiatry had discovered a specific biological cause for a common mental illness. If it could be done once, some people began to say, maybe it could be done again."[7] This miscalculation reinforced the assumption that mental illness was in the brain, which presupposes that consciousness is in the brain, as the symptoms of mental illness manifest as mental states.

Decades of experiments ensued, intent on discovering evidence that mental illness, particularly schizophrenia, was brain related. As image technology progressed countless pictures of the brain activity of the mentally ill were taken in the hopes of finding consistent patterns. The brains of deceased schizophrenics were sliced and examined microscopically. Although some of these experiments showed promising results, those results were not reproducible. The premises of some experiments were subject to question. Conclusions were overdrawn or unsupported by the evidence. "Despite the long tedious hours anatomists spent peering through microscopes of brain slices and searching for patterns of abnormality, no consistent anatomical markers for specific mental disorders were found."[8] Obviously when one reads this one can't help but draw comparisons to over a century of physicalist theories, all making the same assumption – that the brain was the mind. Harrington makes the correct observation "that the brain anatomists had failed so miserably because they focused on the brain at the expense of the mind."[9]

The fact is that through decades of research utilizing fantastic improvements in technology the biology of mental illness remains unknown. The drugs prescribed to treat schizophrenia are based upon drugs prescribed for other patients with similar symptomatic presentation. If they don't work the dosages can be manipulated, other drug therapies attempted, including combinations of different drug therapies. It is no wonder people with mental illness stop taking their meds, as the effects of the drugs can be devastating – sometimes worse than the affliction itself. In many cases the drugs help, but it is hit or miss, based on the statistics of trial and error, with no science behind it. Like electric shock therapy, which is still in use, the drugs affect the brain. If the brain is the locus of the portal into consciousness, then the portal is affected and the impacts to consciousness become observable in the mental behavior of the subject. But the results are not consistent from one patient to the next. The mind is not the brain, and it is almost certain that no successful treatments will be revealed until a subjective science is established that addresses the mind as external to the brain. One might argue that Freudian psychoanalysis was precisely this, and I would be receptive to the idea that it could be a partial solution, but psychoanalytic techniques and diagnostic assumptions tend to be arbitrary depending on the experience of the professional employing them. In any case, treating the symptom with drugs and then standing back to observe the result is just not scientific, subjectively or objectively, being more akin to gambling, but that is where we seem to be.

A different take on the subject of mental illness comes from the postmodernist Michel Foucault. Foucault posited that the so-called mentally ill were actually an oppressed class of eccentrics that experienced and interpreted reality differently than neurotypical people did. This led to their being ostracized by society due to their nonconformity, a reaction much like the response from Kierkegaard's 'crowd', or Nietzsche's 'herd', whenever one of their own departs the mediocrity of the group by seeking authenticity. "The man of madness communicates with society only by the intermediary of an equally abstract reason which is order, physical and moral constraint, the anonymous pressure of the group, and the requirements of conformity."[10] Foucault, disgusted by conditions brought about by the policy of warehousing those people judged insane by others, raised the question of insanity by attacking its reality. Society focuses on trying to make the insane normal again, but what is it exactly that makes a person insane beyond the bearing of that label, and given this, is the illness in the behavior of the insane, or is it in the societal discrimination seeking to silence those who perceive reality in a different way? From this perspective, there is no illness requiring treatment, thus people experiencing nonveridical mental events don't need to be *fixed*. If the result is the inability of the mentally ill to flourish in normal society, then exactly who is to blame for that? "Madness does not represent the absolute form of contradiction, but instead a minority status, as an aspect of itself that does not have the right to autonomy, and can live only grafted onto the world of reason."[11]

The author Ken Kesey held a similar position to Foucault's wherein he posited that institutionalized mental patients were not ill simply because they experienced reality in their own legitimate ways. People diagnosed with ASD (autistic spectrum disorder) also experience reality in their own unique ways, but are they necessarily mentally ill? ASD is a developmental disorder identified with difficulties in social interactions, communication, and limited or repetitive behaviors, and for decades it was considered to be a mental illness, but today the psychiatric community is not so sure. The issue of how sufferers of autism should be classified and subsequently treated "is a difficult one to resolve because there really is no scientific basis on which to separate a psychiatric disorder from a neurological or developmental one."[12] There is a school of thought that ASD is less a mental illness and more a class of people who are simply not neurotypical, which recalls the perspectives put forth by both Foucault and Kesey.

As in the case of schizophrenia, depression, and bipolar disorder, decades of research have yielded no consistent evidence regarding the causes of ASD. Hypotheses range from being genetic or epigenetic to DNA mutations, environmental toxins, illness or injury during pregnancy, malnutrition, and myriad combinations of all the above, yet no conclusive results have been forthcoming. Those diagnosed with ASD are evaluated and treated by both physicians and neuropsychologists, but the variety and combinations of symptoms and the degree of disability vary widely in those afflicted, and *none ever experience remission*. On a parallel with mental illness, more than half of children diagnosed with ASD are prescribed psychoactive drugs, commonly antidepressants, stimulants, and antipsychotics, and again like mental illness sufferers, no known medication relieves ASD's symptoms involving social interaction and communication. As the child psychiatrist Dr. David Rettew (2015) describes in an article in *Psychology Today*:

As science progresses, the neurobiological basis, or at least substrate, of many other psychiatric conditions is increasingly appreciated. And even though there seems something quite medical about autism, we still have been unsuccessful in identifying the specific processes in the brain that underlie the condition, similar to more classic psychiatric disorders. Yet despite these facts and the lack of any solid basis on which to divide various diagnoses into tidy categories, many autism advocates have worked hard to frame it as a developmental or neurological disorder rather than a psychiatric one. The motivation behind the push to label autism as something other than a psychiatric disorder, in my view, comes much more from fears of stigma than any scientific principle.[13]

How ASD is classified unfortunately has a bearing on whether or not health insurance companies will cover the treatments; treatments that will last the lifespan of the patient, just another in a long, endless line of concerns for parents of ASD children. But this classification can also bear on the types of research that can be funded. Again, as in the case of mental illness, could not the focus on the brain be misplaced? Should they be looking at the mind instead? I can only believe that the current assumptions regarding symptoms and treatment are heavily influenced by the stigma that Western medicine places on mental and developmental illnesses.

People with ASD certainly perceive their reality differently than the majority of the human race appears to. Yet even this seems to be a matter of degree. Recently young adults with high-functioning ASD have been hired by corporations to perform operations dealing with extremely large databases of information. Many autistic individuals, most famously Temple Grandin, have the ability to see patterns in what to the rest of us appear as random or common movements in the world. Their *minds* just work differently – not necessarily better or worse – just differently. Preliminary trials of mainstreaming persons with autism into the corporate world have discovered that autistic employees may require solitude, areas free from visual and audial distraction. The guy with the coffee cart just can't bust in on them all of a sudden. Concessions must be made. But the benefits can be incalculable to certain companies willing to make accommodations for people who can perform in ways that few neurotypical people are capable of.

Having worked much of my life in offices and cubicles, as I became an experienced professional in demand and thus in a position to ask for things, I quickly asserted my own preferences for solitude and quiet, and whenever possible, I was accommodated. The difference is that when surprised, or subjected to uncomfortable surroundings, I was able to respond in ways acceptable to society in the workplace. That said, at least in the case of those with high-functioning ASD, how can treating them with drugs that affect the brain and central nervous system, when remission is not an option, possibly be useful? Wouldn't treating them as a class of human beings that simply have a different subjective experience of reality yield more possibilities that might be beneficial to all involved? As with mental illness, those diagnosing and prescribing treatments for people with ASD are groping in the dark, unequipped with any coherent or scientifically borne-out strategy for treatment. Presuming that the mind is the brain, perhaps they are looking in the wrong place to apply their strategies.

On the topic of those that experience reality differently, consider that of the savant. About half of savants are associated with some form of ASD. One does not need to be autistic to be a savant, and I will discuss the phenomenon of *acquired savant syndrome* in the next section. A savant is not necessarily a genius, but all are endowed with mental abilities far beyond the average. These are usually related to memory, rapid calculations, and artistic abilities including music and spatial skills, with the key superpower being memory. Oddly enough, this condition is *not* recognized as a mental disorder. Certainly savants encounter their realities differently than the majority of neurotypical people. Perhaps because they exhibit skills that the majority finds awe inspiring exempts them from this stigmatic classification. Whatever the case may be, between 0.5 and 10 percent of those diagnosed with ASD exhibit some degree of savant syndrome, with human calendars being the most commonly found. Such people have the ability to recall memories from any given date, for example what they had for dinner on March 21st, 1985. Others can listen to Mozart's *Rondo Alla Turca* once and immediately play it with note for note perfection. The reader will recall Dustin Hoffman's excellent portrayal of Raymond, the fictional autistic savant in the movie *Rain Man*, and the famous scene where the waitress spills the contents of a box of toothpicks that scatter randomly onto the floor in front of him. In a few seconds Raymond declares 246 toothpicks. There were four left in the box of 250.

Where I have committed previous paragraphs to descriptions of decreasing mental abilities, savant syndrome is the mind enhanced. Those dealing with mental illness or ASD can experience their realities in manifold ways but what they seem to have in common is that their minds work differently from those of the neurotypical majority. It is true that some of those diagnosed with mental illness and/or ASD exhibit behavioral patterns that cause them to be dangers to themselves or to others, but the association of violence with mental illness is misunderstood and misrepresented, becoming a significant cause of the stigma surrounding it. The evidence shows that violent offenses committed by the mentally ill comprise only a small percentage of that population, while the majority of that violence involves the combination of mental illness with substance abuse, and/or environmental issues. As reported by Harvard Medical School:

> Although a subset of people with psychiatric disorders commit assaults and violent crimes, findings have been inconsistent about how much mental illness contributes to this behavior and how much substance abuse and other factors do.
>
> ... when the investigators probed further, comparing

rates of violence in one area in Pittsburgh in order to control for environmental factors as well as substance use, they found no significant difference in the rates of violence among people with mental illness and other people living in the same neighborhood. In other words, after controlling for substance use, rates of violence reported in the study may reflect factors common to a particular neighborhood rather than the symptoms of a psychiatric disorder.[14]

The facts show that only about 1.5 to 3% of the mentally ill population has been found prone to violence over that of matched controls, when substance abuse is eliminated and other factors are considered equally in balance with the surrounding neurotypical population. When violence does occur it usually takes the form of assault, and is primarily attributed to those suffering from schizophrenia and bipolar disorder; however, these figures can rise significantly when suicide is included as violent behavior.

Examining the evidence, or rather the lack thereof, it is apparent that mental illness is not clearly understood by the medical and scientific communities as they continue to treat it as a biological affliction even though its biology remains unknown. One could ask why these conditions are even looked upon as *illness* to begin with, considering that no biological evidence of disease has ever been found. If there is no consistent biological evidence of disease, then no strategy for its treatment as a disease can possibly be useful. Experimenting with drugs on the non-neurotypical has led to no solutions beyond the temporary tranquilization of the afflicted. Any promising treatment should show some indication of remission, yet none have, possibly because there is no such thing as remission from one's subjective experience of the world. The character of one's subjective experience is what it is. Mental illness and ASD are experienced through the first person and are observable by third person perceptions, therefore they certainly exist, but if they are not things in the objective realm – such as a diagnosable biological disorder – then they must be things in the subjective realm. Perhaps it is time for researchers to begin considering other perspectives and looking in other directions toward a more workable understanding of these mental phenomena. They might start by phenomenologically bracketing off what they think they already know, such as mind-brain identity and the stigmatic assumption that these afflictions are illnesses in the first place. Other than the outward behaviors of those afflicted being inconsistent with those of the neurotypical, by what definition are these people considered to be sick? If the biology of mental illness is unknown, and if no remission is achievable, might not we be seeking a remedy for a state of consciousness less in need of a cure and more in need of a correct and fuller understanding?

Brain Trauma and the Curious Case of Phineas Gage

In the following discussion of trauma and its effect on the brain/portal, I am referring to physical traumatic brain injury (TBI) as opposed to psychological trauma. This latter form of trauma, being an example of subjective stimuli resulting in physical and behavioral manifestations, is addressed in the chapter on mind.

It is well documented that persons suffering head injury, be it concussion, blunt force trauma, gunshot, etc., as a result can exhibit changes in behavior and mental acuity, including deteriorations in the cognitive content of consciousness. As the mind is not the brain, Portalism accounts for this by attributing the cause to degradation in the capacity and facility of the portal mechanism. The extreme manifestation of the effects of cranial trauma would be manifested as a coma, wherein the portal mechanism is completely disabled. Other manifestations of brain/portal impairment could be cognitive in nature, for example aphasia, loss of memory, amnesia, or changes in the character and content of the information passing to the brain from the sensory modalities. As previously stated in the section on age and illness, Consciousness as a fundamental force of nature is unaffected; it is the content of consciousness that is impacted, and in almost all cases of TBI it is a negative impact.

There are cases of TBI where victims have been known to have acquired savant syndrome. These cases are rare but incredible when they occur. Acquired savant syndrome has been documented in people suffering blunt force head traumas, some even after being struck by lightning. The effects include sudden virtuoso abilities on musical instruments by people with no previous exposure to music theory or to the instrument itself. Others become brilliant artists and sculptors overnight. Little is known about savant syndrome, other than that it exists. Theories lean toward the evidence that savant syndrome is the result of parts of the brain associated with creativity and abstract reasoning, such as the frontal and parietal lobes, being severely diseased or traumatized, the reasoning being that this damage acts not as impairment to intellectual functionality, but in the removal of brain imposed barriers limiting intellectual potential. "The skills do not emerge as a result of newly acquired brain power; they emerge because for the first time, the areas of the right brain associated with creativity can operate unchecked."[15]

These possibilities for a reduced or enhanced intellectual potential are compatible with Portalism, as they would directly impact the capacity of the portal into consciousness, where the brain's natural capacity for intellect is actualized. In the case of the man that suddenly found himself gifted with the ability to play the piano, the temporal lobe of his brain which governs creativity and musical awareness was able to comprehend the piano keyboard in a different way. Instead of a simple order of black and white keys he was suddenly able to determine logical patterns. This would make sense, as music is essentially a form of mathematics. This sudden ability is not unlike that of Temple

Grandin's ability to perceive patterns in the movement of cattle in a stockyard. Grandin's visual sense observes the movements of the cattle, but it is her mind that identifies the patterns – the determinate *meaning* of the data it processes exceeds the capabilities of the brain. Only in mind is the context and meaning of phenomenal experience actualized.

Acquired savant syndrome is another case wherein one's brain performs differently than those of the neurotypical. Areas of the brain responsible for creativity become enhanced by having barriers to their potential removed. The sense modalities of sight and sound see the keys and hear the tones, but the piano is an object in the world. It is the portal that connects the two in mind, where the intellectual actualization we know as music takes place. The brain by itself is incapable of assigning any context or meaning to the sounds emanating from the keyboard, or indeed any other sounds and sights from the world that it receives through the senses. Although this expanded creative processing potential physically exists in the brain, it is only in mind that it can be actualized, interpreted, understood and appreciated as music.

This brings us to a short discussion of the curious case of Phineas Gage. Every first year philosophy major is introduced to this bit of history, normally in the context regarding the metaphysical question of that which determines personal identity over time. To recap, Phineas Gage was a railroad construction foreman who, in 1848, was horrifically injured in a blasting accident. Specifically, an iron bar measuring 1¼ inches in diameter and over three feet long, used to tamp dynamite charges down into holes drilled into the rock, was blasted through his lower jaw, exiting from the top of his skull. He briefly passed out and had convulsions, but soon awoke and rode in a cart to the doctor for treatment. He was lucid and talking. He lost an eye and some teeth but was not in great pain and eventually recovered, surviving another twelve years, even driving a coach in Chile before eventually expiring from a grand mal seizure.

The legend is that prior to the accident Gage was a gentle, well-spoken man that led a quiet life, liked by his friends and welcome in society. However, after the accident his demeanor reportedly changed to the extent that his former friends no longer recognized him. He became angry, intolerant, and abusive. His speech became alarmingly foul-mouthed, and he was shunned by society. The philosophical value of this story is in its drawing of the conclusion that TBI can alter one's identity. Post-accident Gage was never the same man again, which begs the question, 'Are our brains our identity?' To argue that they are would be to embrace mind-brain identity.

Outside of becoming an interesting thought experiment there is apparently little other value in the story because its basic truth has been called into question. It is fact that Gage existed and that he suffered the injury described, but the elements regarding the stark changes in his behavior are suspicious. Research conducted by Malcolm B. Macmillan has revealed that the scientific and popular accounts of Gage almost always distort and exaggerate his post-accident behavior well past that attested to by anyone who knew him personally, to the degree that the facts are "inconsistent with the common view of Gage as a boastful, brawling, foul-mouthed, dishonest useless drifter, unable to hold down a job, who died penniless in an institution."[16]

The uncertain extent of Gage's brain damage combined with the suspect and conflicting accounts of his behavioral degradation render him "of more historical than neurologic interest. Phineas' story represents a small stock of facts transforming into popular and scientific myth", the actual lack of evidence having allowed "the fitting of almost any theory to the small number of facts we have". Therefore Gage becomes "a great story for illustrating the need to go back to original sources as most authors have been content to summarize or paraphrase accounts that are already seriously in error."[17] This is yet another example of making a claim of evidence from drawing conclusions based upon erroneous presuppositions. The writer Beryl Benderly (2012) suggests that instead of invoking Gage to imply a link between personality and brain damage, "that instructors use the Gage case to illustrate the importance of critical thinking."[18]

Can TBI cause profound changes in personality? The answer is that we don't know. Personality is subjective, not physically a thing in the world. Surely the phenomenal experience of being-in-the-world influences personality development. Some personality traits may be heritable. Personalities are also not limited to humans, as any horse, dog, or cat owner will testify. To claim that the frontal lobe is the absolute locus of personality implies mind-brain identity, but there can be no personality without subjective experience of the world. As in the case of creativity and memory, the brain may store the behavioral information and impulses that compose elements of personality, but it cannot manifest them in the world. This can only be done in mind, through the mind's experience of being-in-the-world. Besides, personalities only come into existence when observed by the other, thus personality exists only for the other, and is encounterable by the other only in the world. Psychologically, the 'kind' of personality one has is determined by the other from observable traits that fit a preconceived category. The other makes this classification and the other is in the world. Personality only ever becomes a thing through the other's observation of how a person acts and reacts to stimuli that they encounter in the world. Apparently Gage himself never mentioned anything about perceiving his environment or his own behavior differently after his accident. Any credible accounts regarding changes in his personality could only have been noticed by those who had observed him both before and after his injury, and those accounts are inconsistent and therefore suspect. This is not to say that the damage to Gage's brain did not have an effect on his personality, but only that our available facts are insufficient to support claims that it did.

Nootropics and Psychedelics

As claimed in the previous sections, the capacity for mental content is correlative to the intellectual limits of certain relevant areas of the brain and nervous system, and these limits can be affected in many ways, mainly by age, disease, and TBI. Such effects, once established, tend toward permanence. But these cerebral intellectual boundaries can also be temporarily expanded by exposure to certain brain stimulating and mind enhancing drugs.

Nootropics, also known as 'smart' drugs and cognitive enhancers, are a group of drugs taken for the purposes of improving cognitive function, motivation, creativity, and memory. As such they are favorites among students. Students represent a class of people that are periodically and routinely placed under great pressure to perform. In the eyes of Western medicine, these drugs enjoy the same classification as acupuncture, wherein no one can really say how or even if it works, however, it cannot be denied that many users swear as to its benefits.

In the mid-seventies, most students relied upon unlimited quantities of coffee and cigarettes to endure the pressure and maintain the levels of concentration needed to pass their mid-term and final exams. More ambitious students opted for amphetamines originally prescribed for appetite control and weight loss, such as Dexamyl (white cross), Dexedrine, and Benzedrine (Christmas trees). The demand for drugs and their subsequent abuse soared during exam times, and sadly little has changed. In current day these older drugs have been replaced by more sophisticated stimulants such as dimethylamylamine and methylphenidate, which are used most frequently on college campuses, the former being a nasal inhaler (now withdrawn) and the latter used to treat ADHD. While amphetamines still enjoy popularity, there are other options, some even sold over-the-counter, that have become commonplace. These include the racetams – piracetam, oxiracetam, phenylpiracetam, and aniracetam, all of which are sold openly and legally and all of whose properties are not yet fully understood. Another group of popular nootropics are the cholinergics, essentially compounds of acetylcholine that enhance the neurotransmitters and improve memory, at least in older people, as they have not been clearly established to have any effect at all on the young and healthy. What all of these compounds have in common is the word 'enhance'. Again invoking the claim of Portalism that an expansion of the intellectual limits of the brain has a simultaneous effect on the capacity of the portal and by extension the mind, it is therefore plausible to consider that the effect of nootropics upon the brain would temporarily expand the depth of phenomenal experience as well as the intellectual capacity of the mind.

Such a claim is not without evidence. Ex-smokers confess that when they finally managed to quit one prominent symptom that they experienced was the inability to concentrate, causing many of them to take up less harmful addictions to compensate – gum, or hard candies being among the most common. Coffee drinkers can make the same claims. Nicotine and caffeine are stimulants that affect the brain in similar ways, albeit perhaps to a lesser degree than the nootropics popular with the collegiate. As the brain is affected, in these cases not by trauma or disease but by stimulants, the mind's capacity for processing intellectual tasks expands concurrent to the enhancement of its portal connection in response to the drug.

Hallucinogens might seem to be similar to nootropics, but in reality they work quite differently and thus produce remarkably distinctive effects upon both brain and mind. Although there are many compounds classified as hallucinogenic, I need only address two of the psychedelics to make my point – psilocybin, an organic compound found in certain mushrooms, and lysergic acid diethylamide (LSD), an inorganic compound synthesized in the laboratory by Albert Hofmann in 1938, after isolating the psychoactive compound of the *psilocybe mexicana* mushroom. Both of these compounds have been classified as Schedule 1 drugs by the United States government. One of the criteria for a Schedule 1 classification is that the drug has no currently accepted medical use.

Both are also considered to be psychedelics, a Greek word that translates as 'mind manifesting', and both were originally used in research as possible therapeutics for addiction and mental illness, specifically for schizophrenia and depression. This research was halted, at least in the USA, in 1966 when the drugs were put on the Schedule 1 list, but recently both drugs, particularly psilocybin, have been enjoying renewed attention in some medical and psychiatric communities.

As documented in a *60 Minutes* episode that aired on August 16th, 2020, researchers Roland Griffiths and Matthew Johnson, both of Johns Hopkins, "have been giving what they call 'heroic doses' of psilocybin to more than 350 volunteers, many struggling with addiction, depression and anxiety." Griffiths and Johnson obtained permission from the FDA to work with psilocybin in 2020, resurrecting research that had been on hiatus for over 30 years. The 'heroic doses' describe an amount of psilocybin significant enough to act upon a patient for up to six hours, during which time they experience a variety of sensations, images, and experiences within what philosophers would call their reflexive consciousnesses. During these treatments some patients re-experience long forgotten memories or see people long departed. Concepts like the soul or the self may become concrete manifestations that can be altered, destroyed, or otherwise reckoned with. Truths have been revealed, and a few even experience synesthesia, meaning that they acquire the ability to see sound.

The results have been remarkable. "It turns out most of the 51 cancer patients in the Johns Hopkins study experienced 'significant decreases in depressed mood and anxiety' after trying psilocybin. Two-thirds of them rated their psilocybin sessions as among the most meaningful experiences of their lives. For some, it was on par with the birth of their children."[19] People that had smoked tobacco or drank alcohol to excess for decades were able to shed their addictions. Terminal cancer patients suffering from severe depression and anxiety found relief. Several patients were able to come to terms with themselves and create a new and more fulfilling perspective on life.

Research on psilocybin, and more importantly LSD, is being performed by scientists associated with the UK based Beckley/ Imperial Research Programme. Their work with psychedelic science has produced results that indicate the ability of psychedelics to "transiently alter normal brain function and exert their therapeutic action."[20] In 2016 they released a series of stunning fMRI and magnetoencephalography (MEG) neuroimages of brain activity while subjected to micro-dosages of LSD. "The resulting images showed how the brain's visual cortex, which normally receives and processes information from the eyes, begins to communicate with a wide range of other brain regions under the effects of LSD. This means that many brain regions that aren't normally involved in vision suddenly begin contributing to visual processing, which explains why some people tend to experience dreamlike hallucinations when they use the drug."[21] More importantly, this research would seem to offer evidence toward the claim that it is possible to expand the natural boundary limitations for intellectual capacity and by extension affect the content of mind. "The findings show how the drug decreases communication between the brain regions that make up the Default Mode Network (DMN), a collection of hub centres that work together to control and repress consciousness."[22]

Earlier in this chapter, I pointed out that medicine and psychiatry appeared to be pursuing a biological remedy for mental illness where there was no evidence of anatomic pathology. I asked if it might be more productive to focus not on the body but rather on the mind. I present these accounts of the work going on today at Johns Hopkins and the Beckley/Imperial Research Programme as evidence of a hopeful future based on the work of scientists willing to overcome decades of dogmatic assumptions about mental illness, embrace fresh thinking, and produce encouraging, replicable scientific research directed toward exploring the mind. As Amanda Feilding, founder and co-director of the Beckley/Imperial Research Programme summarized, "We are finally unveiling the brain mechanisms underlying the potential of LSD, not only to heal, but also to deepen our understanding of consciousness itself."[23]

I always find it amusing when people that have obviously never actually experienced LSD talk or write about its effects. Having experienced LSD myself on three occasions, I know firsthand what it can do, and therefore I can relate to the descriptions I've read in the accounts of the work mentioned above and know them to be factual. With any street drug the dosages are unknown, and I am prepared to believe that the amounts of LSD that I ingested decades ago were significantly less than what is used today in these clinical surroundings. I have heard the accounts of certain people that have taken LSD, and I can't help but think them to be embellished. For instance, I never experienced a refrigerator walking into the living room and talking to me, or any other such fantasy. I never believed that I could fly, or that I was someone else, or that evil forces were closing in on me. But I did experience things across all three episodes which opened my mind to a wider reality.

While experiencing LSD one does not feel 'high' or doped or sluggish; quite the opposite in fact, one feels sharp and focused. Episodic memory is greatly improved. In normal conversation I often find myself searching for a word, or trying to remember an actor's name – not so with LSD. LSD enhances all of the sensory modalities, and depending on the emotional mood, the dosage, and the quality of the drug, the resulting overall experience has the potential to be good or bad. Although the aftereffects involved with having taken the drug can leave one feeling wrung out and listless for a day, while the drug's effects are active the single most memorable aspect of the experience is that of absolute crystal clarity and a profound understanding about one's self and one's surroundings, experienced because LSD expands the intellectual limitations that the brain naturally places upon itself, allowing one to experience an enhanced state of one's own reality.

I am certainly not advocating taking LSD, as Kesey and Dr. Timothy Leary (1962) did in the sixties, and I mention my own experience only to emphasize my claim that minds can experience reality in manifold ways, and my assertion that people suffering from mental conditions might be better served by a change in the focus of research that places consciousness ahead of the biological assumptions made by mind-brain identity theorists.

What the Brain Does Not Do

Although the brain does not require the mind in order to function, it does require fuel in the form of food and water which it cannot obtain without the mind because it cannot think. When, due to trauma or disease, the portal is disabled to the degree that consciousness is suspended, the brain purrs merrily on doing its job, and will continue to do so until it runs out of fuel. Without consciousness, the brain has no way to signal its needs to the world. Finding food and water is an operation that requires world, and the mind is the only interface to the world that the brain has. Even though bodies are things-in-the-world, all living organisms will eventually die from lack of life-sustaining fuel because without consciousness, be it human or paramecium, they have no ability to comprehend and navigate the world.

Alan Watts (1995) observed that the self is essentially composed of ego, memory, and intellect. Using this definition, the brain's homeostatic needs could be considered as ego, or 'I want this, I don't want that'. The brain manages the ego and memory, and houses the capacity for intellectual potential, but it is only within the mind that the intellect has the capability to achieve agency. Although the components establishing and regulating intellectual potential reside in the brain, intellectual actualization can only occur in the mind.

When making the argument for the consciousness of all living things, I claimed that single celled organisms are conscious for two reasons; they are capable of problem solving, which presupposes intelligence, and they are demonstrably able to navigate their realities. Based on this, one might ask if the individual cells in the human body (or any multicellular creature) are in themselves conscious. Such a question implies some form of panpsychism, so I would answer in the negative as the paramecium, albeit single celled, is a coherent biological system and as such it survives. Single cells in multicellular animals or plants are dynamically synergetic and codependent on each other, forming a coherently cooperative system necessary for their survival. But such 'component' cells, even though they may arguably 'solve' problems, are not equipped to singularly navigate their realities – in effect they have no singular reality to navigate, as they are not conscious. Teed Rockwell addresses a similar problem in his brain-body-world nexus theory regarding individual neurons stating that:

"Even mind-brain identity theorists will acknowledge that the individual neurons are not conscious. Similarly, the claim that the brain-body-world nexus is conscious does not imply that all of the parts of that nexus are conscious. It does imply, however, that each of these objects plays a role in constituting our conscious experience, even though they are not conscious themselves."[24]

Summary

Within these descriptions of what the brain can and cannot do it is certainly not my intention to appear to be downplaying the power of this organ. Considering the mission that it is designed for, it is a miraculously unparalleled creation of biochemical machinery. So miraculous in fact, that it is exceedingly intuitive to assign it qualities that it simply does not possess, qualities that go beyond metabolic management, sensory data processing, and homeostasis. Technical descriptions of the workings of the brain frequently include references to cognition, emotion, and language, when evidence supporting any claim that these are properties of the brain has yet to be shown. These same descriptions ascribe the origins of mental illness to the brain, when the biology of mental illness remains entirely unknown (Harrington 2019). For example, neuroscientists often use dramatic imagery illustrating that the amygdala is the locus of the brain associated with fear conditioning. This process is sequential, beginning first with the brain interpreting the stimulus that signals a fear response, and second with the response itself occurring in the amygdala, as the images show. But there are two problems with this explanation. First, to *interpret* a subjective experience is to assign meaning and context to that experience, which is a function of mind. So to make this claim, one must first assume that the brain is the mind, when physicalism has yet to prove this. Secondly, when I see William James' bear, images of my amygdala may consistently show activity, but to claim that this activity is the experience of *something-like-there-is-to-feel-afraid* would be to assume that it is proof of a conscious cognitive process – a neural activity corresponding to a mental process, when brain imagery has yet to be shown as evidence of cognitive processes. Subjective experience, and the subsequent assignation of meaning to an experience, is a function of mind, not brain. But it is true that most neuroscientists are mind-brain identity materialists, and thus make such claims and draw such conclusions, based upon a premise that phenomenal externalism rejects.

Dissect the brain and its neural networks down to the atomic level and you will never find a thought, an idea, or a belief. Thinking, reasoning, aesthetics, language processing, subjective experience and reflexive awareness are all functions of mind. Consciousness cannot arise or derive from non-conscious matter, which is precisely what the brain is. The brain and mind are existentially codependent upon each other, and in terms of sustaining the life of the complete organism, each has its essential role to play.

Chapter 7

The Mind

While many thinkers agree that consciousness is a single subjective totality, there remain many different perspectives on its component nature. Most philosophers envision different categories of consciousness existing within a single mind. For example, Ted Honderich proposes three in number, these being perceptual, cognitive, and affective consciousness. He defines the perceptual as being the consciousness of perceiving by the five senses while cognitive is the consciousness of thinking. Affective consciousness has to do with wanting things, desiring, hoping, intending, etc.[1] David Chalmers prefers two categories deriving from Ned Block's distinction between phenomenal and access consciousness.[2] John Searle claims that he once distinguished between qualitativeness, subjectivity, and unity, but today believes that all of these taken together constitute the essence of consciousness.[3]

I also agree that consciousness, while arguably composed of different modes or phases largely based upon its intentional focus, is nonetheless an ontologically irreducible subjective totality. For purposes of simplicity, in describing the Portalist perspective on mind I will operate upon the basis that its nature is composed of two distinctions, these being phenomenal consciousness (reaching out), and reflexive consciousness (reaching in).

The 'I', the 'Self', and the 'Soul'

Words matter in philosophy; this is particularly true in metaphysics, and in the philosophy of mind it is important to take care how the pronouns get thrown about. I refer specifically to labels like 'I' and 'self' and for some, the 'soul'. How does one get to be an 'I'? It is clear that subjective experience can only be reported from the first person perspective. For example, 'I' see the fish in my aquarium. *I* have enjoyed watching the fish and *I* am going to feed them later. Regardless of its tense the 'I' always stands as the agent that is my individual localization of consciousness – my mind. As creatures blessed (or cursed) with language, we are constantly having a conversation with ourselves as we navigate our reality, encountering and identifying objects, recounting the past or anticipating the future, the agent in all of these internal dialogues being the *I*. Perhaps Peter Godfrey-Smith illustrates it best: "When we look inside, most people find a flow of inner speech, a monologue that accompanies much of our conscious life. Sentences and phrases, exclamations, rambling commentaries, speeches we would like to give, or wish we'd given."[4] So what *is* the 'I'? Sam Harris has a solid definition: "The pronoun *I* is the name that most of us put to the sense that we are the thinkers of our thoughts and the experiencers of our experience. It is the sense that we have of possessing (rather than of merely being) a continuum of experience."[5]

How does the 'I' originate? When a portal connects into the horizon of Consciousness, a singular localization of consciousness is disclosed as mind, wherein the 'I' is made manifest as awareness of the world brought forth. The world cannot simply be experienced; it must be experienced *by something*. Thus *I* am the first person perspective of mind and the agent of my subjective experience. The 'I' *is* being-in-the-world, the world being necessary to the existence of 'I'. The 'I' is phenomenal consciousness, the mind's awareness of the objective world and its contents.

So what is the difference between the 'I' and the 'self'? Not all minds are sophisticated enough to be aware that they are aware, to reach inward, to become consciousness of themselves, such consciousnesses referring to most non-human minds. But for minds that have this reflexive capability, it is in this mode of consciousness that the 'I' discloses itself to itself, enabling the 'self' to become manifest. If I am typing on my keyboard, the I is conscious of *what* is being typed, while the self is aware of the *intentionality of my act of typing*. The self thinks about itself, reflects upon its acts, its desires, and beliefs. It formulates and strategizes, it creates and composes, it reasons, it decides, and it feels. When I am speaking to another person, *I* might say something stupid and embarrass *my-self* – as the agent 'I' do the talking, but it is the self that feels the embarrassment. I might win a martial arts trophy, but it is the self that feels the pride of accomplishment. I might attend the funeral of a friend, but it is the self that feels the grief. I might see a child walking out in front of a car, but it is the self that decides to act, pulling it out of harm's way. It is the 'I' that encounters things in the world, while it is the 'self' that thinks about them. As Sartre tells us, "The I is the producer of inwardness."[6]

Descartes believed that the soul was *res cogitans*, the thinking substance. Descartes, along with the two other premier rationalists Gottfried Leibniz and Baruch Spinoza, was a man of faith. These profound thinkers developed their theories of consciousness at a time when Enlightenment thinking was in its infancy, and thus it was essential that any metaphysical theory find some role for God to play. To this end, Descartes held that the soul – the thinking substance – survives death, proceeding from there to tie it all up neatly in the *Third Meditation*, wherein he proves that God exists. As an atheist and an existentialist, I have a different view.

The reality is that the *I*, the *self*, and the *soul*, as intuitive as it may be to believe that they exist, are no more than illusions. These terms are not things-in-themselves, but are only words descriptive of the mind's intentional focus at any given instance. All we are is mind, and regardless of whether we are phenomenally *being-in-itself*, or reflexively *being-for-itself*, these perspectives represent only different states within a single, subjective totality – a mind.

Phenomenal Consciousness

The mind is in phenomenal consciousness when it is in the mode of *being-in* the world. The world is the all-encompassing structure in which the mind comports itself to all beings. As *being-in*, the mind subjectively experiences objects that it encounters in the world. Subjective experience is the *something-like-there-is-to-be* sensation of that which is encountered, and whenever the mind is experiencing the world, it does so in phenomenal consciousness.

Phenomenal perception is the means through which we navigate the world, and is primarily achieved through the sensory modalities of sight and touch. Phenomenal consciousness, or 'P-consciousness' as Ned Block (1998) defines it, is composed of raw experiences – sights, sounds, smells, tastes, touches, and feelings manifested by our emotions that we encounter as we move through the physical realm. For example, I go into the kitchen and open the refrigerator door, whereupon I encounter an orange sitting alone on a shelf. Logically, I cannot prove that any of the things that I am seeing and touching really even exist – not the kitchen, the refrigerator, the shelf, nor the orange – but the one thing I do know exists is that I am experiencing *something-like-there-is-to-be-seeing* an orange. In addition, the orange's texture, color, and taste are all sensations whose *experience-of* exceed any physical description. These feelings are also incommunicable, as pointed out by Daniel Dennett (1985), in that there is no effective way that the taste of an orange, the color blue, the sound of a cello, the feel of a lamb's wool, or the smell of coffee, can be adequately described to anyone who has not yet experienced those things themselves. Qualia are entirely subjective and exist only in and as phenomenal consciousness.

Phenomenal consciousness is the mode by which we

subjectively experience the objective realm. Objects and states of affairs in the world that we encounter, and the feelings we experience as the result of those encounters, are disclosed to mind through this mode of consciousness.

Reflexive Consciousness

This second mode of consciousness describes the awareness we enter into when we think, reason, remember, and introspect. It is very like the access or A-consciousness definition of Ned Block, but I prefer to take it a bit further. Block's description implies an awareness of awareness, but to this I would add the concreteness of Hegel's self-reflexivity,[7] that of consciousness being driven back upon itself, to clarify definitively that this mode of consciousness is the medium wherein we become aware of being aware.

The self-awareness I describe in this mode of consciousness is commensurate to contemplation, and does not necessarily require any interaction with the other, although it is very possible to be abruptly driven from everydayness into a reflexive *self-consciousness* by the other, for example through committing an embarrassing act or as a response to another's hurtful comment. In his master-slave dialectic Hegel does use the term 'self-consciousness' as synonymous with self-awareness and in contrast with the self-consciousness of the other, the two distinctions taken as thesis and antithesis leading to the synthesis of a unity of self-consciousness with itself. Hegel describes the meaning of this self-awareness: "in reality, self-consciousness is reflexion out of the bare being that belongs to the world of sense and perception, and is essentially the return out of otherness."[8]

One might think of self-awareness as akin to sitting cross-legged under a tree and meditating, and they would be right, except that when meditating purists seek to clear the mind and not so much to turn it back upon itself reflexively. Still, this is a form of A-consciousness. When I think about writing a song I begin by mentally searching for a melody. When I build a form for the concrete base of my new greenhouse, I take its dimensions and mentally calculate the number of cubic yards of cement I will need to pour. When my aged father refuses to quit driving and trade his car in on a golf cart, I begin to reason how I can frame my argument in the clearest logical terms so that he might be persuaded. These are all examples of abstract thinking, and all that is abstract lies within reflexive consciousness. The brain does not deal in abstracts, only in physical realities. Thinking and reasoning dwell in this realm of reflexive consciousness, as does reflection and introspection.

In his essay *The Transcendence of the Ego*, Jean-Paul Sartre uses the terms 'unreflective' and 'reflective' consciousness to describe his two distinctions of awareness.[9] In effect, when we are moving about the world in what Heidegger would refer to as 'everydayness', we are in unreflective consciousness, where there is no place for the 'self'; we are essentially outside of ourselves in the mode of becoming the world. Imagine that we are walking to 7-Eleven to buy some beer. As we walk through the shopping center we see the items in the shop windows, the colors of the cars parked neatly in their spaces, we hear birdsong and the hum of people talking as they pass. When we eventually arrive at 7-Eleven we reach out to push open the door but it is locked. In Heideggerian terms the door has suddenly become *unready-to-hand* and we are jolted into self-awareness, what Sartre calls reflective consciousness – we have become self-aware. It is the *self* that thinks, "Now what am *I* going to do?"

I once had a professor who told me that radical externalist theories were meaningless because they could not be falsifiable. I realize now that I should have responded that falsifiability, like the scientific method, applies only to the objective universe, but I didn't, and I wonder how he might have responded had I done so. In this example the memory of an event in my past was *recalled* from my episodic memory wherein I *reasoned* an alternative response, felt *chagrined* that I did not think of it when it mattered, *regretted* this missed opportunity, and *wondered* how it could have been different. Thus I remembered, I reasoned, I felt the emotions of chagrin and regret, and using *my imagination* I wondered about a result that never really occurred. Whenever we do this we are in the mode of reflexive consciousness, or A-consciousness in Block's terminology, and 'reflective' consciousness in Sartre's lexicon. Although these different philosophers may nuance their perspectives, in the end the result is the same; we become aware of ourselves as ourselves – we move from the phenomenally outward perspective of the *I*, to the reflexively inward consciousness of our-*self* – two modes of consciousness within the single unity of mind.

Perhaps the most well-known activity within self-awareness is introspection, when we become cognitively aware of our own mental acts, states, beliefs, intentions, and emotional processes. As recounted in Plato's *Apology*, Socrates famously says that "an unexamined life is not worth living" and one could argue that the world might be a much gentler place if more people would take the time for self-examination. After all, it is quite simple, involving putting down the phone, walking outside, finding a comfortable place to sit and beginning the tried and true Cartesian process of doubting everything we think we know, reflecting upon the kind of person we *are*, as opposed to the kind of person we *could be*, or even the kind of person that we might wish to become. This process requires us to *think*, to reflect upon what we believe and to ask ourselves why we believe it, and to allow our reason to guide us to what could be new levels of self-understanding. To follow our reason can lead us to places that many people may find uncomfortable. Questions concerning the preference of a disturbing truth over a comfortable myth can be difficult to reconcile to a person's long held beliefs. Each must decide for themselves if such a journey is ultimately worth making, but regardless of the decision, you were consciously in the mode of reflexive self-awareness when you made it.

Consciousness and the World

The self is not just another entity in the world, but in an important sense it creates the world…
Immanuel Kant

While the chapter on the world described its character and content, this section focuses on Portalism's mind-world relationship. There are two ways of considering the relationship between mind and world. The first is that mind brings the world into existence and the second being that it is the world that actualizes mind. Both claims leave us some unpacking to do in respect to their content.

Kant would favor the former proposition, this keeping in line with his idealism in that we can never experience the noumenal world, only its phenomenal appearance. He describes this ideal world, a world actualized by mind, in the "Antinomy of Pure Reason: Section 1" of *The Critique* where his definitions of world and nature 'coincide': "This same world, however, is called nature if we look upon it as a dynamical whole and consider, not the aggregation in space and time in order to produce a magnitude, but the unity in the existence of appearances."[10] From Kant's perspective, the world presents as a totality of representations that transcend experience. Framed in these terms, it is mind that brings the world into existence, but the term 'existence' in this sense can be confusing. To be sure, a physical objective universe *exists* outside of our perception of it, so the mind does not 'create' the world in that sense; instead it *discloses* the world so that it may be encountered and experienced. So, from that perspective, consciousness can be argued to 'bring the world into existence', for without consciousness there would be no world to be conscious of. But consciousness does not bring the world into *being*, because the world always already was, rather it is consciousness that enables us to know the world by its *being-in*.

The second mind-world relationship claims that it is world that actualizes mind, and Portalism is compatible with this claim, as are most externalist theories. Essentially, Portalism rejects the mind-brain identity of the physicalists while embracing a *de facto* mind-world identity. Given this, Portalism is in accord with the ecologically holistic concepts of Rockwell and Honderich, holding that without world there is no consciousness, as there would be nothing to be conscious of. In other words, in terms of actualization and perception, mind and world are codependent. The nature of this codependence is ontologically critical. The fundamental and irreducible force of Consciousness resides in world, thus mind cannot be *actualized* without world, yet world cannot be *experienced* without mind, and so subjective experience is, by extension, irreducible. Thus the physical realm, or 'world' of objects, is necessary to the ontic being of the 'I', meaning mind, but mind in and of itself is not an object in world; rather, *mind is world* by virtue of its *being-in*. "Being-in is not a property... It is not the case that human being 'is', and then on top of that has a relation of being-in-the-world."[11] By virtue of its experience in and of world, mind *is* world. Consciousness knows the world, and I am consciousness – a mind. As such, mind *is* in the mode of being-in-the-world and the world is brought before mind through mind itself – so in the sense of the former claim, world did not exist (become available and encounterable) before mind, which discloses world as the all-encompassing structure in which the ontic 'I' comports itself to all beings, and which contains all of its possibilities.

Given these explanations and clarifications, if we now return to the two relationship claims as originally stated, an argument could be made that they are not mutually exclusive, and in light of these definitions, *are in fact both true*. What needs to be understood is that when a portal manifests a localization of consciousness, an identity between mind and world is autogenically established, the portal and the all-encompassing horizon of Consciousness representing the necessary and sufficient conditions for actualizing mind and disclosing world.

The Content of Consciousness

The term 'content' refers to that which differentiates specific states of consciousness that we may find ourselves in at any given time, and the subjective impressions that we experience therein. For example, the phenomenally conscious state of encountering an object in the world, or the mode of reflexive consciousness when thinking about something. Each of these mental states will have content of some nature. As Chalmers states: "Most conscious states seem to have some sort of specific representational content that represents the world as being one way or another."[12]

The subject of content inevitably moves us into the realm of epistemology where careers have been made dealing with the complexities regarding whether or not we can actually know anything about what we phenomenally perceive, and that if we can, explaining the mechanics of exactly how that process works. For example, beliefs are intentional and involve propositional statements. How then does one go about determining the truth value of a belief? Or, if I observe a grapefruit, how can I be sure it is real? Is it a veridical experience that I am having, or a hallucination? How can we determine if what the world reveals to us is the actual reality? When it's all said and done, all I am left with is a feeling *of something-like-there-is-to-be* experiencing a grapefruit, as I cannot logically prove that anything else is real. David Chalmers, among others, has done considerable work in this field, and on this subject he observes that: "Human beings are conscious beings; there is something like there is to be us. Human beings are intentional beings: we represent what is going on in the world. Correspondingly, our specific mental states, such as perceptions and thoughts, often have a phenomenal character: there is something like there is to be in them. These mental states also have intentional content: they serve to represent the world."[13]

Portalism holds that Consciousness is a fundamental force of nature, an all-encompassing horizon in which subjective experience becomes possible. Although as a force of nature, much like gravity being ubiquitous throughout the world, it contains no content in and of itself. All living things have the ability to manifest a localization of Consciousness through their respective portals resulting in the actualization of mind. Only in the mind is world made accessible, manifest, and encounterable to living things through their *being-in*, wherein a *de facto* identity between mind and world is established. As such, only mind can have content, the expansiveness and quality of this content being correlative to the sophistication of an organism's portal. Things are as conscious as things need to be. In organisms capable of self-awareness, content is created both from the mind's being-in-the-world as well as being-for-itself.

Regarding mental content, I certainly do not minimize the important contributions made by analytic philosophers in epistemological thought and cognitive science, and my decision not to explore them deeper stems not only from my lack of training in psychology but from the observation that regardless of where the truth lies, either in the extracranial mind of the externalists, or the mind-brain identity of the physicalists, the cognitive aspects of mental content would function the same, as cognition requires only the *existence* of a mind. The locus of mind, as far as the mechanics of cognition go, would be irrelevant as long as there exists a world to cognate and a mind to disclose it.

Hallucinations, Illusions, and Déjà Vu

The subject of hallucination and illusion has been addressed by every book on consciousness that I have ever read, and although it is primarily presented as a topic of perception and cognition, there are important elements that I feel should be addressed that pertain to my previous discussion on realism. The phenomenon is particular to sighted people or people who, once being sighted, have lost their vision. The question is this: if consciousness is being-in-the-world, and the world is the reality of physical objects, then how do we account for visual manifestations of things that are not real?

The answer depends on how one defines reality, and this inevitably collapses back to perception and the debate over naïve and representational realism. As I shall discuss in the next section, mind experiences two realities, a shared reality in wake state and an unshared reality in dream state, wherein the shared reality is defined as perceptions of the world that are veridical and verifiable, while the unshared reality of dream state is, in physical terms, unreal. If reality is so described, then I would submit that neither definition is correct.

Reality does not require veridicality in order to be real. If something is perceived, then it is real to the perceiver. The fact of whether or not it is similarly perceived by other perceivers is irrelevant. Hallucinations are a perfect example of this, being very real to the observer yet not veridical. The fact is that the phenomenology of hallucinations and veridical perceptions are identical. Disjunctivists dispute this, holding the position of direct realism wherein the presence of a physical object is required for perception, and as there is no physical object present in the case of hallucination, there cannot be commonality between the two experiences.

A.J. Ayer's *Argument from Hallucination* would show this conclusion to be erroneous. This ingenious case has been framed in many different ways, but the basic logic of it is:

P1. Fred perceives a camel.

P2. There is no camel in front of Fred – it is a hallucination.

P3. The camel that Fred perceives is something mental.

P4. Fred's hallucination is phenomenologically identical to the veridical perception of a camel.

C1. No camel, nor any other material object, is required for perceptual experience.

C2. The immediate object of perception is something mental.

This argument would be incompatible with the direct realism of the disjunctivists, and compatible with representational realism, which holds that we can never see the object-in-itself, but only the object-as-itself. Kant famously refers to this definition of perception as Transcendental Idealism; that we can never see the world as it is, but only how it presents itself to us – his concept of the noumenal world as opposed to the phenomenal world. This is consistent with any philosophy of idealism, in that we don't actually perceive an object, only an ideal, or image, of that object, in mind.

As with any historical debate in philosophy this gives us a lot to unpack, but fortunately we don't have to do that here. That which regards the nature of perception I shall leave to the epistemologists while focusing back upon the meta-question of: *What is reality?* If the phenomenology is identical in both hallucinatory and veridical experience, then Fred's subjective experience of the camel is real. It is real to Fred, because that is how reality is objectively presenting itself – to Fred.

A hallucination is defined as the experience involving the apparent perception of something not present. But *not present* is not the same as *not real*. Hallucinations are explicitly concrete to the perceiver, and although the immediate object of the hallucination is not present, the hallucination in and of itself is definitely not unreal, as Searle observes: "The perception in the hallucinatory case was not veridical, but all the same in this case you were still *conscious of something*. Indeed you were *aware of something*, and we could even say – though we might have to put 'sneer' quotes around 'see' when we say it, you did *see something*."[14]

John Searle points out that actual hallucination is extremely rare. In his argument against Disjunctivism, he quotes the psychiatrist D.H. ffytche (2012), "What goes on in the brain when you hallucinate? It's the same as when you experience real things." Searle, a defender of direct realism, dispenses with Disjunctivism by showing that its assertion that no commonality exists between hallucinations and veridical experience is false, whereupon he concludes that: "If you deny that the hallucinatory experience and the veridical experience can be phenomenologically and intentionalistically exactly the same, then you know you have made a mistake."[15]

Although hallucinations can be induced by drugs, the majority of people that experience them are non-neurotypical. I refrain from using the words 'mentally ill' as I am not convinced that what these afflicted people experience necessarily meets the definition of an illness (see chapter 6). Focusing again on what constitutes reality, while engaged in the performance of research on the possibility of psychedelic drugs as treatment for schizophrenia, the English psychiatrist Humphry Osmond made this interesting observation in 1952: "Osmond realized with a shock that when schizophrenics spoke of seeing boiling skies, having strange beasts stare back at them in the mirror, and feeling menace all around them, they were not delusional or simply talking nonsense – they were describing the world as it objectively appeared to them."[16] When one makes such a characterization of their world, it must stand as an explicit description of *their* reality.

Illusions are entirely different from hallucinations, and all of us experience them on an everyday basis. Probably the most common illusion is when we look into a mirror. We perceive our image in the glass before us, but the image isn't in the mirror at all, as that would mean that the reflected image would be a property of the mirror. All we are seeing are light rays being reflected off the silvered glass. If we are at the carnival we might see mirrors that make us look fat or huge headed, or otherwise distorted, none of which is the truth.

In philosophy, the gold standard for illusion has to be the bent stick. With this illusion we come upon a crystal clear pond and see a stick protruding from the water. Closer observation reveals that the stick bends at a noticeable angle at the point where it enters the surface of the pond. Our sensory modalities are capturing this perception faithfully – there is a stick in the water, and our brain processes this data correctly into consciousness. And here is where it goes off the rails. Our minds perceive the stick in the water as an image collected by the eyes and disclosed to mind by the brain via the portal connection to consciousness, but that is all that is perceived – neither the rods and cones of the eyes nor the processing and filtering lobes of the brain ever attached a perceptual tag to this image claiming that the stick is bent. Such tags are created by the mind, the subjective realm where interpretation and meaning are assigned to the sensory information. That which is offered by the brain to the mind is only information, and information is not knowledge. True, when we see the bend in the stick we are seeing something other than the truth about the shape of the stick, and yet what we are seeing, as with the example of the mirror, may not be the truth, but it is nevertheless the reality. The stick appears bent. The externalist Ted Honderich describes it best: "the bent stick is what a real physical stick is; it is exactly something that looks different under different conditions. If it didn't… it wouldn't be a real physical thing. If a tree didn't look smaller as you got further away from it, it wouldn't be a tree. It would be something like the number 66 or a dream-tree or whatever."[17]

In reality a thing appears as it is, although that appearance manifests differently under different conditions, but it is not within the powers of the brain to *know* what those conditions are. As mind, most educated persons understand the refraction of light, and anyone that has had a course in photogrammetry has performed the equations that determine the angle of light refraction through water and crown glass. Any and all assignment of relevance, context, definition, relationship, and meaning to sensory data collected and processed by the brain is a function of mind. The world is reality, and the contents of the world are exactly as they appear.

Honderich's pronouncement upon the bent stick illusion is reminiscent of the famous battles between the perceptual idealist David Hume with his 'thoughts and impressions', and Thomas Reid, a proponent of direct realism and also the founder of Scottish Common Sense Realism. For example, Hume is mystified that anyone can believe that what we see is anything more than an image or impression of the actual object, in this case a table: "The table, which we see, seems to diminish, as we remove farther from it: But the real table, which exists independent of us, suffers no alteration: It was, therefore, nothing but its image, which was present to the mind. These are the obvious dictates of reason, and no man, who reflects, ever doubted, that the existences, which we consider... are nothing but perceptions in the mind, and fleeting copies or representations of other existences, which remain uniform and independent."[18] To which an equally mystified Reid replies: "I observe that Mr. Hume's argument not only has no strength to support his conclusion, but that it leads to the contrary conclusion – to wit, that it is the real table we see; for this plain reason, that the table we see has precisely that apparent magnitude which it is demonstrable that the real table must have when placed at that distance. Let the table be placed successively at a thousand different distances, open your eyes and you will see a table precisely of that apparent magnitude, and that apparent figure, which the real table must have in that distance and in that position. Is this not a strong argument that it is the real table you see?"[19]

Philosophers in the 18th century tended to be wordy, while Honderich got it right in only a few elegantly concise lines. The bitter feud between Hume and Reid continued for decades, only ending with Hume's death in 1776. This very same gauntlet was then picked up by Kant in 1788 in *The Critique of Pure Reason*, and the debate between direct and representational realism, specifically the nature of reality as determined by appearance and perception, continues on to this day.

The sensation of dèjá vu is arguably better documented than that of hallucinations. Some believe that déjà vu is a duplicative re-experience of a situation encountered in dream state, while others insist that it is a phenomenon of split perception, wherein an original series of sensory data was for some reason incomplete or occluded, while a second perception of the identical data results in an accurate set of data, this act of duplication resulting in a feeling of having been there or done that before. Still another explanation holds that the brain is constantly processing and filtering data coming in from the senses and on occasion may store information that we are not consciously cognizant of, in other words, a memory that we don't remember. This is called cryptomnesia, and when this information is successfully recalled, it having been previously stored causes a déjà vu.

One explanation that I favor is dual neurological processing, proposed by Robert Efron in 1964. He explains how the brain sorts incoming sensory signals in the temporal lobe, but that sometimes they can enter twice, once from each hemisphere, wherein they can become unsynchronized. When this happens the signals are processed twice, with a delay of only milliseconds between each instance. As the results become cognitively available, a feeling of déjà vu is manifested.

I like Efron's concept because it reminds me of a discussion of déjà vu that I had with a colleague of mine a few years ago. Dr. Richard Wahrer is a biologist out of Texas A&M and one of the scientists whose work I supported as a GIS programmer/analyst and cartographer at the Kentucky Department for Natural Resources. His elegantly simple theory is that sometimes the brain just *stutters*.[20] Mechanistically, this is not significantly different than Efron's explanation, Wahrer's stutter being roughly equivalent in process to Efron's unsynchronized incoming signals. Yet there is an implication of temporality in Wahrer's perspective that could indicate a slight divergence between the two explanations that I find compelling. In dual neurological processing, the information itself enters the processing center at two different points in time, where in Wahrer's hypothesis, the sensory information enters the temporal lobe for processing only once, but then the brain stutters, the result being that the brain is not linearly processing the experience twice, but duplicating it by spatially stacking the experience twice upon a single moment in time. Cognitively, the mind perceives this aberration as a stutter in time itself, disclosing the two events to itself as a temporal singularity manifested phenomenologically as the *something-like-there-is-to-have-been-here-before*.

This explanation would seem to be compatible with the fact that two-thirds of people have had the experience of déjà vu, while the remaining third has never experienced it at all. This could be attributed to the fact that in one-third of human beings, their brains simply don't stutter. If the split perception model or cryptomnesia are correct, then everyone should experience déjà vu at some point, as it would be inherent in the mechanics of the brain going about its performance of sensory information processing and memory management, and yet everyone does not. Déjà vu has been established by the medical and psychological communities to be a neurological anomaly, but exactly what it is and how it happens is still a matter of conjecture. People suffering with epilepsy are reported to experience it frequently, but déjà vu has not been scientifically linked either to mental illness or personality disorders, nor has any genetic origin been discovered. People that travel often or watch lots of movies seem to have them more frequently, and the frequency of episodes has been discovered to diminish with age. Speaking from personal experience, I have always had episodes of déjà vu, some of them quite intense, and I have also noticed a decline in their number as I have aged. I will conclude that the next time you feel that you have been here before, you have – twice in the same place while only once in time.

There is nothing in Portalism that is incompatible with hallucinations, illusions, or déjà vu, as the locus of the mind has little to do with what are essentially perceptual and cognitive events. Phenomenologically, hallucination and veridical experiences are identical, and illusions caused by nature, distance, and the physics of electromagnetism are exactly as they appear, the issue being not with the presentation of what we see as illusory, but the meaning that we choose to assign to those presentations.

Wake State and Dream State

Whether we are awake or asleep we are still conscious. In fact, unless we suffer a traumatic brain injury, go under total anesthesia, or die, we are in some state of consciousness at all times.

The subjective realm has two states – wake state and dream state. In wake state the mind is either in the phenomenal mode of being-in-the-world, or in the mode of self-awareness, otherwise known as reflexive consciousness. In wake state, we are phenomenally conscious of our own bodies in the world. As physical objects our bodies are governed by the laws of physics and bound in space and time. Whenever we are awake and in the world, our minds are also bound in space and time, because although the mind is a localization of Consciousness it is nevertheless tethered to a physical body, which like all objects, is pinned in space and time.

But in dream state (REM sleep) although we are not consciously aware of our bodies we nonetheless remain absolutely conscious. While we sleep, the brain operates at a reduced level of energy, recharging itself and taking care of the housekeeping responsibilities of sorting out the events of the day, categorizing, time stamping, and storing memories, basically reorganizing itself like the biological machine that it is. It even disables the body by temporarily paralyzing it, allowing the muscles and organs to recover their energy. This is accomplished through the neurotransmitters gamma-aminobutyric acid and glycine causing REM sleep paralysis by switching off the specialized cells in the brain that allow muscles to be active (Brooks and Peever 2012). While in dream state, our minds become untethered to the body and are no longer in the world; no longer subject to its physics, and unbound in space and time. The portal, like the brain, operates in a reduced state as memories of experiences pass through to consciousness and fuel our dreams.

When our consciousness is in the mode of being-in-the-world, we exist in a shared reality, wherein our experience is veridical and verifiable, but while in dream state we operate within an unshared reality, wherein our experiences are non-veridical and unverifiable. Which is real? We cannot say for certain, because in dream state our experiences are every bit as authentic as those in wake state. While dreaming, if I stub my toe on the leg of a dream coffee table I feel pain, I stumble, perhaps fall. If I fall off a dream cliff, the thrill of falling is the same. If I am bitten by a dream dog I feel the sharpness of the teeth and the pressure of the jaws, I become emotionally frightened, I am in pain, and my quadriceps strain from running away. Nightmares can be even more terrifying than wake state experiences as I can hear the dream monsters chasing me down hallways of closed doors, and when I am caught, the effects of their claws and teeth meet every definition of reality.

On a brighter note, as mind is no longer bound by physics I can fly and even breathe under water, unrestricted by any physical limitations. Although I 'have' a body in dream state, I can change it at will, becoming someone or something else; perhaps I am young again, enjoying the company of family and friends long passed out of my life yet here with me once more. I am also unstuck in space, able to be at any place simply by imagining it. Although I might wake up and get some water, I can usually go back to sleep and pick up the dream where it left off. Time, as I experience it in wake state, does not exist. My only limitation in the dream state reality is that I am unable to experience anything the elements of which I have not previously experienced in wake state, and this is the phenomenon that unifies the two realities as a conscious singularity. I cannot be 'wake state Jeff' or 'dream state Jeff', I can only be *conscious* Jeff because consciousness is all I am and can ever be. Whether consciousness dwells in the subjective reality of being-in-the-world or that of the unbound existence of dream state, I can never *be* any more or less than my mind, regardless of what conscious reality, shared or unshared, I am experiencing. In wake state, mind is in the world and its acts are confined by the world's physical limits, but in dream state, mind is boundless.[21]

Fields of Perception and Inattentional Blindness

The sensory modalities that gather information about the world belong to the body, itself being a thing in the world. It is the body that moves through the world, and the external mind is tethered to the body in an existential relationship of codependence. Physical objects in the world become disclosed to the mind through perception, that perception being limited by the range of the body's senses. At all times, wherever our bodies are in the world, this range represents our available field of perception.

This perception can also extend to non-physical entities in the world such as verbal communication, for example if I hear a person say, "I just love sand in my bathing suit," I can perceive the sarcasm, yet the voice, as sound waves, is a thing in the world and so is within my perceptual field. For the sighted, the field of perception is a function of space. When I go outside and view my backyard I see the objects present within it, the fences that bound it, and my neighbor's house, and I also see the jet airplane flying above me. Space is defined by distance, and I perceive the various distances between me and the objects whose reflected light my eyes are sensing. The tree line is forty feet away, the barbecue is ten feet away, and the jet is 20,000 feet away from my body's current position in the world. Of its physical objects, all I can know of the world is that which is encounterable within my current field of perception. If I, as mind, wish to know about the Yankees game, I must direct my body to take me to the stadium so that I may 'see' it, or else to a device or person capable of communicating the information I seek. In a field of perception, proximity governs the availability of objects that can be known to the knower.

Fields of perception are quite different for the blind, particularly for those that have never known sight. Other than the square foot of ground beneath their feet, the role of space becomes diminished if not irrelevant because visual distances cannot be ascertained. In the reality of the blind, the distance between me and the front door of the bank becomes a meaningless equation. The distance to the bank is however long it takes me to find my way to it. Distance becomes no longer a function of space, but a function of time. For the blind, the sensory modality of touch largely replaces that of vision, although greater emphasis upon hearing and smell is also brought forth. In many cases the loss of one sense, say vision, increases the magnitude of the others as the brain rewires itself by redirecting the energy previously spent on vision to the other sense modalities. For the blind, distance is manifested by touch. Being blind, my laser cane taps upon an object. I reach out and identify it as a tree. This action manifests a distance, as I now understand the tree to be an arm's-length away, but as soon as I move away from the tree, the distance, as a spatial phenomenon, is once again unknowable. If I hear birdsong I can identify it as a blue jay, and I can turn in its direction, but what that direction is in relation to true north I can only estimate. "The whole significance of our life, from which theoretical significance is merely extracted, would be different if we were sightless."[22]

Intentionality plays an interesting role in fields of perception because all perceptual experiences have intentional content. Intentionality is the power of mind to be *about* something – one cannot simply be conscious, they must be conscious of something. Perhaps the Zen masters can clear the mind through meditation, but if you think this is easy I invite you to try it. The vast majority of us are thinking about something at all times, even in dream state. There are two components to any perceptual field; the thing I am focused upon, and background. Imagine you are standing on a rocky beach looking out at the sea. You are focused on as much sea as your vision can take in – a rather large area of ocean running out to the horizon. You are not focused upon the rocks, or the lighthouse in the distance, or the birds crying overhead, although you may be aware of them. Suddenly your vision detects a disturbance on the surface, which you identify as a dolphin making her way along the sandbar 100 yards out. To the mind, the dolphin has become salient, and our intentional consciousness becomes narrowly focused upon it while everything else becomes background by default.

It seems simple, but we must remember that consciousness

is in the world, and part and parcel of everything that the mind comprehends to be world. While we are mentally focused on the dolphin everything else in our perceptual field becomes background but it certainly doesn't disappear. The mind is still assigning context and meaning to everything within that field of perception even though our intentional consciousness is on the dolphin. The object of mental focus can be determined by mind or brain, the former voluntary, and the latter involuntary. As willing agents, we are able to choose what we focus upon, but evolution has instilled various survival reflexes that override choice. These can appear as responses to sudden or irregular movements, such as the shift of my focus to the dolphin breaking the surface of the sea. They can be loud or uncommon noises, or particularly foul smells, all of these examples having in common the property of being 'out of the ordinary' in respects to the contextual nature of our current field of perception. For example, if I am at a zoo watching the monkeys, I might not 'notice' a zebra to any degree that might promote it from background into the focus of my perception as zebras are common objects at zoos and as such it is not out of the ordinary to see them. But if I am in my backyard with my friends grilling bratwursts and a zebra walks by, its *out-of-the-ordinariness* in this environment would cause it to come to the forefront of my attention.

Mind is in the world, conscious at all times of everything regardless of where the mind's *immediate* focus is directed. If this were not the case we would not be able to perform such tasks as driving or hunting. Searle explains it best: "All conscious perceptual experience occurs as part of a total conscious field. It is important to remind ourselves of this because some authors who write about perception treat it as existing in isolation. It does not. I cannot consciously see the glass of beer in front of me without having a whole lot of other conscious states as part of my total subjective conscious field."[23]

If so, then one might ask what about 'phone blindness' – the case where one is so focused on their phone that they become oblivious to surrounding stimuli, in some cases to their own peril? This question drifts into the subject of cognitive deficit, so I will abbreviate the answer by addressing only its perceptual ramifications. Phone blindness is actually a form of inattentional blindness. The next time you are waiting for a flight at the airport, take notice of the men and women standing and holding phones to their ear. In many cases you will note that they are slowly turning in circles, absolutely oblivious to their surroundings or to the fact that they are rotating in place. They are in the mode of ready-to-hand, focused upon the tasks of thinking and conversation. When the attendant announces their flight, or another passenger accidentally caroms into them, they become unready-to-hand as their consciousness moves from reflexive to phenomenal and back again. One of the most famous experiments linked to inattentional blindness involves people walking along a busy urban street talking on their phones, listening to headphones, or otherwise focused on a non-walking personal activity. On the same street travelling in the opposite direction is a clown riding a unicycle. Experiments revealed that the people on their phones were least likely to notice the clown.[24] Tragically, due to inattentional blindness, when automobiles injure or kill cyclists, it is commonly the case that driver of the car never 'saw' them.

Inattentional blindness has been well studied, and like many neurological researches the results consist of a myriad of cognitive and neuropsychological theories and speculations. These include late and early processing of stimuli by the brain's filtering, or gating, systems; inattentional amnesia, visual neglect, inattentional agnosia, expectation, perceptual cycles, and stimulus overload reactions. Portalism is not a theory of cognition, as all of these listed above are, nevertheless they are important to Portalism because their premises make assumptions regarding the filtering of sensory information and the disclosure of that information to consciousness.

It is important to understand that the theories of inattentional blindness which I have listed have one trait in common; they all assume the same starting physicalist premise, that the mind is the brain. A common thread among these theories is that brain filtering mechanisms, meaning the neural process of sensory gating, chooses what information to disclose to consciousness based upon what the mind is concentrating upon at a given time. The differences in the theories amount to speculations over how the brain actually accomplishes that action, and what it does, if anything, with the information that never reaches consciousness. Because these theories subscribe to mind-brain identity, they are not too concerned about causal pathways, assuming that since the brain is the mind, the causal path will always be upwards. Portalism rejects this assumption. The reason inattentional blindness is important to Portalism does not involve its cognitive aspects; it is important because it highlights not only the fallacy of mind-brain identity, but also that of single path causation.

It is the function of the brain to gather and process sensory information. The brain then filters out redundant and/or flawed and defective data and makes it available to consciousness. Where the theories on inattentional blindness fall down is in claiming that the brain either discards, withholds, forgets, or commits to some temporary memory buffer (the precise excluding action being dependent on the particular theory), all processed information that is *irrelevant to what the mind is concentrating on at that given moment*. Portalism asks, 'How exactly does the brain know what the mind is concentrating on at all?' The answer is that it doesn't – it can't – because the brain can't think. To theorize that the brain is aware of the context and content of the mind's intentional focus would be the same as claiming that my wristwatch knows what time it is. True, the processed information disclosed to consciousness does have irrelevant information filtered out in deference to whatever the mind is concentrating upon at any given moment, but as the brain is not in the world, this can only occur by the mind's disclosing of that focus to the brain.

Imagine that there are two men playing chess in the park. Chess requires immense concentration within a narrow perceptual field. Both men are consumed in thought and immersed in reflexive consciousness. As a result they don't see the attractive girl roller-skate by in her bikini. Suddenly one of them gets hit in the back of the head with an errant Frisbee. Concentration then shifts into phenomenal consciousness within a much broader field of perception as he turns to behold a young boy begging his forgiveness. Once again he turns and focuses upon the game. From the visual sense the brain receives the reflected light from the black and white pieces, and from memory it can make available the rules of chess and furnish previous experiences acquired by years of playing the game, but it does not 'know' how to play chess and it cannot decide what the 'best' moves might be, because it doesn't 'know' that it is even playing chess – it is simply processing sensory input. Consider the analogy of typing data into a database. The computer accepts the ASCII letters typed in from a keyboard acting as a passive sensory data collector, translates the data into machine language, stores them and makes them available to addressable memory if I require the data. At no time does the computer know why I am typing this particular data in, or how I intend to ultimately use the data, or how the data fits within the overall scheme of things. Similarly, how can a brain, being inside the skull and removed from the world, possibly determine what the mind is focused upon unless it is the mind that discloses it? I will make the argument for downward causation in a later section where I will take up the obvious questions that this claim raises, but for now simply remain open to the idea of downward causation.

The fact is that consciousness is always in a state of inattentional blindness to some degree because it is impossible to focus intentional consciousness on more than one thing at a time. Depending on the intensity of concentration, this can range from ignoring that which is not an impending threat, as when we are driving (trees passing, parked cars, etc.), to not seeing the clown on the unicycle. In other words, this blindness can extend from the indifference toward simple background to the complete omission of something (the clown) that never became salient due to the presence of a level of concentration that causes the brain to filter out peripheral distractions. If I am just walking down the street in the everydayness of unreflective consciousness, mentally on hold until my destination is reached, I would have seen the clown on the unicycle because in that context his out-of-the-ordinariness would have caused it to become immediately salient within my expansive field of perception. But making the same trip while reading my e-mail or thinking about breaking up with my girlfriend (reflexive concentration), my field of perception is correspondingly altered by its focus having turned inward, and the brain filters out irrelevant information from background accordingly, with the result that I never 'notice' the clown. Thus what we are able to perceive becomes codependent upon the dimensions of the field of perception, and our level of focused concentration on an object or thought within that field.

Aesthetics

Aesthetics is arguably the most obvious manifestation of qualia, and thus the biggest thorn in the side of materialists struggling to find neural correlates for it. This is largely due to the fact that aesthetics are radically inconsistent from one person to another, therefore one mind to another, with the added complexity that such feelings and preferences often undergo changes over time within each individual.

The philosophy of aesthetics deals with the appreciation of beauty and the principles of artistic taste. To hold that viewing a painting by Botticelli correlates to the firing of a specific neural network would appear to be ambitious. Is this the neural network for a certain Botticelli or for all Botticelli's works, as type identity might warrant, or is this the neural network for all Italian Renaissance painting, as per token identity? Images of neural activity for such stimuli vary from brain to brain. And what if I don't happen to like Botticelli, or I am uneducated in fine art and don't know who Botticelli was, or what his art even looks like? Do these Botticelli neural networks go unused? If this were the case then Botticelli networks would be innate, which would be absurd, thus all such networks must be established at perception time. If so, then how are these neural network correlates explained in the case when my tastes change over time? When, as a child I first heard Tony Bennett sing I didn't care for him, mainly because he was not-Beatles, yet today you will find not only Bennett, but Astaire and Sinatra in my library, right next to a complete Beatles collection. Are new neural network correlates created to reflect this change in taste, and further, are these new neural networks causally responsible for my change in preference? The implied complexity is enough to make a physicalist embrace hard eliminative materialism, as it's so much simpler to claim that aesthetic taste, being qualia, doesn't really exist and therefore doesn't need to be accounted for.

Aesthetic taste is subjective, not physical, so it cannot be accounted for in physical terms. Take the example where you and I are both educated, well-travelled individuals brought up in places where exposure to art, music, and theater were available. Perhaps at first our parents forced it upon us, as in my case with Tchaikovsky's *Nutcracker* and a performance of *Macbeth* at the Kennedy Center, but eventually we, as individuals, decide what we admire, as opposed to what the other says we *should* admire. Imagine we are now both at the Metropolitan Gallery, both looking at a still life by Paul Cézanne, or a landscape by John Constable. I am intrigued by the use of different perspectives in the compositions of Cézanne, but you just see a bowl of fruit. Observing the Constable, I claim that if I believed in heaven, that this is what it would look like, while you are unmoved. In the very next room is a Jackson Pollock that you find ecstatically thrilling in its boundless possibilities, while I start to think about lunch.

Tastes and preferences change over time. It is likely that very few people enjoy their first oyster or their first beer, yet for many a taste for them is acquired over time. I have never tasted cottage cheese – I just can't stand how it looks, but my wife loves it. Together we both enjoy oysters and beer, but we do differ over things – cottage cheese for me; pudding for her. She loves The Doors, while I find them okay but appreciate the genius. I like to read plays by Ibsen and Chekhov, while she doesn't like to read plays at all. Music appreciation represents perhaps the most divisive category when it comes to personal preference. Out of the seven billion of us, not many appreciate jazz, but those that do tend to be energetically adamant fans of that style of music. In the world, everyone that can hear has heard music, be it Bach, birdsong, or sticks banging on hollow trees. Age and culture play a huge role in influencing our preferences for just about everything from food and drink to music and theater. The choices are so myriad and plentiful, the nuances so subtle, and the changes in taste over time so common, that the phenomena of aesthetics should be proof apparent that a realm of subjectivity exists at least in some form. Another undeniable effect of the arts is to evoke emotion. Ultimately, as aesthetic preferences are subjective, to claim that they influence our emotions means to embrace the concept of downward causation. For a materialist to insist that these *feelings*, these artistic preferences, have neural origins and are epiphenomenally causal would seem to be a case of desperation in trying to fit an enormously complex and shifting set of speculations into the framework of a preconceived theory. But in the interests of continuing this discussion of aesthetics, let us take a leap of faith and assume that feelings exist.

Aesthetics being a subjective theme, I can only speak for myself, but I can state with certainty that there are examples of artistic creations that can change the way I feel at any given moment. When I hear Beatles music my mood improves. I understand that this is because of the melody, being an amateur musician myself, still it is a simple fact that this music makes me happier when I hear it. The art of Edvard Munch disturbs me, and when I see the paintings of Edward Hopper I feel cold, remote, and disassociated. When I hear the first movement of Beethoven's *Sixth*, or the fourth movement of his *Ninth*, I am frequently moved to tears. I don't know why – there is no corresponding event in my life associated with Beethoven that should invoke such a response, but it does. I am descended from Scots-Welsh, and the first time I ever heard bagpipes I loved them. If my evolutionary ethnicity – if that's even a thing – has anything to do with that I could not say, but I can say that now, after all these years, when I hear bagpipes I'm good for about thirty seconds before I am ready to move on. There are countless scenes in countless movies that also invoke tears, joy, laughter, pity, empathy, and anger. I am sure that this is the case with most people in the world, as it is the primary reason that movies are so popular in the first place.

My point in presenting these examples is to illustrate that aesthetics, being subjective, can and often do evoke physical response. Take the case of the movie *The Elephant Man*, and the scene wherein John Merrick is invited to Dr. Treves' home to meet his wife in an effort to establish a feeling of normalcy in Merrick's life. Of course the children have been sent away so as not to subject them to Merrick's startling deformity. Merrick shows a portrait of his mother to Mrs. Treves who comments upon her beauty. In response Merrick looks again at the picture and agrees that she is indeed beautiful, and then says softly that, "I must have been a great disappointment to her." I have watched this scene many times, and the hopeless unfairness of it never fails to move me. But what is actually going on here? True, my sensory modalities of sight and sound detect the light and sound waves from the television which are subsequently processed by my brain, but there is no possibility that the brain, removed from the world, can assign the meaning necessary to affect my mood or cause my tear glands to activate. Interpretation of sensory input and the subsequent assignment of context and meaning is a subjective activity occurring only in mind. At this point I, as mind, react emotionally manifesting a *feeling* of empathy, passing it causally downward from mind to brain, which accordingly stimulates my tear ducts. Artistic taste, or the lack of it, is entirely subjective. The brain has no ability to prefer one thing over another, because doing so would require reason and the brain can't think. Any emotional responses that aesthetics engender are actualized only by encounters with physical stimuli, and all such stimuli are in the world. Art, music, poetry, drama, romance, and tragedy are things in the world, and our preference for or against them can only be manifested through the mind's connection with the world. This explanation is thus compatible with Portalism, as the mind becomes the world through its *being-in*. As such, a phenomenal externalist theory accounting for the phenomenon of aesthetics will enjoy superior plausibility over any reductive materialist explanation.

As I have previously stated, in this work I do not intend to delve deeply into cognition as my only goal is to demonstrate plausibility for the theory of Portalism by describing the nature of consciousness, yet any discussion of aesthetics presupposes cognition. In order to feel removed and remote at seeing Hopper's *The Nighthawks* I must first be cognitive of it. Precisely how the mechanics of cognitive processes function I leave to the psychologists and epistemologists to explain. Qualia are *prima facie*. Aesthetics are about *feelings*, and I have presented this section not to hypothesize upon cognition but to demonstrate how downward causation is necessary if aesthetics and the feelings that they engender in the form of emotion exist. The reader is free to draw their own conclusion, but if they have ever *felt* themselves moved by a song, a painting, a poem, a sunset, a lover's gaze, the loss of a pet, or the first sight of their newborn child's face, then any doubt that qualia exists must be removed.

Pathways of Causality

At this point it becomes obvious that the plausibility of Portalism is contingent upon the concept of dual-path causality, specifically downward causality wherein mental events can causally interact with physical events. Science and physicalism assume the reductionist explanation of causality, in that every physical event has a physical cause. Yet many are skeptical, holding that we can never 'see' the cause, a cause not being a thing in the world. I cannot hold a cause in my hand, it has no mass, form, extension, number, charge or spin. In David Hume's opinion the best we can ever do is to *infer* the cause of an event. Although it is certainly true that all effects have a cause, and it is also true that causality is necessary to the manner in which we temporally order events, it nevertheless remains that the cause simpliciter amounts to no more than a form of intuition. In opposition to the empiricism of Hume and Locke, Schopenhauer argued that causality is actually understood *a priori*: "the fact that we always associate a cause to an effect is an innate process and could not be otherwise, since it is the only way to give a meaning to all empirical experiences. By experience alone, we would perceive only a temporal succession of unconnected states."[25]

If the physicalist argument for causality is that all physical events have physical causes, then there would seem to be a dependency established between the event and the cause, as there could not be one without the other. If that is the case, then to argue causality at all would be to claim that physical events (that have causes) are events that have causes, which would be tautological. Nevertheless, I have no problem granting that causality exists in the objective realm, albeit either as an unobservable physical property, an intuitive understanding, or an inferred act. Why then should physicalists be resistant to granting the same admission to mental events in the subjective realm? The answer is that they reject the existence of such a realm, continuing to insist that mental events, if they exist at all, arise from and can be correlated to neurological activity, and they continue to cling to this intuition despite the lack of any scientific evidence to support it.

Most physicalist or property dualist theories embrace mind-brain type/token identity wherein the locus of consciousness is embodied inside the cranium. Reductionist theories search for neural correlates to mental states while others uncomfortably admit that although mental states may exist, it doesn't matter because they can have no affectual influence whatsoever upon physical events. This school of thought is called Epiphenomenalism, and it represents the last theoretical straw to be grasped by a mind-brain materialism drowning under the weight of its own dogma. Epiphenomenalism holds that mental states are dependent upon physical functions but are not causally reducible to physical states. However, because mental states cannot cause physical events, they are therefore meaningless causal dead ends. Causality is a one-way path only, from the physical – meaning the brain – to the mind. If mental events exist at all then the brain must cause them, but it can never be the other way around, as to entertain such a thought would be dualistic, amounting to the admission of the existence of something non-physical outside of the physical world – specifically a realm of subjective experience – and that this subjective realm is causally empowered to initiate events within the physical world through causal pathways that can, and do, travel in both directions. Epiphenomenalists reject this possibility and are wrong to do so.

If causality is, as the epiphenomenalists hold, a one-way path and mental events are unable to cause physical effects, then some awkward questions are brought forth. If true, then Beethoven's *Ninth* was a neurological event, meaning that one day this grey mass of cells in Ludwig's head conceived the melody, commanded the hand to write it down, adapted Schiller's "Ode" into lyrics while abiding by all the rules of Western music theory. Additionally, given the subject matter of the *Ninth*, we must conclude that Ludwig's brain was inspired by God prior to its decision to undertake this labor. This is to say that the brain is capable of composing music in much the same manner in which it receives chemical information from the kidneys that the body needs water and causally directs the body to go find some and drink it. If this explanation is too much to ask one to believe, then what is the alternative? The answer is that Beethoven spent much of his early life learning music and composition, the rules of which were dutifully stored in his explicit and procedural memory. At the same time Ludwig was in the world, experiencing the uncertainties of late 18th and early 19th century Europe, cultivating a religion and forming an understanding of the role of God in the world. One day he sat down at the piano and created a masterpiece – from mind, as a mind was all Ludwig was, and all any of us can ever be.

To believe that the brain, while processing sensory information, suddenly became compelled to compose the *Ninth* is a long reach, but that is exactly what must have happened unless we embrace the idea of dual-path causality, meaning that Beethoven at his piano conceived the melody in mind (including parts from snippets of earlier work he was saving), causally recalling the rules of composition from the neural connections in the brain's long-term explicit memory, and proceeded to write his last symphony. This is an example of dual-path causality in task performance, initiated from mind, carried out simultaneously in milliseconds, seamlessly and evenly manifested as *thought*.

There is a strong thought experiment along these same lines that demonstrates the existence of dual-path causality. In this research study, a healthy woman participant is placed into a room by herself. The room is empty, windowless, and the walls, floor and ceiling are painted white so as to be free of any sensory distractions. A piece of notepaper is slid under the door. She picks up the note, reads its contents and collapses in a faint. We presume that the note held some horrific news, perhaps something like, 'your daughter has been hit by a car', or some other phrase sure to invoke overwhelming emotion. Within a split second she becomes upset, fearful, and distraught to the degree that her blood pressure plummets and she goes into shock. The brain, ever homeostatically watchful of the body with an eye towards self-preservation, detects a sudden lack of oxygen getting up to the skull and immediately pulls the plug on consciousness, shutting down the portal and causing the body to fall unconsciously into a prone position so as to make it easier for blood to reach the brain. Nothing too surprising here, as everything happened just as it should have. Except that the brain can't read. In memory, it stores the rules of English syntax and semantics, but language processing – the task of assigning meaning and context to sounds, text, or hand signals – occurs in mind; the brain can't do it. The woman reading the note interpreted its meaning which caused the subsequent events to unfold. If instead, the note had said, 'Hi there, I think you're cute,' other emotions may have been invoked causing a different set of hopefully less dramatic events. This thought experiment is demonstrative of the existence of downward causality, wherein a mental event can cause a physical result.

A far more sophisticated argument for downward causality was put forth in 1980 in a paper by Donald Davidson where he famously introduces the *Theory of Anomalous Monism*, which in its first principle asserts:

> ... that at least some mental events interact causally with physical events. (We could call this the Principle of Causal Interaction.) Thus for example if someone sank the *Bismarck*, then various mental events such as perceivings, notings, calculations, judgements, decisions, intentional actions and changes in belief played a causal role in the sinking of the *Bismarck*. In particular, I would urge that the fact that someone sank the *Bismarck* entails that he moved his body in a way that was caused by mental events of certain sorts, and that this bodily movement in turn caused the *Bismarck* to sink.[26]

Davidson further hypothesizes that mental events can have relations with other mental events, and through these events have causal intercourse with physical events. This relaxation of the formerly rigid idea of causal pathways assumed by physicalists opens a considerable amount of blue sky in terms of explaining how thoughts can influence behaviors such as creativity and emotion, the results of these manifesting as physical events like laughing, weeping, or Beethoven's *Ninth*. Although Anomalous Monism resembles materialism, it creatively expands the boundaries of identity theory through its identification of at least some mental events with physical events, a direction that flies in the face of traditional type/token identity definitions of causality. He notes correctly that in the physical world events have causes, and that those causes correspond to some deterministic law, while at the same time proposing in the third principle that there can be no such 'psychophysical' laws that would operate similarly in the context of mental events: "The third principle is that there are no strict deterministic laws on the basis on which mental events can be predicted and explained (the Anomalism of the Mental)."[27]

Although Davidson's idea of dual-path causality is necessary to Portalism, he does not abandon monism for either dualism or phenomenal externalism, opting instead for framing his theory in terms of non-reductive supervenient physicalism. There is something about the intuitiveness of cranialism that monists just can't seem to let go of. Still, Davidson's out-of-the-box thinking some forty years ago yielded this truly elegant theory based upon a bold rethinking of causal pathways and the new possibilities they can unveil.

Underpinning the existence of the comfortable box-frame reality of the materialist is the concept of causal closure. Although it has its strong and weak forms, its basic premise is that only physical states exist and thus all physical states have only physical causes. In short, no physical event has a cause outside of the physical domain, because nothing outside the physical domain exists. Nothing outside the physical realm can exist because all of the energy in the universe is already accounted for. To start, I will admit my astonishment at materialism's unquestioning acceptance of causal closure as a bedrock fact, when in itself it is only another theory. To science, the concept of causal closure works so well with Newtonian physics that to question it would be ludicrous. But they have a lot riding on causal closure being true, because if it is not then some very sticky problems will need to be addressed. Chief among those would be acknowledging the possibility of the existence of a non-physical subjective realm; a realm where the scientific method is bereft of the tools necessary to explain its content and workings. The concrete certainty of physics, impressive with its

Portalism

explanations of the physical world, cannot explain subjective experience and so is of little use in metaphysics, and causality is a metaphysical concept.

Not all questions concerning the validity of causal closure originate from metaphysics or even from philosophy. For example, causal closure doesn't work in quantum physics. In a 2018 experiment using a polarizing beam splitter, photons of different polarizations were sent along different paths:

> In their experiment, Romero, Costa and colleagues created a 'quantum switch', in which photons can take two paths. One path involves being subjected to operation A before operation B, while in the other path B occurs before A. The order in which the operations are performed is determined by the initial polarization of the photon as it enters the switch. The two paths are then recombined, and the polarization of the photons is measured. The operations A and B are designed such that the order in which they are applied to the photons affects the polarization of the output photons – if the system has causality. The team did the experiment using several different types of operation for A and B and in all cases they found that the measured polarization of the output photons was consistent with there being no definite causal order between when A and B was applied.[28]

If one embraces the idea of dual-path causality, then by extension one embraces the idea that something non-physical is able to affect physical events, and causal closure is false. But the quantum is physical, and causality is clearly not closed within that physical reality. I fail to comprehend how any admission that causal closure is not the case makes the heavens fall for the scientific world. If it does, then perhaps science needs to reexamine its assumptions regarding the boundaries of reality. Assuming causality actually exists, and I believe it

160

does if only as a necessary intuition, then it is common sense to say that a cause takes up no space and consumes no energy. To borrow Hume's analogy of the pool cue striking the cue ball which then strikes another ball, the action of the pool cue and the impacts upon the balls all consume and release energy, but the cause in and of itself does not. The ball at rest begins to move when acted upon by an external force in the form of a cue ball. The impact of the cue ball puts the target ball in motion, but the 'cause' of this motion is not the ball; the cause is only an intuitive idea, ideas being subjective thoughts unbound by the laws of physics.

My point is that if downward causation exists, as I believe it must, then Davidson's dual-path causality is true while nothing in the physical universe changes. Reality remains as it always has been; that being a physical realm, a subjective realm, and pathways of causality between them that always already were. Channeling Alfred North Whitehead, at some point one has to ask the question: "Why should consciousness exist at all if it has no effective or affective power?"[29] There are no physical properties in the world that would preclude the mind directing the brain to perform an action, or to retrieve and furnish a memory. Portalism holds that there is a necessary codependency between the external mind and its internal brain, thus causal pathways existing between them are an integral part of this codependency. This dual-path causality extends only between the brain and its individualized localization of Consciousness, and not to the world totality. If this latter was the case then mentally I could levitate my coffee cup, or cause my eighth-grade gym teacher to burst into flames, but no serious person is proposing such fiction. Downward causality as I have described it in this section exists *prima facie*, and the fact that it does is necessary to Portalism and entirely compatible with the physical world.

Portalism and Free Will

Many books have been written regarding philosophical questions surrounding free will and determinism, and this is not one of them. Although some consider the subject unresolvable in view of its depth, I believe it is straightforward enough to make this section brief.

Portalism holds that there are two realms in the world, the subjective and the objective. Consciousness, being a fundamental force of nature, is the all-encompassing medium of subjectivity, while the objective realm is the domain of physical things. The objective realm is determinate, but consciousness is indeterminate, not being subject to physical laws. Free will is the unrestricted ability to select from a range of possible courses of action. Mind-brain identity materialists tend to deny the existence of free will citing causal closure, although some supervenience physicalists can be receptive to compatibilism. As consciousness is the realm of subjectivity it is therefore indeterminate and unbound by the laws of physics; hence causal closure does not apply to consciousness.

I am mind, and thus I have no innate essence or physical limitation that can restrict my ability to choose or not to choose an action. Although the possibilities for action that are open to me may be dependent on physical states (I cannot walk on water, I cannot eat bread if there is no bread), those possibilities that are open to me are entirely subject to my choice. As there is no thing and no one to determine my actions, I possess complete agency, and so become subject to the consequences that this incurs, meaning that I take responsibility for my choices with the knowledge that I, as mind, can ultimately become no more in life than the ensemble of my acts. In this fashion, Portalism is an existentialism, and Portalism embraces free will.

Temporality

Time is "not an object of our knowledge, but a dimension of our being."
Maurice Merleau-Ponty[30]

In this section I will describe the relationship of the external mind in time. I shall begin with a short discussion of the concept of time, and conclude with an explanation of time and the nature of its consanguinity with Portalism.

The vulgar conception of time is that of Newton's absolute linear time, wherein events happen in orderly succession from future to present to past, the present acting as a gateway for the transformation of the future into the past. This is likely the most popular conception of time, due to its apparent intuitiveness, and thus has become the idea held by most people who have never committed themselves to an examination of the phenomenon.

Augustine was not one of those people. Written in the 4th century, Book 11 of the *Confessions* represents one of the most astounding works of temporal reasoning in all of philosophy. For example, if Newton is correct, and time passes uniformly without regard to events in the world: then time is linear. If time is linear then it is implicit that it has a beginning and will at one time have an end. To wit: "The future diminishes as the past grows, until the future is completely gone and everything is in the past."[31] If this is correct, then it also implies that there was a time before time began, when time did not exist. Not so, as Augustine reasons: "You created all times and you exist before all times. Nor was there a time when time did not exist."[32] He goes on, the cadence of his reason so clear and methodical it is as if he is working it out for himself quietly over a beer across the table from you.

If nothing passes away, there is no past time, and if nothing arrives, there is no future time, and if nothing existed there would be no present time. How can they 'be' when the past is not now present and the future is not yet present? If then, in order to be time at all, the present is so made that it passes into the past, how can we say that this present also 'is'. The cause of its being is that it will cease to be. So indeed we cannot truly say that time exists except in the sense that it tends toward non-existence.[33]

Immanuel Kant had a different take, holding that space and time are only formal features of how we perceive objects in the world, and that time is an ideal whose ideality is manifested intuitively by mind. For Kant, time and space are only conceptual tools, a systematic framework that our brains use to order our world. Time does not exist in and of itself as it is not a property that adheres to things we encounter, nor does it "remain when abstraction is made from all subjective conditions or our intuition of them. Time is nothing but the form of inner sense, that is, of our intuition of ourselves, and of our inner state."[34] Instead, time is the formal *a priori* condition of all appearances in general and is intuited *a priori* through synthetic propositions. For Kant, time is not an objective entity. Time discloses itself *a priori* through the subjective experience of a thing's appearance wherein time obtains an 'objective validity'. When we sense an object we intuit time *a priori*, which enables us to comprehend the object in space and time, but take away the object and time loses its existence. "Time is therefore merely a subjective condition of our human intuition, (which is always sensible, that is, so far as we are affected by objects), but in itself, apart from the subject, it is nothing."[35]

J.M.E. McTaggart's thoughts are also in line with the concept of time being no more than an ideal. He introduced two temporal series known as 'A'-series and 'B'-series. The A-series represents the common notion of time in terms of events being past, present, or future, while the B-series divests itself of those vulgar temporal assignments, casting events in either an earlier-than or later-than relationship. I believe that his B-series is representative of how the brain establishes its temporal flags when it stores long-term (explicit/episodic) memories. For example, I don't remember the exact date when I went to Paris, but I know that it was after I stayed in London, but before I visited Nova Scotia. On the other hand, if I had immediately written an account of my adventures in those places and stored them in a file on my computer, it would have time-stamped the file with the precise date in strict A-series fashion. The problem with A-series was that an event can never be past, present, and future at the same time, nor any combination within, a curiosity known as 'McTaggart's Dilemma', which demonstrates that A-series, or Newtonian absolute time, is incoherent while B-series, similar to Leibniz's relative time, is in and of itself insufficient to account for the overall nature of time. Mirroring Kant, McTaggart's final pronouncement was that time is 'unreal', as he observes: "If time is anything at all, it is merely an effect of the mind, a subjective quirk rather than an objective fact."[36]

Consciousness being a subject of metaphysics, it is natural that it would be closely associated to time and causality. It is therefore fitting to give brief mention to the perspectives of the presentists and eternalists. Presentism holds that the only time that exists is 'now', and that the past and the future do not exist as objective realities. Most presentists agree that the now is the simultaneous moment wherein present and future meet, the now being a device for making the future into the past, and that therefore it progresses along some tensed-time version of a linear continuum.

Eternalists hold that the past and the future do exist, one group believing that everything that will ever happen, has happened, while others embrace an expanding future. Both envision time as a four dimensional 'block' wherein all events occupy a unique coordinate position. This implies that all events are related, and would support ideas regarding the necessary sufficiency for travelling in time. For example, if you knew the positional coordinate for the Battle of Tours within the block, and the means for doing so was available, then theoretically you could travel to that position. If block time were true, then the reasoning for events such as described in Kurt Vonnegut's novel *Slaughterhouse Five*, wherein a man becomes 'unstuck' in time, would be valid.

Both of these positions tend to create more questions than they answer, and they have more to do with the physical world than with subjective experience. I only mention them in brief to illustrate the existence of additional schools of thought regarding the metaphysics of time.

In terms of Portalism and its concept of temporality, the thinking of Martin Heidegger renders the closest approximation to the truth. Invoking the *cogito*, I am mind, therefore I exist, and any existence implies a *future*. This future is an essential quality of existence, because if one has no future then one has no possibilities, and if one has run out of possibilities, then one is dead by definition. Being human, I await my future with anticipation, because if the future exists at all, then it can exist only as expectation. As a thinking human being I am constantly projecting myself into the future as the *ahead-of*, or as Sartre says, "I await myself in the future," and as such my existence can never be particularly characterized as past, present, or future in terms of the vulgar understanding of time. While I factically exist, I am at all times always already *having-been*, *making-present*, and *ahead-of* (the Heideggerian ecstasies of temporality). This dynamic extends into the future while returning from the past – moving toward itself – the present thereby synthetically arising as a result of the tension between the two. But Heidegger's 'present' is not some "pure succession of nows, without beginning and without end,"[37] but rather is expressed as the moment (augenblick) in which I, as the *letting-myself-come-toward-myself*, come back on myself in a way that the future *in-the-process-of-having-been*, releases the present from itself.

This is representative of the cryptic style of Heidegger that drives analytic philosophers crazy, but when examined closely the elegance of his reasoning is brought forth. What he is positing is that the past, present, and future exist as a single unity that comprises the temporal totality. But time is only measurable as long as I am in the world, and my existence is finite. As I progress through life I expend myself for the sake-of-myself and eventually use all my time up, whereupon death overtakes me as the final possibility, and time dissolves. So in Heidegger's view, *we are time*. As Merleau-Ponty accurately describes: "Time is, therefore, not a real process, not an actual succession that I am content to record. It arises from my relation to things."[38]

Augustine, Kant, McTaggart, and Heidegger were each at least partly correct in their reasoning. The past exists only in our memories, and the future doesn't exist because it hasn't happened yet. Even though the future represents only as expectation, we nevertheless intuitively feel as though we can influence it, even though we concede that we cannot change the past. We can always go forward, but we can never go back. The past is lost to us, even to the degree that forgetting an event in memory is identical to its never having happened. When I visited my grandmother in the late stages of Alzheimer's, she did not recognize her only grandson, or even the fact that she had one. Disease was causing her portal connection to diminish, so that within her receding reality there was never a time when I existed.

Time is an illusion, and like space, only a tool that enables us to cognitively order our reality. Consciousness is not temporal, the untethered mind being unbound by space and time, as demonstrated in dream state. The phenomenon often mistaken for time is actually change, the case being where if nothing changes, then no time has passed. This concept is borne out by the effects of total anesthesia and coma. During my last colonoscopy, I was talking to my doctor about why he chose medicine as he introduced fentanyl analgesia into my IV. Suddenly my perceptual background was different and I was talking to a different person. I had picked up my conversation at precisely the point in mid-sentence where I had been rendered unconscious by the complete shutdown of my portal, but it presented to me to be an uninterrupted dialog. Although by the clock it was 25 minutes later, nothing had changed, so effectively, no time had passed.

I am mind, and the mind resides in the subjective realm. My body resides in the objective realm, pinned in space and time and subject to physical laws. I, as a localization of Consciousness, am tethered to my body through its portal. The body ages – changes – over time, but the mind does not 'age'. Time has no claim on mind because mind is an entity outside of time. Although it is all too well aware of the aging of the body, as the subjective realm is not bound by time, the mind itself cannot age. The content of consciousness appears to 'grow', as the limited reality of the infant progresses to the inquisitive nature of the child, the skilled and experienced adult, then again to the limited reality of advanced age, but these transformations are indicative of the health and capacity of the portal, not the mind. Being the horizon of consciousness in which subjective experience takes place, consciousness simpliciter is thereby ageless and immune to the effects of time. "In this sense I am my past, I do not have it; I am it."[39]

We see photographs and videos of when we were very young and wonder, 'Who is that?' We cannot connect to the physical presence of the past. Once retired from our labors and careers, we walk along the street in our conscious state of everydayness. Turning toward a large store window we suddenly see our reflection and it shocks us, because the mental image we carry around of ourselves is often a much younger and stronger version of the physical reality, causing us again to ask, *'Who is that?'* The physical, objective realm ages, we confront it every day in the mirror, but the mind, dwelling in the subjective realm, is, was, and always will be, changeless. I, as mind, do not move through time, as from some beginning toward some end. I, as mind, am stationary, while it is time that flows through me. Mind does not *move* through anything; only physical things can *move*. As a localization of the ubiquitous force of Consciousness, the possibility of mind always already was, the missing piece being 'which' mind, in terms of the individuality of the localization. While mind is *being*, time is only an idea, and as such it has no essential nature. While mind is subjective and ontologically irreducible, time is only a condition of appearance.

Death

After your death you will be what you were before your birth.
Arthur Schopenhauer

I like to believe that Descartes was essentially correct about a lot of things, but his idea of the *res cogitans*, that which he considered to be the 'soul', surviving after the death of the body was not one of them. In Portalism, the localization of Consciousness in which the individual mind becomes actualized is dependent upon the physical portal mechanism, whatever form or biochemical construct that mechanism might take, and by extension is therefore dependent on the life of the host body.

Life in the body can survive without the mind, as demonstrated by total anesthesia or coma, but without the living body there can be no portal and thereby no localization of Consciousness, and the mind, like a guttering flame, is simply extinguished. In most cases of total anesthesia, the mind is revived, and as the memories, ego, and intellect that defined the mind's personality are stored in the brain, the mind just picks up where it left off, appearing as if time had stopped for that brief period of unconsciousness. Even for comatose victims that regain consciousness after years of unconsciousness, they may or may not be able to remember everything right away, but as far as time is concerned, it is like the accident that caused the coma happened only a moment ago and no time has passed. In the case of death, the mind dissolves into the nothing as if it had never existed.

The early externalists had interesting takes on death, particularly the rationalists Leibniz and Spinoza. Leibniz explained that after death the body dissolves into its component monads, while the soul as spirit, by virtue of his theory of pre-established harmony, moves from the kingdom of nature into the kingdom of grace, as spirits, being copies of God, get reabsorbed by God. "... while souls in general are living mirrors or images of the universe of created things, spirits are also images of the Deity himself or of the author of nature. They are capable of knowing the system of the universe, and of imitating some features of it by means of artificial models, each spirit being like a small divinity in its own sphere. Therefore spirits are able to enter into a sort of social relationship with God."[40] Markku Roinila explains it best: "The rationality of human beings makes them images of divinity itself, that is, moral beings. They have access to God in a special way: Through their reason they are able to imitate actions, as there is only a difference of degree between human beings and God."[41]

Spinoza had a simpler theory. As a pantheist he held that although God had many attributes that are not present in the world, the material universe and everything in it is God. In this explanation, death becomes simple as no one can really die, at least in terms of the commonly held notion of death, since they are essentially already God. Death amounts to no more than a change of state, like water becoming ice – it's all still H_2O. If true, then this means that the soul doesn't go anywhere after death because there isn't anywhere else to go – you are already there – you always already were there.

I have previously mentioned Merleau-Ponty's analogy of the wrinkled sheet, wherein consciousness is merely a wrinkle that disappears when the sheet is straightened. As Portalism holds that the mind dissolves when the body dies and the portal closes forever, it follows that Portalism embraces an atheistic perspective. To paraphrase Soren Kierkegaard – the end is death, and death is the end.

Brains in a Vat and More?

The brain-in-the-vat thought experiment has drawn the attention of many philosophers, especially since the very successful *Matrix* movie trilogy brought the dilemma before the masses, causing millions of nonphilosophers to ponder metaphysics for the first time, perhaps many of them completely unaware that they were actually doing philosophy. It is considered to be a problem within the philosophy of mind, but it also begs epistemic questions, including the skeptic assertion that it is never possible to truly know anything, and solipsism, wherein we are unable to logically prove that our consciousness is the only consciousness that there is.

Basically, the question put forth is, 'How do you know that you are not just a brain in a vat?' Although the question is simple the philosophical implications can be profound. Imagine that 'you', along with all your subjective experiences, everything you believe, all your friends and family, your education and career, indeed your entire reality, are only electrical stimuli generated from complex programs and algorithms housed within a colossal master computer. So instead of being a sales manager from Philadelphia that enjoys bass fishing and has a degree in marketing from NYU, the reality is that 'you' are a brain in a vat of liquid hooked up to a computer and everything you *think* you are, know, love, and aspire to, is only an illusion.

The discussions that this experiment engenders span a wide range of perspectives. I have heard more than one person ask how this scenario is any different from Christianity. Others ask what difference does it make, being that we are all mortal and thus any existence is therefore meaningless, vat-brain or otherwise? Among philosophers, some exceptional thinkers have tackled the question with plausible solutions based upon their own clever perspectives.

John Searle addresses the problem from the standpoint of intentional content and phenomenology. He begins by making it clear that we are all essentially brains in vats, it's just that our vats are our skulls and we can walk about in the world. Earlier in the discussion on realism I described Searle's theory holding that objects in the physical world intrinsically possess the causal capacity of causing experience in the mind of the perceiver. He observes that although the phenomenology would be the same in both cases, the intentional content is different. That is, if a zebra is perceived either because the computer program sent 'zebra' code to the vat-brain (a hallucination), or because the skull brain perceives an actual zebra standing in front of it (the veridical), the brain in the vat and the brain in the skull still enjoy the same phenomenology in that both experience *something-like-there-is-to-see* a zebra, but for the vat-brain there is no zebra actually present, a real zebra being a thing-in-the-world that would have the intrinsic causal capacity to actually cause the experience, and that is the difference.[42]

Although Searle is no externalist, Portalism is compatible with his perspective because, as in all externalist theories, consciousness is in the world. The vat-brain has no world to be conscious of, and it would seem unlikely that stimuli from a computer, however advanced, could create a world, and even conceding that it could, its created 'world' would be empty of things with the property to cause experience. In short, the computer generated vat-brain world would be philosophically insufficient for causing experience. In order for mind to be in-the-world, the body must take it there; any other explanation would seem to invoke solipsism.

So as long as we are doing thought experiments let us consider this – why have a brain at all? According to Portalism, Consciousness is always already there; all that is required for an actualization of mind is a portal. Up to this point we have been dealing with the realities of a world of living organisms and speculating upon their biological, chemical, or biochemical portal solutions. Pulling from functionalism, if what we should be focusing upon is the *function* of the portal, we can speculate that through the process of evolution over millions of years, a non-corporeal portal mechanism could emerge, and that if so, then the existence of conscious non-corporeal beings could be possible. This is certainly not an original idea. *Star Trek* season 1 episode 26 "Errand of Mercy" (1967) featured incorporeal beings interfering with the competing efforts by Klingons and the Enterprise crew to foment revolution among a peaceful people. Such beings were presented as *pure mind*, the ultimate externalist theory. A common complaint from cranialism regarding phenomenal externalism is with the envisioning of a mind just floating about out in the ether on its own. Such is not the case with Portalism, as mind and body are existentially codependent albeit the locus of the mind is extracranial. But in the case of pure mind beings, the cranialist's dread is realized. In addition, as these non-corporeal beings have no physical bond to the objective realm, they are thereby unpinned in space and time. For example, to be at the edge of the galaxy, all a pure-mind being needs to do is think it and it would be so. As entities with no mass, extension, form, number, charge or spin, space becomes irrelevant. Kant and Schopenhauer both held that space and time are only tools within a framework required by the brain in order to make sense of our world.[43] Beings of pure mind would seem to prove them correct. And if this speculation should ever become the case, the theory of Portalism would remain entirely compatible with it.

Chapter 8

In Defense of Portalism

To explain experience, we need a new approach.
David Chalmers[1]

In this chapter I make the case for the plausibility of Portalism and illustrate how it meets the challenges and questions that must inhere upon all theories of consciousness.

Fundamentals of Portalism in Review

Portalism is a theory of consciousness premised on the principles of radical phenomenal externalism, and like all metaphysical theories it makes certain critical assumptions. The following is a reprise of the six assumptions of Portalism as originally described in chapter 3:

1. A nonphysical subjective realm exists, as does a physical realm independent of our perception of it.
2. The mind is not the brain. The locus of the mind is entirely external to, but causally connected to, the *res extensa*.
3. The horizon of Consciousness is a fundamental force of nature and is ubiquitous throughout the universe. It is ontologically irreducible and precedes the distinction between subject and object. Consciousness is the all-encompassing structure that enables the possibility of subjective experience. The horizon of Consciousness is devoid of content, it being the subjective ground and not the subject.
4. All living organisms harbor an innate and intrinsic bio-mechanism capable of facilitating an individual

connection, forthwith known as a 'portal', into the horizon of Consciousness.

5. A portal/Consciousness connection is necessary and sufficient to manifest the localized, individual state of consciousness actualized as mind. Such a connection is the necessary condition before any mind can be.

6. Only Mind has content.

In case the reader has skipped to this section first off, it will be important to recall the semantic difference between 'Big C' Consciousness and 'Little c' consciousness. When capitalized within a sentence, Consciousness refers to the ubiquitous force of nature that is the all-encompassing horizon of subjectivity and the ontologically irreducible subjective ground, whereas an actualization of mind resulting from a portal's connection into Consciousness is synonymous with 'little-c' consciousness, this form of consciousness being the subject.

Portalism draws a distinction between portal, Consciousness, and mind. The portal is an embodied biological and/ or biochemical mechanism that facilitates access into the horizon of Consciousness. Each living thing, every biological system, inherently possesses one. When a portal connects to Consciousness, a localization of the horizon of Consciousness is manifested. This resulting consciousness (little 'c') is actualized as 'mind', its locus external to the *res extensa* while tethered to it via the physical portal connection.

As the subjective agent, only the mind has the potential to realize experiential content, whereas Consciousness simpliciter, being the enabling horizon, is an irreducible ontological ground in and of itself devoid of content. Different minds will experience different levels of awareness based on the sophistication of the portal mechanism. The depth, capacity, and quality of an agent's subjective experience are dependent upon the sophistication of its portal mechanism, while the all-encompassing horizon of

Consciousness remains constant as the ontological ground. The potential for experiential content is in turn dependent on the dynamic potential of the portal connection. The terms 'mind', 'subjective experience', and 'consciousness' (little 'c') are held to be synonymous.

Let us further examine the assumptions in more detail. They reduce to five basic ideas composed of four entities. First on the list is the subjective realm. I chose to use the term 'realm' as opposed to 'substance', even as physical and mental substances are the traditional terms of dualism, the term 'substance' implies a thing whereas 'realm' implies a state of being. As mind cannot be defined in physical terms, it cannot be physical, and although as its locus is external to the body it must still reside somewhere. Physical things are objective. Mind, by being non-physical and therefore not a thing in the objective world, must then be subjective, and therefore existing *in*, and within its individualized state *as*, the medium of subjectivity. This assumption is nothing new and is certainly not beyond plausibility, where if materialism is false and mental states do exist, then it follows that some other mode of reality must exist for mental states to exist in, regardless of what one might call it, and the term 'subjective realm' would seem to be as good as any.

The next assumption is that although the locus of consciousness is extracranial, its existence remains dependent upon the physical body. This ties in with assumptions 4 and 5, wherein mind becomes actualized through an organism's embodied portal mechanism, and the quality of the content of consciousness is determined by the sophistication of the portal, which explains why different organisms have different realities – for example, the conscious reality of a Siberian Husky is very different from that of a crab, yet both are conscious nevertheless. The mind's existence is therefore dependent upon the portal connection, tethered to the body, and as the body is a physical object subject to physical laws and anchored in time and space, so then is phenomenal consciousness pinned in spacetime. Here I make the distinction between the phenomenal consciousness of the world and the reflexive consciousness of the self, which is purely subjective and so unbound by space and time. The mind being tethered to the body, if the body dies, or the portal is otherwise closed due to damage or disease, the mind dissolves.

Assumption 3 represents the fundamental philosophical underpinning of the theory of Portalism, wherein Consciousness is assumed to be a fundamental force of nature, on a par with the weak and strong nuclear forces, electromagnetism, and gravity. Of these four forces of nature, Consciousness shares the greatest similarity with gravity for two reasons. First, being ubiquitous in the universe, it can be invoked anywhere at any time; gravity by the presence of a mass, and consciousness by the connection of a portal. The second similarity that the two forces share is that no one knows exactly what they are. Physicists can calculate gravitational fields, and cognitive scientists can predict patterns of child mental development, but neither knows exactly the *nature* of what it is that they are dealing with. They know, at least to some degree, how they behave, but can only speculate as to their natures.

Portalism – Phenomenal Externalism Meets Dualism?

Philosophers from Aristotle to Kant to Chalmers seem to derive significant enjoyment from classifying and categorizing things. So as a theory of consciousness, where does Portalism fit within traditional philosophical characterization? Because the locus of consciousness is extracranial, it is therefore a form of phenomenal externalism, but because it assumes both subjective and objective realms, and as these ideas can be argued to be at least conceptually parallel to Cartesian substances, Portalism is also a form of dualism. Specifically, it is a form of 'Type-D' dualism, as defined by David Chalmers in *The Character of*

Consciousness, where the 'D' is for Descartes but also stands for 'downward causality'.[2] In the case of Portalism, the 'D' would correspond less to the former and absolutely to the latter. A dualist himself, Chalmers has a considerable respect for this view, observing: "Still, if we have independent reason to think that consciousness is irreducible, and if we wish to retain the intuitive view that consciousness plays a causal role, then this is a view to be taken very seriously."[3]

The materialist's positivist view that the physical is all that exists has been solely responsible for causing metaphysics to run in place for over a century, while waiting patiently for science to uncover definitive proof that the brain is the mind and that nothing 'mental' exists. They are still waiting, and still running on their dogmatic treadmill going nowhere, their scientific expectations having failed to produce even the thinnest evidence, while theory after theory, from Positivism to Behaviorism to Type Identity are consigned to a growing pile of materialist theoretical wreckage. Indeed, the idea that consciousness is in the head, either 'emerging' from physical stuff or as a yet unknown phenomenon of the brain/central nervous system/body dynamic, is almost irresistibly intuitive, much like a flat earth, or a geocentric solar system. But that 'feeling' of intuitiveness is the extent of the materialist's metaphysical reality, causing thinkers like Donald Davidson to move toward anomalous monism, or even New Mysterianism, as in the case of Thomas Nagel.

As materialism has yet to provide any empirical evidence of mind-brain identity and as the analytic tradition tends to dismiss *a priori* reasoning as a source of knowledge, philosophy and science must look elsewhere for answers, as evidenced by a renewed embrace of phenomenology by neuroscience, manifested in recent philosophical theories of non-reductive supervenience, dual-aspect theory, mind-world identity, enactivism, and phenomenal externalism. The fact that these philosophies are arguably dualist to some degree or fashion amounts to absolutely nothing, as the metric is not what metaphysical category a theory might be in, but in what it can plausibly explain. Being metaphysical, the strength of any theory of consciousness ultimately lies in its explanatory power.

Held to such a standard, materialist explanations of reality have been found to be woefully inadequate. In fact, when considered with an open mind, the explanatory power of contemporary monist idealism is far more robust. In consideration of the traditional problems within the philosophy of mind, such as that of other minds, the mind-body problem, the hard problem, etc., monist idealism successfully overcomes many of them by denying their basic premises. For example, we don't need to show how mental states cause physical effects if all that exists is mind, and the 'hard problem' is easily solved as we no longer need to account for how brain matter engenders feelings – qualia and intentionality – because there is no brain if reality is only a state of mind. Thus we are left with a materialism that explains little if nothing, and monist idealism which explains nearly everything but rejects a physical reality that persists outside of our perception of it. What is needed is a theory that has the explanatory power of idealism but that embraces a physical world, a world that is all too real and that conforms to the principle of the apparent uniformity of nature. For such a theory we must look elsewhere, and for many new thinkers 'elsewhere' is phenomenal externalism.

In the following sections I will address the problems inherent in dualist theories of consciousness and attempt to justify Portalism based on its explanatory power. I leave it to the reader to judge how successful I have been.

The Hard Problem of Consciousness, the Explanatory Gap, and Bridging Principles

As I reflected earlier in the introduction to this work, I listened to a TED talk given by David Chalmers that opened my mind to ideas that led me to phenomenal externalism, and having proposed a theory of consciousness within that framework, it becomes incumbent upon me to answer the challenge manifested by the famous 'hard problem'. For the nonphilosopher, Chalmers' definition is as follows: "The hard problem of consciousness is that of explaining how and why physical processes give rise to phenomenal consciousness. A solution to the hard problem would involve an account of the relation between physical processes and consciousness, explaining on the basis of natural principles how and why it is that physical processes are associated with states of experience."

Chalmers supplies four possible forms of explanation that could meet this challenge[4] – they are:

1) The *reductive* explanation which would involve purely physical principles with no appeal to consciousness.
2) The *materialist* solution in which consciousness is a physical process.
3) The *nonmaterialist* solution wherein consciousness is nonphysical.
4) The *non-reductive* solution in which consciousness becomes an integral part of the explanation.

Given this selection to choose from, the answerable form(s) that Portalism would correspond to are options 3 *and* 4. Portalism assumes a nonphysical subjective realm in addition to an objective reality, and so is a *nonmaterialist* solution, while it is at the same time *non-reductive*, the horizon of Consciousness being established as an irreducible fundamental force of nature and the ontological ground of subjective experience, therefore qualifying as 'an integral part of the explanation'.

Regarding the question pertaining to "how and why physical processes give rise to phenomenal consciousness", if it is true that the locus of mind is outside of the body then the answer from phenomenal externalism is that *they don't*. Consciousness, as a fundamental force of nature, always already is, and being ontologically irreducible it therefore cannot 'rise' from anything, as doing so would contradict that irreducibility. That said, it does not mean that this explanation does not bring forth problems of its own, but such is always the way with philosophy, and so it falls to me to present solutions to them. Many of the difficulties associated with consciousness stem from the presupposition that the mind is the brain. Phenomenal externalism invalidates these problems by denying their premise. This does not mean that the brain and nervous system, at least in humans and higher animals, is not an important and necessary element in Portalism – it absolutely is – but not in the way that physicalism holds that it must be.

The hard problem of consciousness also requires an answer for the explanatory gap, referring to the problem that materialist theories encounter in explaining how physical properties give rise to the way things feel when they are experienced, a problem famously introduced by Joseph Levine (1983). This difficulty must be addressed not only by materialists, but by all theories of consciousness, although it is materialism that has the greatest challenge with it due to its presupposition of mind-brain identity. To solve the explanatory gap, one or more 'bridging principles' would seem to be necessary, or as Chalmers states, "... we simply need to add further bridging principles to explain how experience arises from physical processes."[5]

Regarding the Chalmers quote, since Portalism holds that experience (as consciousness I am assuming) does not arise from physical processes, then this would seem to be a non-problem, but I don't believe I can get off so easily in this case. The context of Dr. Chalmers' quote was made within a wider discussion of non-reductive naturalistic dualism in the light of James Clerk Maxwell's expansion of the ontology of physics, the point being that the non-reductiveness of a given theory does not release it from the obligation of bridging principles per se, only that a *different kind* of principle might be required to account for the subjective experience of the world, and that since these new kinds of principles will not be derivable from physics, "they must be taken as *explanatorily* fundamental."[6]

Again, as we are dealing in metaphysics while burdened with empirical tools that do not work well in that environment, we are left with the appeal to explanatory power. Yet explanatory power is in fact quite powerful, just ask any monist idealist – to have a theory with explanatory power is significantly preferable to having a theory without it. All David Chalmers is asking of us is to explain our bridging principles, whatever they may be, fundamentally.

But bridging principles become necessary only when there is a need to show a causal path between stimulus P and experience Q, thus they become inconveniently critical in all reductive physicalist theoretical propositions. In his 2003 article "Phenomenal Concepts and the Explanatory Gap", Chalmers invokes Frank Jackson's (1982) famous thought experiment of Mary's Room, a classic thought experiment wherein Mary has spent her entire life in a room devoid of color while at the same time becoming an authority on the physics of vision. At this point Mary does not 'know' the color red (just imagine describing red to a person blind from birth – it can't be done). So in this case 'P' is Mary's comprehensive understanding of the entirety of microphysical knowledge, while 'Q' is the experience of seeing red things. Chalmers' point is that the truth of Q is not derivable using *a priori* reasoning from truth P, and as such the material implication $P \supset Q$ is not knowable *a priori*.[7] So from the standpoint of bridging principles, for me to merely claim that no bridging principles are needed to explain experience because the mind is external to the brain and in the world is insufficient. Regardless of *where* the locus of consciousness may be, this problem still requires some plausible explanation of how stimulus P incurs experience Q, which I shall now present in terms of the theory of Portalism.

Given that gravity and Consciousness are both irreducible fundamental forces of nature and both phenomena occur autogenically, it would follow that anything with mass has gravity, and anything with a portal has consciousness. In all living things, mind is actualized as an individual localization within the horizon of Consciousness, manifested via this portal connection. The mind is external to the *res extensa* and therefore must have its locus in the world: "Consciousness... belongs to the world, as something which emerges from nature, and it makes the world into the object of knowledge and action."[8] As the world is the medium of reality, and consciousness is the necessary condition for the subjective experience of that reality, a *de facto* relationship of identity between mind and world manifests. The mind is external to the body, not to the world. I think Merleau-Ponty characterizes the concept best: "Would I know that I am truly caught up and situated in the world, if I were truly caught up and situated in it? I should then merely *be* where I was, as a thing, and since I know where I am and see myself among things, it is because I am a consciousness, a strange creature which resides nowhere and can be everywhere present in intention."[9] As mind, we do not 'look out' upon some external reality, observing and encountering things that are *not* us. Truly each of us, as mind, is *absorbed* into world through our *being-in*, so in effect: the world is something that we, as mind, always already are. "'World' is ontologically not a determination of those beings which Dasein essentially is not, but rather a characteristic of Dasein itself."[10]

This concept of a mind/world totality appears in the different perspectives of phenomenal externalist thinkers. One of the most extreme perspectives is Manzotti's spread mind theory, wherein "we represent the world by being made of the world we experience."[11] For Manzotti and for most externalist thinkers including myself, the world is exactly as it appears, so there is no need for any intermediate interpretive inventions: *"Consciousness is where and when the physical objects that one experiences take place."*[12] In spread mind theory, the apple I encounter in the world *is the experience*. In another example I discuss in chapter 4, John Searle's theory that any encounterable object in the physical world intrinsically possesses the causal capacity of causing the experience of that object in the mind of the perceiver. Both Manzotti and Searle are physicalists, but note how the two theories account for experience from very different perspectives. There are other examples but they all claim some version of mind/world uniformity, so it can suffice to say that Manzotti and Searle are emblematic of two great thinkers having found uniquely plausible ways to account for the explanatory gap.

In Portalism, the external mind is absorbed into world such that a relationship of *de facto* identity is established. This identity collapses the distinction between object and subject, with the result that the knower and the known become a single unity. 'I' exist only as consciousness, and my consciousness is tethered to my body through its portal mechanism. As my body is an object in the physical world it is pinned in time and space, which in turn pins me, as mind, also in time and space. As the body moves about in the world, I, as mind, encounter objects and states of affairs within my perceptual field disclosed to mind via my body's sense modalities, and because, as mind, I am *being-in-the-world*, these encounters are consciously intentional and concurrently manifest as phenomenal content – *my feelings about* – enabled by the singularity of a mind/world unity actualized by my *being-in*. I believe that this account of experience qualifies as 'explanatorily fundamental'.

As far as any cognitive mechanics are concerned, whether the experience is identical to the object, or the object has the intrinsic property of causing an experience upon its being perceived, the result is the same – if, as Portalism claims, there exists a relationship of *de facto* identity between mind and world, then the perception *is* the experience. If perception is experience then there is no gap to explain, and if there is no gap there is nothing to bridge. This is Portalism's response to the problem of the explanatory gap and the necessary bridging principles it implies.

Oh, and if the nonphilosopher is still worried about Mary, fear not – one day she leaves her colorless room and sees placed upon a table a crystal vase containing a single red rose. The ultimate value, if any, of this experience is still being debated by the epistemologists, but the fact remains that having once had the experience of red, she can now *imagine* it, whereas before she could not.

The Problem of Other Minds

The problem of other minds is again a problem of epistemology. I have said repeatedly throughout this work that it is my intention to leave cognitive and epistemic issues to others while focusing upon the nature of consciousness. However, this particular problem needs to be at least cursorily addressed by any theory of mind, if for no other reason than that tradition calls for it.

For the nonphilosopher the problem is stated as this: Given that outward behavior is all that I can observe in others, how can I know that other minds exist? Due to the nature of subjectivity, I can only report my experience in the first person, wherein the experiences of others, if they even exist, can only be revealed to me from the third person, like that of a narrative story. Simply put, if I step on a nail I experience the pain in the first person, but if you step on a nail you can certainly describe what you are going through, but I can never actually *experience* what you are feeling. I can be empathetic, I can compare your account of the pain to similar situations that I myself may have had in the past – your pain can even affect my emotions, for example it can cause grief – but when it's all said and done only you can 'know' your own mind and 'feel' your own experiences. So in light of this fact, how can I be absolutely certain that my own mind is not the only mind that there is?

Just as it happens in ethics, epistemic inquiries tend to generate more questions than answers. Thus my reply to this problem will be terse and to the point as I leave philosophical zombies, solipsism, skepticism, and infinite regress, all worthy and interesting topics in their own right, for another day.

Thus, assuming that radical subjective idealism is false and that a physical universe exists outside of our perception of it:

1. As I can sense their presence with all five of my sense modalities, I am justified in the belief that other human beings exist. Since I have a body and a mind and I can perceive that other humans have bodies similar to mine, I then have a reasonable expectation in the belief that other bodies also have minds.

2. Portalism holds that Consciousness exists as an ontologically irreducible fundamental force of nature and that all living things are innately possessed of a bio-mechanism that facilitates a portal of access into this horizon. Such access manifests as an individualized localization of consciousness.

3. As Consciousness is ubiquitous and available at all times and in all places, the existence of a functional portal *is* the necessary and sufficient condition to the actualization of mind.

4. Given a functional portal, individual actualizations of mind are immediate, involuntary, autogenic, and invariable within the sphere of living things.

5. Given this, there can be no question of whether or

not other minds exist as given any functional portal mechanism *consciousness becomes the default state* for all living systems.

Therefore, *ipso facto*, other minds must exist if Portalism is true. To be sure, when any organism is possessed of a functional portal, mind cannot *not* exist.

The Binding Problem of Consciousness

Just as the problem of other minds diverts us into epistemology, the *binding problem of consciousness* points us toward cognitive neuroscience. There are actually two separate problems that qualify under this heading. The segregation problem (BP1) asks how brains can take complex patterns of sensory input and break them down into discrete elements, while the combination problem (BP2) is the problem of how objects, background and abstract or emotional features get combined into a single experience.

Although in many cases the two problems overlap, strictly speaking BP1 seems to be entirely within the realm of neuroscience. The very description of the problem presupposes mind-brain identity and embraces the analytic tradition of reduction, seeking to distill comprehensive sensory input into discrete objects, in the search for neural correlates and the identification of the different parts of the brain and central nervous system that are responsible for processing the isolated components of a gestalt perception. In addition to the mind-brain identity assumption, the methodology in many responses to BP1 are framed in the terminology used by those who still assert that, through sensory perception, the brain uses the incoming data to create an ideal 'copy' of the external reality which it can then operate upon. Many fine thinkers, Daniel Dennett (1981) included, simply reject this idea claiming that consciousness is not unified to begin with and thus no binding problem exists.

The combination problem, BP2, is more interesting. Like BP1 it assumes a mind-brain identity but it does not lie entirely within the realm of neuroscience, having been previously addressed by philosophical worthies going back to Descartes, Leibniz, and the pragmatist William James. The crux of the issue involves the problem of how brain mechanisms construct the phenomenal object. How do data from sounds, sights and smells combine in the brain to create the phenomenal experience of sitting outside a café in Madrid enjoying a cold beer with my wife?

The answer is that they don't. Portalism is phenomenal externalism. As the mind is in and of the world, so is phenomenal experience. The identity relationship is between the mind and the world, not the mind and the brain. The brain does receive and filter sensory input, but it cannot assign the meaning or context necessary for an understanding, and it cannot determine the object of intentional focus without causal direction from mind. For example, while I am walking through the woods lost in unreflective consciousness, my brain is busy processing, repairing, and filtering sensory input, yet 'I', as mind, am thinking about last night's Bears game, thus the brain is also locating and furnishing those appropriate short-term memories (STM) because the Bears game is what 'I' choose to think about at that moment. Suddenly, attracted by movement and a splash of color, I am startled out of everydayness as a beautiful scarlet tanager swoops by in front of me. My mind is now intentionally conscious of the bird, and my brain begins to store STMs of the event as well as directing the muscles, rods, cones, etc., necessary to follow the bird as it flies out of my perceptual field. All of this action I have described, plus countless other details I won't bother to go into, occurs within a split second.

Neuroscience can publish pages about the neuron firings, acetylcholine neurotransmissions, distributed neural connections, and color images of brain activity, and all of it is valuable in its proper context, but none of it is evidence of the *experience* itself; the *feeling* of *something-like-there-is* to see a scarlet tanager. The brain only processes its sensory data, and it stopped accessing STMs of a football game to begin storing active memories of the experience of the bird when I, as mind, became intentionally conscious and aware of it. In effect, it is my experience in the world that alters my brain's active mission, 'passed' to it through a downward causal path from the world, 'through' the portal. At no time can the brain understand who the Bears are, what scarlet is, what beauty is, or even what the concept of 'bird' is, because it is incapable of assigning any meaning to the sensory data being reported to it. Only mind can assign meaning and context, because only the mind is capable of cognition. The brain being cranially embodied can never experience the world, unlike the external mind, which is in and of the world. *Experience* is not what a brain does; it's what a mind does.

Binding problems only present difficulties for materialists that continue to embrace the mind-brain dogma. If the mind is the brain – if mind truly 'rises' from some unknown arrangement of matter – then exactly how objects, background, and emotional features are combined into a single holistic experience must be accounted for. Such a cranialist position would have to explain how a brain that never experiences being-in-the-world, goes about deriving *experience* from copies of reality spawned by sensory data.

Portalism holds that the external mind always already is being-in-the-world, and that phenomenal experience manifests autogenically from the *de facto* relationship of identity between mind and world. If Portalism is true then there is no premise for binding problems.

The Argument from Brain Damage
In an effort to discredit dualism while promoting materialism,

Paul Churchland, the eliminative materialist and Professor of Philosophy at UC San Diego, introduced his famous *Argument from Brain Damage*. Elegant in its simplicity, he points out that whenever some manner of brain damage is sustained, whether by disease, automobile accident, drug abuse, etc., it is *always* the case that the mental substance and/or properties of that person are significantly changed or compromised. He reasons that if the mind were separate from the brain, as dualism holds, how could it be possible for it to be injured whenever the brain is injured? In fact, it is often the case where the character and extent of such injuries to the mind, such as in the case of stroke, are predictable, and therefore dualism is false and the mind is the brain.

Churchland's argument is quite fair, and in cases of dualism where the mind is embodied, as it is with Cartesian cranialism, it can present quite the challenge for a dualist to respond to. But Portalism, being an externalist theory, is entirely compatible with this argument. Damage to the brain may affect the intellectual limits of certain areas of the brain, simultaneously reducing or increasing the capacity of the portal mechanism, and making it more or less efficient as I have previously described, but it can never directly impact the mind. The all-encompassing horizon of Consciousness being constant and mind being an individualized localization ontologically grounded in that horizon, only the quality and capacity of the portal mechanism is subject to impact by damage or disease, that affectation being manifested in the reduction (or enhancement) of the phenomenal content and cognitive possibilities of any particular localization of consciousness. Brain/portal damage impacts the content of consciousness, never the nature of consciousness.

Therefore, if viewed functionally, Portalism would be compatible with Churchland's premise that brain damage invariably, albeit indirectly, affects the mind, while at the same time rejecting his conclusion that the mind is the brain.

The Argument from Biological Development

This argument against Cartesianism rests upon the idea of ontogeny. Its premise is that since all living things begin their existence as entire physical or material entities and since nothing outside of the domain of the physical is added later on in the course of development, then we must necessarily end up being fully developed material beings, and as such, there is no opportunity nor any need for anything nonphysical, like a mind, to be *added* at some later time. In short, we get everything we need from the start to become whatever it is we are.

True, an embryonic snail growing inside its egg can only become a snail. Ontogenically, its DNA carries only the essential structures of snailness, and because of this snail essence, it is biologically unable to become a tiger, or a rat snake, or a sycamore tree. Given this, the argument assumes that if dualism is true, then somehow mental stuff gets 'added' to the finished physical product, becoming embodied within the physical, as Descartes envisioned. The conclusion is that since living organisms are *already* possessed of the materials necessary to become what they are, to hold that anything additional must be added would be superfluous and redundant; therefore dualism is false.

This is another argument predicated on mind-brain identity in that consciousness inheres within the basic ontogenic mix at creation-time, because if consciousness exists at all, then it must be contained in those original components, and based on neurological research (not evidence), this would most likely be the brain. From my perspective, it is a thin argument against dualism and one that does nothing to advance our understanding of what consciousness *is*; nevertheless Portalism is compatible with it.

The portal mechanism is part and parcel of every organism's ontogenic blueprint, regardless of how sophisticated an organism might be. Mind is not 'added later', as consciousness is established immediately and autogenically through the portal's connection into the horizon of Consciousness – the ubiquitous and fundamental force of nature that always already is. The fact that Consciousness is perpetual and consistently available to portal mechanisms supports the original premise of the argument, that being where all organisms are ontogenically equipped with everything they require to become that given organism, thus Portalism is compatible with this premise. At the same time, the argument's conclusion that such would require *something to be added later*, although possibly true under Cartesianism, is false under Portalism. As per Portalism, nothing needs to be *added later* because everything necessary and sufficient for consciousness is *already there* – that being the organism's portal together with the fundamental force of nature that it accesses. Portalism accounts for consciousness with no need to 'add anything later'. The argument then claims that to add anything more would be superfluous and redundant. Portalism is compatible with this premise as well, adding nothing and in agreement that nothing needs to be added, but that if it were, it would indeed be redundant and superfluous. This argument fails in its conclusion, as for dualism to be false something additional must be added. Portalism adds nothing, and yet is a form of dualism. In the case of Portalism, the conclusion of the argument from biological development is contradictory rendering the entire argument unsound.

The Argument from Neuroscience

This argument against dualism is predicated on a phenomenon known as Readiness Potential, or (RP). The argument claims that evidence in the form of scanned imagery of brain activity indicates that decisions a person makes can be detected up to ten seconds in advance, including subjective experience and covert attitudes. Its conclusion is that this stands as empirical evidence that cognitive processes have their locus in the brain and therefore dualism is false.

Without getting too far into the weeds on what amounts to a cognitive issue, Benjamin Libet's (1983) famous free will experiment involved a number of researchers sitting in front of an oscilloscope/timer with EEG (electroencephalogram) electrodes affixed to their scalps. They were then instructed to execute a simple motor activity like pressing a button or lifting a finger. As they executed the task each participant was asked to note the position of a dot on the timer when they were first aware of the wish to act. Pressing the button or lifting the finger also resulted in the electronic recording of the dot's position on the timer. The difference between the two marked the time between the volition to act and the action itself. Analysis of the EEG recordings indicated mounting brain activity before any conscious will to act, and concluded that the conscious will to act was preceded by an unconscious increase in electrical activity in the brain. Libet believed that he had shown considerations that "would appear to introduce certain constraints on the potential of the individual for exerting conscious initiation and control over his voluntary acts."[13]

Such a controversial conclusion, if valid, has implications beyond challenging dualism. If our supposedly conscious acts are actually decided unconsciously beforehand, regardless of what the time interval might be, then determinism is true, free will is false, and agency is an illusion. Libet denied this implication, citing that an RP indicates only the *awareness* of a decision, but that this does not necessarily indicate that a decision has been carried out, meaning that the agent always has the choice to change their intentions.

In Libet's defense, we must recognize that the equipment he was using some 40 years ago was vastly inadequate in terms of supporting his conclusions, but his research methodologies have also been called into question by several fine thinkers, among them Daniel Dennett and Patricia Churchland (1981);

the former challenging ambiguities in the timing mechanisms and the latter objecting to possible implications of downward causation (conscious initiation). There is no question as to the existence of RP being a fact; instead the question lies in what it reveals to us, if anything. As Gerard Verschuuren notes: "In other words, the RP demonstrates that expected brain activity always occurs *before* a decision but does not reveal the *result* of the decision."[14] The general consensus among scientists and philosophers appears to be that Libet's conclusions are overdrawn in that they would seem to be insufficient either to argue for, or against, determinism or conscious initiation. "Considering the human organism, there is no reason to question whether the brain is the 'agent' of consciousness. Perhaps it is not the 'agent' of consciousness, but rather the 'instrument' of consciousness. If that is the case, the brain could very well be receiving instructions from elsewhere to execute choices. Part of these instructions could be stored somewhere in memory, but only *after* the instructions have been executed."[15]

Libet's experiment was reexamined by the Australian biostatistician Judy Trevena in 2010, wherein the evidence supporting his conclusions was found to be scientifically lacking. "We tested that assumption by comparing the electrophysiological signs before a decision to move with signs present before a decision not to move. There was no evidence of stronger electrophysiological signs before a decision to move than before a decision not to move, so these signs clearly are not specific to movement preparation. We conclude that Libet's results do not provide evidence that voluntary movements are initiated unconsciously."[16] These findings do not reject Libet's assertions, they only show that his conclusion lacks the empirical evidence necessary to support it.

So what does all of this mean in terms of Portalism? The argument from neuroscience, as stated in the first paragraph, is another argument against dualism predicated on an assumption of mind-brain identity. As we have seen, although the phenomenon of Readiness Potential has been scientifically established, in no way does it prove that cognitive processes have their locus in the brain. To make such a claim would represent a logical bridge too far. Thus, the conclusion that 'dualism is false' being predicated upon this unsupported and overdrawn claim renders at least this particular argument from neuroscience, unsound.

The Argument from Causal Interaction

In this section I will reply to the argument from causal interaction while at the same time answering the challenge proffered by Ted Honderich, wherein "a decent theory of consciousness will allow, respect and in fact explain the fact that consciousness is causal – has physical effects."[17]

In considering all of the arguments against dualism, the argument from causal interaction ranks among the most important. This is because dualism is a metaphysical position, and causality is it itself metaphysical. This situation renders answering the argument problematic as nothing metaphysical can be characterized empirically. In light of this, David Hume took roughly the same expressivist approach to causality as he did to morality, positing that it simply doesn't exist. That said, he admitted that we nonetheless absolutely depend upon causality in order to make the predictions necessary for the navigation of our reality.

Books can and have been written on this subject, and all theories of consciousness must account for it. Portalism is no exception, and as tempting as it is to commit pages of text to this fascinating topic, I am concerned only in illustrating how causality is characterized within my theory, and will do so by responding to specific questions while happily leaving any further argument to the academicians.

Portalism is a phenomenal externalist form of dualism, and

as such will be expected to reply to the following traditional questions:

A. Answer the basic problem of causal interaction: How can something totally immaterial affect something totally material? Explain how something without any physical properties can cause physical effects.

B. In dualism "the mind" is assumed to be non-physical and by definition outside of the realm of science. Thus the mechanism which explains the connection between the mental and the physical would therefore be a philosophical proposition as compared to a scientific theory. Explain this mechanism and exactly how interaction takes place.

C. How are physical memories created concerning consciousness?

In reply to question (A): The existence of immaterial things that affect material things is not unknown to science. The term 'material' describes something made of matter. Gravity is immaterial, yet it affects material things. Gravity is a field – a totally immaterial force – that acts upon anything with mass, and things with mass are considered to be 'material'. Portalism holds that the all-encompassing horizon of Consciousness is, like gravity, a fundamental force of nature, ubiquitous throughout the universe, and that it interacts autogenically and invariably with all living things through their portals, just as gravity interacts autogenically and invariably with all things having mass. This description stands as the explanation of how something totally immaterial can affect something totally material, and should be sufficient to satisfy question (A).

In reply to question (B): This question makes two assumptions; the first being that the mind is assumed to be non-physical and by definition outside of the realm of science; the second being that the explanation of the mental/physical connection will be a philosophical proposition and not a scientific theory. Portalism agrees to both of these assumptions. The locus of the mind is external to the body and is indeed non-physical, but its existence outside of the realm of science is a limitation placed upon it not by Portalism, but by science itself. There is nothing precluding science from expanding its horizons to include a subjective science, in much the same way that physics expanded its ontology in order to adopt Maxwell's characterization of electromagnetism. Yet, in regards to the original question, the current state of science and its self-imposed limitations would indeed place the phenomenally external mind outside of it, by definition. Given this, it follows that an empirical characterization of consciousness as per the scientific method would not be a possibility, leaving us with a philosophical proposition. But in response it is worth pointing out that, being metaphysical, *such is the case with any theory of mind.* As I describe in the next chapter, Manzotti and Rockwell would disagree with me on this point, as their respective theories claim a fundamental basis in physicalism, but their claims become plausible only after making a leap of faith that the assumptive (albeit compelling) premises of their externalist perspectives are indeed the reality. To be sure, Portalism is no different when it comes to its own dualistic theoretical assumptions. So all that is left now is to explain the 'connection between the mental and the physical, and how this interaction takes place'.

Portalism holds that mind is manifested within a localization of the horizon of Consciousness individualized to a respective organism through its portal. To restrict the explanation to the syntactical confines of the question, this portal mechanism is the connection between mind and brain, but it is at the same time so much more. Consciousness, as mind, is in-the-world, and through this *being-in*, affects a relationship of *de facto* identity through which mind *becomes* the world. The world is disclosed to mind through the sensory modalities of the body, and the data they in turn provide to the brain for processing becomes disclosed to mind via the portal. Phenomenal experience of the physical realm is therefore instantaneous to the mind, as the world is exactly as it appears. Causal pathways between brain and mind/world are bidirectional, and downward causality exists (I make this case in chapter 7). The sensory modalities are always providing data in unreflective everydayness but can be focused at any time by the intentionality of the mind via its portal, directing the brain to move the body and/or perform any acts necessary in response to the intention of the mind. The mind has agency, and all of these processes are perpetual and ongoing, involving only milliseconds, whether in wake state or dream state, as long as the portal is open. In answer to question (B), this is how the interaction takes place.

In response to question (C): The brain stores, organizes, time-stamps, and establishes necessary neural relationships to other memories, whether they be active, episodic, procedural, or semantic. Neuroscience has proved this by showing how the same neural connections fire when the memory is retrieved that fired when it was first captured. Through downward causality, mind can retrieve any memory it chooses through reflective consciousness. Many memories are accessed unintentionally as a result of encountering objects in the world as we go about living in our everydayness, but when my consciousness turns reflexively inward, I, as the agent, can retrieve or search for specific memories on demand. There are of course limitations, as I discuss in an earlier chapter. For example, on April 10, 1970, I could remember what I had for dinner on April 8th, but I can't recall that memory now. Just the same, I remember very well what I was doing when I first heard that John Lennon had been killed. The brain seems to understand the significance of a memory, if not the meaning of it, as that is imparted to it through degrees of emotion engendered by the mind. For example, I was never emotional about whatever I had for dinner on April 10, 1970 (probably a grilled cheese), but I can well remember how that croissant I bought in Strasbourg last year melted in my mouth, although I couldn't tell you the exact time and date without some research. For the exam I have coming up, it is essential that I remember the details surrounding the regicide of Charles I, although after the exam is over it is almost certain that I will forget or misremember the finer points of that historic event only months from now. The point I am making is that the brain is incapable of assigning any meaning to that which it stores as memory – only mind can do that – and it is mind, and the emotions that originate from its experiences in the world, that can elevate one memory over another. I can see his face, but I can't remember the name of the kid that sat next to me in Cartography 220, and yet I can remember in every detail my first physical act of love with a woman, my aged cat that died in my arms, and the first time I ever skydived. The brain has no capability of differentiating one memory from another, as memories have meaning and context which can only be assigned by the mind, communicated instantaneously through the portal, and stored by the brain. Loss of memory, loss of chronological order, and the inability to store active memory is therefore never a function of mind, but a function of either the reduced intellectual limitations in the lobes of the brain (see chapter 6), or more common, the deterioration of the portal mechanism due to age, damage, or disease. Memory was discussed in more depth in an earlier chapter, but this description should be sufficient as a response to question (C).

I believe that I have responded adequately to the argument from causal interaction, and in so doing defended the plausibility of Portalism as a dualism in respects to causality. In reference to the criterion set by Dr. Honderich, I believe that I have allowed, respected, and explained how consciousness can be causal, thus I submit that in light of the criterion he imposes, Portalism can be considered to be a 'decent' theory.

The Argument from Simplicity

This argument should not be confused with Occam's razor, an issue which I will address further on. Instead, the argument from simplicity appeals to heuristic techniques. Basically, the question for the dualist amounts to 'why have two ontologically distinct entities when it would be so much easier to explain consciousness in terms of only one'. In other words, why unnecessarily complicate matters by insisting that the mind is *not* the brain?

There are several problems with the heuristic approach, as it is defined in this way. True, *one* is simpler than *two*, unless *one* is unable to sufficiently explain the problem, wherein subjective experience is the problem waiting to be explained. A similar argument might be to claim that four tires on a car are overly complicated when one will do. But one won't do, and neither will mind-brain identity theories that struggle to explain how subjective experience rises from physical matter. Heuristic strategies derive from previous experience with similar problems, but there is nothing 'similar' to consciousness. There are no pre-established methodologies to employ in our search for the nature of subjective experience. As proof one simply has to look at the record of materialism, accentuated by one rejected theory after another. In terms of an argument from simplicity, one could claim that the explanatory power of having two ontologically unique substances at least answers some questions, wherein the heuristically 'simple' solution of only having one explains nothing at all.

Heuristics is a tool for finding satisfactory solutions where optimal solutions are not possible, but it is a tool that has been honed to operate in the objective, empirical realm. Heuristics can also be a valuable tool in a subjective science, but only if the satisfactory solution has not been preconceived to be one of mind-brain identity. When we bracket off what we think we know about the objective and subjective realms, and in so doing leave materialism behind, the way may then be clear to pursue fresh, new, and workable heuristic hypotheses of consciousness.

In regards to Portalism in view of the argument from simplicity, the concept of a portal into the horizon of Consciousness manifesting as an actualization of mind, establishing a *de facto* relationship of identity with the world through its *being-in*, is arguably much simpler than the pursuit of complex neurological correlates to discrete mental states, while at the same time being possessed of far greater explanatory power. Thus I would hold that Portalism *is in itself* an argument from simplicity.

In the sections above I have shown how the theory of Portalism is able to respond to the challenges posed by the hard problem, as well as to the traditional arguments against dualism. In the sections that follow I will present arguments intended to justify the plausibility of the theory itself.

Tools for Exploring a Subjective Realm

Consciousness, as mind, exists. To even think this presupposes mind. The existence of mind is therefore self-evident, requiring no further argument, as to engage in the act of argument would be to presuppose mind. The *cogito* is correct; mind is all that *I* am and all that *I* can ever *be*. It is here that monist idealism draws the line in terms of that which is necessary and sufficient for reality, a position for which that philosophy makes a compelling case for the open-minded thinker. I know because I was once one of them, before I became uncomfortable with what I perceived as an inability to credibly account for the world and the apparent uniformity of nature. To my sense of things, to deny the existence of a physical world existing outside of our perception of it is as unreasonable as denying the existence of consciousness. Monist idealism, positivism, and illusionism all share different perspectives on the same basic untruth, being that only the subjective exists, or only the physical exists, or else that we are all simply mistaken and profoundly deceived about our reality. In fact it is both rational and reasonable to conclude that mind and world clearly both exist, and that dualism in some form must be true. To justify this conclusion, all that need be explained is an equally rational and reasonable description of the interaction between these two mediums. There are several theories that attempt to provide this description, and Portalism is one of them. It is hoped that in the future science will expand its ontology and develop a subjective science with new tools and methods, but lacking this at present I will argue the plausibility of Portalism using a process that includes synthetic *a priori* propositions and abductive reasoning.

Kant states that by definition, all metaphysical propositions are synthetic *a priori*. Epistemically this translates that the justifications of such statements do not rely on experience (although they can be validated by experience) and that their predicate is related to but not contained within their subject. In a more meaningful sense, if *a posteriori* reasoning is necessary to obtaining empirical knowledge, and empirical knowledge is only justified by experience, then *a posteriori* reasoning is inapplicable within the subjective realm, as nothing subjective can be empirically understood. Since our choices are limited, as per Kant, to *a posteriori* and *a priori* reasoning, then *a priori* reasoning, by omission, would seem to be the correct tool for exploring the subjective realm. Kant's definition for the analytic/synthetic distinction is best described using his famous 'bachelor' example. The analytic proposition is given as "all bachelors are unmarried", the predicate of this proposition being contained in its subject, and the proposition being tautological. This is opposed to the synthetic proposition given as "all bachelors are alone", wherein the predicate 'alone' is not contained in the subject 'bachelor', and neither is it a definition of a bachelor. It is, however, descriptively more meaningful, as it tells us something about our world. In addition, it is also an *a posteriori* claim that can be verified through experience. What is important to take away from this extremely cursory foray into epistemology is that analytic propositions are true by virtue of their constituent terms, while the truth of synthetic propositions is dependent upon *how their meaning relates to the world.*[18] Thus, in the search for tools to characterize consciousness, the propositions and claims that will best fit the purpose are those reasoned *a priori* that are justified by how their meanings relate to our reality, as that reality appears to us.

Abductive reasoning was introduced into modern logic by the pragmatist philosopher Charles Sanders Peirce in the late 19th century. Abduction is a form of inductive reasoning. Given that the premises are true, inductive arguments are intended to show that the conclusion is *unlikely* to be false – hence establishing a *plausibility* that the conclusion *could* be, indeed is *likely* to be, true. Unlike the deductive arguments used in empiricism, when formulating hypotheses within the subjective realm their plausibility is as close as we can come to empirical fact (if indeed we are to be held to that objective metric), thus the credibility of such arguments becomes a matter of degree, wherein the degree is established through a given theory's explanatory power.

Abduction takes inductive logic a step further as, according to Peirce, it essentially amounts to guessing. Yet abduction is an important tool as it promotes a flexibility of thought unbound by dogma, or in other words, thinking 'outside of the box'. As Peirce himself claims: "Abduction guesses a new or outside idea so as to account in a plausible, instinctive, economical way for a surprising or very complicated phenomenon. That is its proximate aim."[19] The ability of inductive logic to deduce new theories from existing knowledge can be a valuable tool for formulating new theories of consciousness. In addition, a hypothesis can be abductively validated if it can be argued that its explanation is the best possible considering the alternatives. This process of abductive validation brings us again to the recognition of the importance of explanatory power in the establishment of a theory's plausibility, best exemplified by Occam's razor.

Occam's razor is a common abductive heuristic used by science that can operate equally well in the defense of theories of consciousness. Those that claim Occam's razor holds that between any two theories the simplest one will always be the best fall victim to a common misunderstanding, the fact being that the razor applies only when the two theories *are of equal explanatory power*. When such is the case, the simpler of the two will always be the best. But this definition also allows for one theory to elevate above the other through the enhancement of its explanatory power, even if by doing so it becomes more complex. Therefore, the decision metric in Occam's razor lies not in a given theory's simplicity, but in its explanatory power, and it is by this metric that I will show the plausibility of Portalism to be as good as any and better than most.

The Explanatory Power of Portalism

Any theory of mind must be a theory about human beings interacting with each other and with their environment.
W. Teed Rockwell[20]

Within the world of contemporary metaphysics, theories of consciousness that embrace phenomenal externalism, although having recently achieved some gains in recognition, remain by far in the distinct minority. This is especially true within the Anglo-American university system, where the analytic tradition still enjoys the overwhelming influence achieved originally through the Vienna Circle's positivist embrace of science and empiricism nearly a hundred years ago. The resulting meteoric ascent of monist materialism succeeded in establishing the dominate contemporary perspective that nothing non-physical exists and that therefore the mental states we think we experience are either illusions or else have some unknown biological explanation. The conclusion being that what we mistakenly consider to be mental processes are in fact physical processes – in other words, the mind is the brain.

Mind-brain identity theories have evolved by generally softening their original rigid positions of eliminativism, illusionism, and logical positivism, methodically moving toward non-reductive explanations. Several of these theories fall within property dualism and can range anywhere from the boldness of non-reductive supervenient physicalism to a retreat into the safe harbor of epiphenomenalism. But my point is that after a hundred years spent on attempts to retool, reshape, and remodel the physicalist explanation into these multivariate forms, there has yet to be shown any verifiable or reproducible empirical evidence that the fundamental theoretical concept of mind-brain identity is in fact the case.

So why does this type/token identity theory of mind persist, and what are the ideas that make it such an attractive position? Mind-brain identity theories tend to commonly embrace the following arguments:

a) Mind-brain identity is intuitively compelling. The feeling that I am a conscious self moving through an external physical reality encountering objects and states of affairs would appear to be self-evident; to the degree that believing otherwise would seem contrary to the principles of common sense. I am a thinking being, alive in a universe of things which I observe and come to some understanding of. Such cannot be denied; it is a fact of the world.

b) Invoking Occam's razor, why introduce an unverifiable non-physical world of supposed subjective experience, when a single physical world will do. Mind-brain identity is thus the simpler solution.

c) Assuming that 'mind' even exists, the current inability to explain the interaction between mind and brain is insufficient for denying mind-brain identity. Absence of evidence is not evidence of absence, and science will eventually evolve to the point where all is revealed.

d) The universe is causally closed and all of its energy is accounted for. Therefore there is no energy left that could account for anything non-physical. If anything non-physical did exist, there would be no unallocated energy by which it would be able to causally act upon anything physical. Thus nothing non-physical can exist.

In citing the arguments above I have resisted the temptation to present them in terms that can be readily and easily attacked. I believe that they fairly describe the materialist mind-set as per basic identity theory. That said, I will address the arguments in terms of their explanatory power.

As far as argument (a) is concerned, I absolutely accede to its claim of intuitiveness. The feeling that we are sitting in a little chair behind our eyes navigating our way through the world is overwhelming. This intuitive feeling, however, does not rise to the level of argument. It is not sufficient to say that a thing is a certain way just because it just feels that way, for to claim such amounts to belief which is no more than faith.

Conversely, Portalism is genuinely counterintuitive, as one must be willing to embrace possibilities that can appear to be impossible. But regardless of which way one leans toward an explanation of consciousness, intuitiveness is not an argument. Intuitiveness is an unempirical emotional response which the analytics would discount scientifically, while the continental approach would be to dispose of it phenomenologically. Intuitiveness explains nothing.

Before proceeding with the consideration of physicalist arguments it is perhaps best to remove eliminative materialism and illusionism from the mix, for the simple reason that if subjective experience either does not exist or is mistaken for what is actually a biological process, then such a situation doesn't leave us much to argue about. If the mind is the brain, then only the physical exists, and that's that. Eliminative materialists and illusionists point out that there is no evidence that mental states exist (which if they did would presuppose a non-physical subjective realm), regardless of how intuitive it might seem. In this claim they use the same argument against the intuitiveness of mind that I make above against mind-brain identity. The problem is that if my conclusion is correct in that intuitiveness explains nothing, then their claim would amount to saying that absence of evidence is in fact evidence of absence, which would be an argument from ignorance wherein nothing is brought forth. I am aware that there are degrees within the eliminative materialist position, that not all perspectives are 'hard' and that a distinction between mental states and qualia can be drawn, but to argue that mental states or qualia *don't* exist (or are misunderstood) while providing no evidence is no stronger a position than arguing that mental states and qualia *do* exist while providing no evidence. Although eliminative materialism and illusionism cannot be disproved outright, they nevertheless promote the properties of elimination versus those of explanation, which conceptually makes them lonely and barren islands of materialist non-positions. It is much more challenging and interesting to explain why a thing is or how a thing could be, than it is to simply deny its existence in an effort to make it fit conveniently within an ossified physicalist ontology.

It is perhaps best to consider the remaining three arguments taken together, as each tends to overlap the others. Having set illusionism and eliminative materialism aside, we can move forward with the assumption that consciousness, actualized as mind, exists. Such an assumption would presuppose a realm of subjective experience – a non-physical realm in some form or fashion. Given this, it becomes necessary for both physicalist and dualist theories to account for the interrelationship of the physical with the non-physical, as well as for the phenomenon of experience – the *feeling-like-there-is-to-be* something – and it is here that the difficulties with traditional analytic explanations reveal themselves. Theories of consciousness tend to break into two camps; those of phenomenal externalism, versus those of mind-brain identity. I use these terms instead of dualism versus monism because some recent externalist theories are so original in their concept that the lines of demarcation between monism and dualism can become blurred, even irrelevant, as I will discuss further in the last chapter.

Before embracing phenomenal externalism, one must first reject type/token mind-brain identity theory. This might be easier than it appears, because if one accepts the existence of subjective experience, it becomes incumbent on the mind-brain identity materialist to account for how mental states emerge from physical matter, and how a grey blob of organic matter in the skull accomplishes experience. There exist all manner of creative explanations for how this might be the case, from emergentism to supervenience, and from functionalism to property dualism, all of them seeking to justify how an embodied mind derives experience from an external world. Such is the mind-body problem, but this famous problem applies to all theories of consciousness, monist and dualist alike. And since there is no current science of subjectivity, theorists must use the investigative tools that they have, which are those of empirical science. This has created a new merging of science and philosophy into the discipline of neurophilosophy, wherein the most recent areas of research include neuroscience and the search for the physical correlates of consciousness.

It is a desperate search and the stakes are frighteningly high, for if physical correlates of conscious experience cannot be mapped and/or explained, then mind-brain identity is false, which by extension makes materialism false. But what is important here is the relationship that this emphasis on neuroscientific research bears upon our original three arguments. Remember how the original mind-body identity theorists claimed Occam's razor – the sheer 'simplicity' of the single substance concept – the 'elegance' of a single physical universe. But one can make the argument that the elements of this theory have now become victims of complexity, as evidenced by a profusion of distributed neural pathways, mono-synaptic reflexes, c-fiber firings, re-entrant neural loops, axons, synapses, excitatory and inhibitory neurotransmitters, etc.; these concepts being only the thin end of the neuroscientific wedge employed in the search for the physical correlates of consciousness. Still, in the light of all of this intense research and the participation of a lot of very smart men and women, the fact remains that we are no closer to any real understanding of the nature of a thought, or of the feeling one has when their son hits a home run – yet this is not my point. In lieu of all this scientific research based upon the assumption of mind-brain identity, research which I still believe is valuable in its own right, my question here is simple – what happened to the original claim of Occam's razor? Apparently, the 'simplicity and elegance' of single substance mind-brain identity theory has gone out the window. If compared to the external mind/world concept of Portalism, which theory now has the stronger claim to simplicity? As I will argue later, I believe Portalism has not only the stronger claim to elegance, but also to explanatory power.

The second part of this argument is the belief that science will one day evolve to where an empirical characterization of consciousness will be revealed. Some of our finest thinkers, including Searle and Churchland, have taken this position. But it might seem that making such a claim is at best only faith, while at worst is an argument from ignorance. For example, when I say that 'there *could* be someone behind that door,' I am essentially admitting that I am ignorant of whether or not there is anybody behind that door. I do not necessarily disagree that science will one day be able to explain consciousness. However, I do believe that science as it exists in the confines of its current ontology will never be able to explain consciousness, for the simple reason that current science is objective and consciousness cannot be explained in objective terms. But I also recognize that there is nothing holding science back from expanding its ontology – scientists have done it before, and they can do it again.

The final argument that mind-brain identity theorists commonly embrace is that of causality, in that the universe is causally closed, and that downward causality cannot exist, as nothing non-physical can possibly affect anything physical. I discuss my position on this subject in detail in the previous section of this chapter subtitled *The Argument from Causal Interaction*. To recap briefly, I hold that the universe is not causally closed, that downward causality does indeed exist, and that the mind is fully capable of agency, and as such this commonly held physicalist causal argument makes conclusions that do not follow from its premises and is therefore unsound.

Having addressed these arguments commonly held by physicalists, what then is the explanatory power of mind-brain identity theories? On the plus side, mind-brain identity is certainly intuitive, and unlike the type-identity version of the theory, token identity theory supports multiple realizability and so avoids charges of neural chauvinism. These are credible attributes, but they are far outweighed by the theory's inability to account for subjective experience. Like all cranialist theories, the world is experienced through the body's sensory modalities. These are vision, sound, smell, touch and taste for humans, but these by no means represent the limits of sensation. Mind-brain identity holds that the senses detect the properties of an encounter with objects and states of affairs in the world, sending the data to the brain for processing, and up to this point this explanation would be correct. But where the theory falls down is in its assumption that the brain is the mind. If the locus of the mind is a part of the brain and/or central nervous system, then what the mind is conscious of about the world, what it experiences within any given field of perception, is in fact only a copy existing *inside the brain*. This means that the mind can never know reality, only an ideal copy of the world driven by sense-data stimuli processed by the brain. If this is the case, then the locus of experience is in the head. As such we would never experience the world, being limited only to a stitched-together reframing of reality.

Given this, it falls upon mind-brain identity advocates to provide an explanation of how phenomenal experience arises, derives, projects, or somehow becomes conscious content from this processed ideal. That the brain receives and processes sense data can be demonstrated by a process of elimination akin to the argument from brain damage or even Fred Dretske's observation wherein experiences are in the head: "why else would closing one's eyes or stopping one's ears extinguish them,"[21] although this would apply only to phenomenal consciousness and not to reflexive consciousness, where one could still be conscious – still be a thinking mind – even when deprived of any physical sense modalities. This is highlighted by Bishop Berkeley's claim "that neither our thoughts, nor passions, nor ideas formed by the imagination, exist without the mind, is what everybody will allow."[22] But within this mind-brain model, where is meaning and context assigned to this brain generated ideal? To this, Dretske further posits that "phenomenal content could depend on *something elsewhere*."[23] But in mind-brain identity, there is no *elsewhere* to be, because the locus of the mind is cranial – so whither cognition?

To make the mind-brain identity case, a connection between processed sensory data (or thought, in the case of the reflexive) and phenomenal experience must be shown. Take for example my aged pet cat, which having been given a shot by the vet dies in my arms. As a result I feel overwhelming grief and begin to weep. How does this series of events, reported to the brain via touch, smell, and sight, progress to the phenomenal experience of grief? Neuroimagery can show the activity within the different parts of my brain that scientists have associated with emotion, but there is not a shred of evidence that this activity amounts to cognition, nor is such activity identical from brain to brain, nor have any physical correlates to any conscious experience ever been mapped. The brain is faithfully performing its task, which is the assembly and disclosure of the sense data, but how does it attach the meaning of loss? It can't, because that's not what the brain is designed to do. Mind-brain identity theories have no explanation for how the brain creates consciousness, or how it fills that consciousness with phenomenal content. The best they can do is claim that one day science will figure it all out, amounting to a last straw to cling to for those that dogmatically resist thinking beyond the self-imposed limitations of a causally closed, deterministic physical reality. And they are self-imposed. There is no rule that a subjective realm cannot exist, or that downward causality and the non-deterministic agency it promises cannot be the reality. Such are the false barriers mandated by the remnants of logical positivism and a science unreceptive to expansion. Returning to the idea of using the metric of explanatory power to gauge the strength of a metaphysical theory, how does mind-brain identity measure up? Beyond the admission that the theory is seductively intuitive, it is clear that it has little if any power to explain the nature of consciousness.

Where mind-brain identity assumes that consciousness is the brain, Portalism assumes that Consciousness is a fundamental force of nature. Each of these assumptions is crucial in its role as the single most fundamental, important, and necessary philosophical underpinning upon which these theories are built. Nevertheless, both premises are reasoned abductively, each intended to support the likelihood of a conclusion. Yet when it is all said and done, there is no empirical evidence supporting either case, thus together they ultimately amount to no more than guesses. But this does not mean that they have no value, as abductive reasoning, as a form of inductive reasoning, can be a weapon against dogma through its ability to entertain explanations that may appear unorthodox and counterintuitive. And science often advances, at least collaterally, from these kinds of ideas manifested within rationalist thought.

Portalism is a radical phenomenal externalist theory of consciousness. It explains the character of consciousness as follows:

a)   The horizon of Consciousness is a fundamental force of nature, ontologically irreducible, and the medium of subjective experience.

b)   The means of accessing Consciousness inheres in all living things and can take many different biological and/or biochemical forms. In this theory, any given organism's enabling means of access to Consciousness is referred to as its 'portal'.

c)   Provided that the portal is functional and unimpaired, access to Consciousness is immediate, involuntary, invariable, and autogenic, and remains so until the portal is closed by damage, disease, a brain induced act of self-preservation, anesthesia, or death.

d)   Portal access to Consciousness creates an individualized localization within the all-encompassing horizon of Consciousness, manifested as consciousness and actualized as a mind, specific and particular to the individual.

Mind is existentially codependent upon the *res extensa*, and when the body dies, the mind, as both 'I' and 'self', dissolves. Consciousness is subjective and in itself not bound by space or time, but mind, with its relationship of bodily codependency, becomes pinned in space and time through its portal connection to the body. To encounter objects and states of affairs, the mind is dependent upon the body's ability to move through the world of objects, while the body is dependent upon the mind to find those things in the world necessary to sustain it, such as food, water, shelter, and a mate. Without mind, the body cannot navigate its reality, nor can it survive unassisted.

The locus of consciousness is external to the *res extensa*. Mind is in and of the world – since it is extracranial, where else could it be? As the body navigates the physical world, mind encounters objects and states of affairs through the body's sense modalities, to which it assigns meaning and context. Causal pathways are bidirectional and the mind has agency, directing its body in navigating the world, while the brain maintains homeostatic equilibrium, processes sensory data, categorizes and stores memories, communicates egocentric needs to the mind, and establishes intellectual limitations.

The mind is the agent, not the brain, and the subjective realm is indeterminate. The 'I' is possessed of free will and is therefore wholly responsible for its choices. The 'self' manifests as reflexive consciousness, as self-awareness, within an entirely subjective realm, purely mental, independent of the sensory modalities, and unbound by time and space.

Phenomenal experience occurs through the encountering of objects and states of affairs in the world, and Portalism allows for multiple ways in which this phenomenon can be realized. As mind is in and of the world by its *being-in*, a *de facto* relationship of identity is thereby established, and through this property it is able to experience the world. I also favor John Searle's concept of a property inherent in objects through which they can *cause* experience, yet these two concepts are not mutually exclusive, in fact, they could be argued to be mutually supportive, thereby strengthening the likelihood of the theory. The cognitive mechanics of subjective experience may conform to this description, or they might be something else entirely, but this only serves to illustrate the multiple realizability of Portalism, which must considered as a point of strength. Should the reader find this explanation of phenomenal experience insufficient, they should know that at least it is a serious consideration of what *could* be the case, which is a stronger argument than the hopeful materialist claim that one day science will be able to explain it.

It is critical that the relationship of the portal to consciousness be understood. It can be symbolized logically as:

Given that P is an individual localization of the horizon of Consciousness actualized as mind, and Q is a living organism's functioning biological/biochemical portal mechanism, we can make the material implication that $P \supset Q$, or whenever there is mind, a portal mechanism is implied. The existence of P presupposes Q as (if P then Q). Logically, the obverse will not work, as it can be possible to have Q without P (a portal without mind), as in the case where the portal is damaged or diseased, or for reasons of self-preservation when the brain overrides and shuts the portal connection down. In the case where the portal is disabled (closed) for whatever reason we would understand this as $\sim Q \rightarrow \sim P$, or if not Q (portal) then not P (mind); mind being dependent upon a functioning portal. As Consciousness always already is as a fundamental force of nature, existing at all times and in all places, the portal mechanism is sufficient to the actualization of mind, and is the necessary condition before any mind can *be*. The strength of this relationship can also be expressed as a material equivalence, as in $P \equiv Q$ or [P (mind), if and only if Q (portal)], demonstrating that mind has an existential dependency upon the viability of the portal mechanism. Again, the obverse statement will not work, as it could be possible to have a nonfunctioning or impaired portal, wherein although *existent*, is nonetheless insufficient to the actualization or the sustainability of mind.

Throughout this work I have been resistant in straying into the cognitive and epistemological aspects commonly addressed by other theorists. Having a sparse background in psychology and little interest in epistemological philosophy, semantics and the like, my purpose has been to characterize how body, mind, and world *could* work within the metaphysical framework of phenomenal externalism, having found materialism and idealism to be insufficient theoretical perspectives. To this end I have limited my arguments to address the nature of consciousness as phenomenon. As such I am prepared to accept any explanations of cognition as well as epistemological ideas because the ultimate validity of such explanations is independent of the locus of consciousness. Whether mind-brain identity is the case or Portalism is true, explanations concerning cognition will work or not work equally as they depend only upon the existence of a mind and not upon its locus.

One area where Portalism will almost certainly be attacked is on the issue of falsifiability. For a statement to be falsifiable one only needs to think of a single observation that would make the statement untrue. The famous example is the proposition that 'all swans are white'. Basically, this proposition is true until it's not, occurring when someone eventually sees a black swan. But falsifiability presupposes that an idea is verifiable by observation, and observation implies experience. Consciousness cannot be verified by experience, because it is experience.

Therefore any attempt to apply falsifiability to consciousness begs the question and leads to circularity and skepticism. Falsifiability is a child of the analytic tradition, replacing the verificationism of the positivists, and although it has become the gold standard for validating the claims of science, in the realm of metaphysics it is of little use. This is no problem for most analytic philosophers, as the analytic tradition considers metaphysical subjects to be meaningless. And yet here we are, watching as philosophy transcends traditional schools of thought to explore more interesting radical alternatives, phenomenal externalism being among them. Portalism is certainly not falsifiable, but I don't believe that this situation is enough to reject the theory, as there exist no metaphysical theories of consciousness that are falsifiable, including mind-brain identity. In regard to the materialist's presumption of mind-brain identity, Teed Rockwell makes the same observation: "Unless experiments are performed that are expressly designed to falsify the claim that the mind is the brain, we cannot say that this claim has been scientifically established, no matter how natural it may seem so."[24] So to charges of non-falsifiability I would reply that this test is not applicable within metaphysics and thus irrelevant, and that a different set of exploratory tools and metrics will need to be devised, most likely within a science of subjectivity, before any such verification can be meaningfully applied to theories of consciousness.

While I hold that the explanatory power of Portalism, which far exceeds that of mind-brain identity, is an indicator of the strength of the theory, Ted Honderich has proffered another metric for justification claiming: "One criterion is that a good theory will include a clear and good answer to the mind-body problem, the problem of the relation of consciousness to the brain."[25] Portalism is compatible with this principle, answering the mind-body problem by removing the premise of the argument requiring an explanation of how the brain gives rise to consciousness because Consciousness *always already is*. The subjective realm therefore exists in harmony with the objective world, and the locus of the mind is in the world. If it is in the world then it is of the world, the experience of the encountered object is the object, and the world is exactly as it appears. Brains do what brains do, minds do what minds do, and dualism, as a phenomenal externalism, is true. As I have shown in earlier sections in the chapter, Portalism can respond cogently to all of the arguments levelled against dualism by demonstrating its compatibility with them, or by rendering them unsound. In addition, embracing Portalism has no negative impact on cognitive science, and it is here I make the distinction between psychological explanations of human mental development and understanding, meaning cognitive science, and neuroscientific research that presupposes mind-brain identity in its relentless search for the physical correlates of consciousness.

The explanatory power of Portalism is further strengthened by its ability to account for how all living things are able to navigate widely disparate realities. In doing so it simultaneously accounts for other minds while rejecting skepticism, solipsism, pantheism, and panpsychism. It demonstrates compatibility with the ideas of several brilliant contemporary thinkers, ranging from the dualist Chalmers to the materialists Searle and Churchland. Portalism denies the false dichotomy of analytic versus continental, embracing ideas from both traditions with emphasis on the standpoint of *what works* while rejecting dogma. Within a science of subjectivity, both the empiricism of the analytic and the intellectualism of the continental will be needed in order to overcome the difficulty that Merleau-Ponty so well describes wherein: "Empiricism cannot see that we need to know what we are looking for, otherwise we would not be looking for it, and intellectualism fails to see that we need to be ignorant of what we are looking for, or equally again we should not be searching."[26]

Portalism is an assembly of ideas, some of them Pre-Socratic, all considered with no deference to the philosophical tradition they may have originated within. As I stated in chapter 2, I claim no originality for Portalism outside of the name, and philosophers that consider this theory will have no trouble recognizing the ideas of Heraclitus, Democritus, Augustine, Hume, Descartes, Kant, Leibniz, Schopenhauer, Nietzsche, Heidegger, Sartre, Peirce, McTaggart, Chalmers, Searle, and many others, and I have striven earnestly to credit all of them properly in my citations. I believe that many of these thinkers have formulated important pieces to the metaphysical puzzle of consciousness, and that Portalism is the result of a workable combination of those parts that offers a cogent explanation of consciousness.

As a final argument for plausibility, I claim that Portalism meets the requirements of Occam's razor. I have shown that the explanatory power of Portalism significantly exceeds that of mind-brain identity theory, emergentism, epiphenomenalism, and supervenient physicalism. It is not neurally chauvinistic and is compatible with multiple realizability and functionalism. It has an answer to the hard problem of consciousness, the problem of other minds, and each of the traditional arguments against dualism. No other Cartesian, property dualist or materialist theory is able to make similar claims.

In the spirit of a contemporary version of continental Rationalism, I have used synthetic *a priori* propositions, arguments from analogy, and abductive reasoning in defending the theory of Portalism, but these tools cannot deductively or empirically prove its truth. Inductive arguments can never be sound because the truth of the premises cannot be determined from experience. But such is the nature of subjectivity, and by extension, of all things metaphysical. If we assume that the premises of Portalism are true, those premises being that Consciousness is a fundamental force of nature, that portals enabling access into this horizon inhere in all living things, and that any presence of a functional portal, no matter how unsophisticated, autogenically manifests an individual localization of consciousness actualized as mind, then it becomes justifiable to believe that the conclusion, being that the locus of mind is in the world and accounts for subjective experience through a *de facto* relationship of identity with the world – therein becoming world – is *probably* true. Given this, the argument for Portalism is cogent, meaning that as a theory of consciousness it is *plausible*, and plausibility is the best I can do given the metaphysical environment that I must operate within.

I believe that I have adequately demonstrated the plausibility of Portalism, through its explanatory power, its elegance and simplicity, its arguments appealing to *a priori* powers of reasoning, its premises being reasonable, and the truth of its conclusion sufficiently persuasive. These are the criteria of the cogent argument. I therefore submit that Portalism, as a radical phenomenal externalist theory of consciousness, is possible, likely, and justified.

Chapter 9

Phenomenal Externalism and the Future of Philosophy

As my explanation of the theory of Portalism draws to a close, it might be useful to compare and contrast it to other contemporary phenomenal externalist theories offered by some very original thinkers. To rephrase, phenomenal externalism rejects the mainstream physicalist mind-brain identity and supervenience positions so prevalent among contemporary analytic neurophilosophers and psychologists, instead embracing the concept that cranialism is false and that the true locus of consciousness lies outside of the body. Most externalist theories are arguably dualist, as any position wherein one claims an extracranial realm or horizon of subjective experience is likely proposing the existence of non-physical things. That said, there are theories that reject dualism outright, holding that if certain assumptions are made, their versions of externalism are indeed compatible with empirical physicalism. Regardless of the metaphysical category they might belong to, they certainly represent perspectives quite different from that of either property dualism or Cartesianism.

The theories that I have chosen to briefly examine all have unique perspectives regarding perception, the role of the world in consciousness, and the manner in which they seek to solve the hard problem. These theories include W. Teed Rockwell's 'brain-body-world nexus', Ted Honderich's 'Actualism', and Riccardo Manzotti's 'spread mind'. In addition, I have included a few paragraphs on the thinking of Alva Noë, because I believe it makes a very good introduction to these types of theories. All of these perspectives share certain elements with Portalism, but none go so far as to claim that Consciousness is a fundamental force of nature. For the reader interested in fresh, alternative approaches to the philosophy of mind, the books of all four of these thinkers are listed in the bibliography at the end of this work. They are inexpensive, thought provoking, and surprisingly quite readable.

Alva Noë

Alva Noë is a Professor of Philosophy at UC Berkeley, a neuroscientist and cognitive scientist. In his book *Out of Our Heads*, he presents a series of compelling arguments against orthodox materialism, holding that the mind is not the brain. Himself a neuroscientist, he argues that although technological advances in brain imagery have yielded stunning and colorful images of brain activity in response to certain stimuli, the results in many cases have either been misrepresented or misunderstood, and that some of the conclusions subsequently drawn have been incorrect, erroneous, unreproducible, or otherwise do not follow from the data: "The pictures we see in the science magazines are not snapshots of a particular person's brain in action. Brain scans are not pictures of cognitive processes in the brain."[1] Noë implies that science has begun to view itself as having taken over the search for a definition of consciousness from philosophy, having become excited about the recent advances made in neuroscience that they believe indicate strong possibilities of eventually mapping the neural correlates of consciousness. Noë reminds us that, as dramatic as the images are, the fact remains that there is not even the thinnest evidence that mind-brain identity is the case, yet this concept remains the standard base assumption of materialism. He characterizes the issue succinctly: "In a way our problem is that we have been looking for consciousness where it isn't. We should look for it where it is."[2]

Noë holds that consciousness requires more than just the brain – it requires the world, as he describes: "The causal processes that enable us to talk and think and find our way around are not confined to what is going on in our skulls. But that is just a way of saying that the machinery of the mind itself is not confined to the skull. The head is not a magical membrane. We are involved in the world around us. We are in it and of it." This concept represents a consistently recurring idea fundamental to phenomenal externalist theories – the role of the world in actualizing the mind. Many theories, including Portalism, take this to be Heideggerian in origin, but Noë's position is more in line with enactivism, wherein mental processes are entwined with the body and the environment. Many of Noë's positions are compatible with Portalism, in fact, of the theories I present in this section, his is the only one that extends consciousness to other organisms in the world, in one example – the snail: "... the world can act on us and provide opportunities for us to act. But like the snails we are bound to the world, and what we are and what we can accomplish depend on what is done to us as much as on what we do. We share this with the snail: like the snail, we are not autonomous. We are in the world and of it."[3]

Should the reader be considering exploring further into theories of phenomenal externalism, I strongly recommend reading Noë's book first. Afterwards they will it find easier to grasp the counterintuitive perspectives that they will encounter going forward.

Ted Honderich

Ted Honderich is a Canadian born British philosopher whose latest theory of mind is called Actualism. In his book *Mind: Your Consciousness is What and Where?* Honderich claims that there is one subjective physical world per perceiver and goes on to ask us what is 'actual' in our perception of our particular world. For example, I perceive the room I am in. The room is a thing in the objective physical world, but that explanation falls short. What is 'actual' is in fact my perception of the room –

my perception 'actualizes' the room. This perspective collapses orthodox conceptions of a subjective and objective world into the single unity of a subjective physical world, which manifests itself through perception – in other words through the *being-in* of consciousness. "Subjective worlds are dependent on several things, one being the objective physical world."[4] Honderich's subjective physical worlds are our reality: "We spend our lives in our subjective physical worlds."[5] His approach, as well as some of his language, is near Heideggerian in that the subjective physical world is the all-encompassing horizon in which objects are disclosed to mind. Our ontological consciousness is being-in-the-world – the world being our personal subjective physical world. Honderich's claim that "Subjective physical worlds are subjective in that they cannot conceivably be separate from consciousness for various reasons, one being that they are the existence of perceptual consciousness" is refreshing and reminiscent of Merleau-Ponty.[6]

Actualism, although distinctly different, does have some conceptual compatibilities with Portalism, perhaps the most important being downward causality. Another interesting parallel is the idea that although an objective physical universe exists outside of our perception of it, Honderich's subjective physical worlds are private to each perceiver. In Portalism, there is indeed one objective physical world perceived by all beings in their own way, yet each individual's localization of Consciousness is tethered to that perceiver. Thus in Actualism, there would be as many subjective physical worlds as there were perceivers, while in Portalism, there would as many localizations of Consciousness as there are organisms. In both theories, the world is absolutely necessary to consciousness. Although Honderich is listed as an analytic, I found his appeals to continental thinkers invigorating, and I strongly agree with his call to abandon the dogmatic orthodoxy of Ayer and the positivists in favor of Husserl's epoché, starting over with fresh thinking and following wherever reason may lead us.

W. Teed Rockwell

W. Teed Rockwell is a Professor of Philosophy and cognitive research at Sonoma State University. Interestingly, he is considered to be a subscriber to both the continental and analytic traditions, and cites the pragmatist John Dewey as a bridge between the two paths of reasoning. In Rockwell's book, *Neither Brain Nor Ghost*, he presents what he terms as "A Nondualist Alternative to the Mind-Brain Identity Theory". This alternative "sees the mind not merely as a network property of interacting cranial neurons, but rather as being equally dependent on the interactions among a brain, a nervous system, a body, and a world."[7] This idea, which understands consciousness in the context of it being a component within a system requiring more than just brain, posits that although physics continues to accurately describe our world, "the fact of multiple realizability guarantees that the physical story cannot be the whole story."[8]

In Rockwell's theory we again see a familiar thread common within externalist theories, which is the idea of dual-path causality: "So why assume that the brain is a closed causal system that creates mind and thought all by itself? Why not say that the mind is dependent on the causal interactions of the brain, the body, and the world?"[9] This concept of a brain-body-world nexus of a codependent consciousness is the foundation of Rockwell's theory and, as with Portalism, embraces the idea of downward causality, opening the possibility of mental events precipitating physical effects. A further similarity between the ideas of Portalism and the brain-body-nexus concept is the necessity of the world and the critically indispensable role it plays in consciousness: "there can be no mind without a brain-body-world nexus."[10] Channeling Heidegger, as many externalists seem to do, Rockwell rightly claims "that no self is strictly distinct from the world in which it dwells." Rockwell spares no room for equivocation as regards the importance of the world to consciousness, even to the extent wherein he borrows from enactivism, noting that previous externalists have simply not gone far enough: "I am not merely repeating the slogan of Putnam 1975 that 'Meaning ain't in the head.' I am also saying that consciousness ain't in the head. All experience is, I claim, completely and irreducibly intentional, and thus gets its meaning from relationships that the living self maintains with the outside world."[11]

One significant area wherein Rockwell's thought and Portalism diverge is in his unwillingness to extend consciousness to all living organisms, as expressed in his argument against panpsychism: "But there is one form of panpsychism I will unhesitatingly renounce: the far-fetched speculation that consciousness is also possessed by rocks and trees and toasters..."[12] He is certainly not alone in this resistance, and I am in total agreement with him as regards the rejection of panpsychism, as I am with not extending consciousness to non-living objects, but I see no reason in discriminating between human beings and other living organisms, although in fairness he does admit the possibility of dogs and cats. It appears to me that the basic concept of a brain-body-world nexus is flexible enough to be compatible with life across the board. But Rockwell's discernment is a significant distinction, as Portalism holds categorically that all living things possess consciousness to at least some degree and that all particular organisms are as conscious as those particular organisms need to be in order to navigate their realities. So I am fully prepared to give him the rocks and the toasters, yet respectfully recommend that he might reconsider the trees.

Rockwell shares another thread with other externalists, particularly with Riccardo Manzotti, in his desire to view his theory as empirical, thus maintaining important ties to the physicalist and scientific camps: "Nor, for that matter, can my suggestion that the mind is distributed elsewhere be any more than a suggestion until experiments are performed that are designed to falsify it. My only claim is that a noncranial mind is a genuine empirical possibility."[13] If we unpack this statement not only do we detect an homage to the analytic, but also a call echoing Chalmers' appeal for a subjective science. At the same time Rockwell's prose can simultaneously invoke the continental tradition, as shown in this elegant summary, perhaps reminiscent of Heidegger himself:

> All of our experiences are experiences of our relationship to our world, and because both ourselves and the world are real, there is no reason that this fact supports skepticism, or the belief that our experiences are illusions. On the contrary, our experiences become the realest thing we have, because they are constituted by our relationship with the world. Insofar as we are at home in the world, and what we encounter is ready-to-hand, we *are* the world. And insofar as reality impinges onto our world in ways that we cannot cope with, we experience the world as being different from ourselves. In either case, however, our experience is constituted by our relationship with the world, not just by the neurological activity in our brains or the sentences in our heads.[14]

Riccardo Manzotti

Riccardo Manzotti is an Italian philosopher and a Professor of Theoretical Philosophy at the University of Milan. He is an analytic with a strong background in science, specifically robotics and artificial intelligence. His theory of consciousness is called the 'spread mind', and although unique on many levels, what stands out about it is the manner in which the construction and presentation of the theory in his book, *The Spread Mind: Why Consciousness and the World Are One*, is consistently empirical, requiring no metaphysical appeals, inventions, or devices. As he claims, this refreshingly radical theory lies entirely within the realm of physicalism. It is important to Manzotti that the reader understand with crystal clarity that his is a scientific hypothesis and not *a priori* philosophical idealism nor is it semantic manipulation: "From the onset, I want to stress that spread mind is an empirical hypothesis... It is a strong physicalist framework aiming to place consciousness in the physical world. Such a hypothesis is capable of generating predictions that are amenable to falsification. Therefore, the theory of spread mind qualifies as a scientific theory about the nature of consciousness."[15]

Almost at the 'meta'-Metaphysical level, if you will, Manzotti rejects the dichotomies surrounding subject and object, mind and world, and philosophy and science that have served for centuries as the assumptive ground for metaphysics. From Manzotti's perspective, nature is all that exists, everything is physical; hence a non-physical subjective realm becomes no longer necessary as the experience is identical to the experienced. Instead of the dogmatic orthodoxy of type/token mind-brain identity, Manzotti posits a mind-object identity wherein: "One's conscious experience of an object is the object one experiences." In short, the mind-object identity dissolves any relationship between the knower and the known because they are not related; they are the same thing identically.

The elegance of the mind-object concept solves a lot of problems, but like all theories of consciousness it raises others, for example in the case of veridical experience versus hallucinations, which Manzotti spends the rest of the book resolving in clever and unconventional ways. One of the problems intrinsically solved by the theory is causality, because if the experience is identical to the object perceived, then questions concerning epiphenomenal or bidirectional causal paths simply go away. The mental does not cause physical events, nor does the physical cause mental events; there is only the physical, so it "revises the notion of the object in the physical world. The object is no longer a passive entity but it is instead an active cause."[16] If this is true, then causal speculations such as Searle's idea of a property of causing subjective experience inhering in physical objects, or Davidson's dual-path concept, become unnecessary. A mind-object identity renders the debate over direct/naïve versus representational realism equally moot, because if the subject is the object, then traditional ideas about perception don't follow. Traditionally, my perception of an object triggers an experience of that object – if I open the refrigerator door and perceive a grapefruit, then I am feeling *something-like-there-is-to-experience* a grapefruit – and this process implies at least a two-step event as well as a cause. If mind-object identity is true, then the perception and the experience are a single physical unity and a cause unto itself. The mind does not perceive the kitchen, the refrigerator, and the grapefruit as separate experiential events because it is 'spread' throughout the world, experiencing it as a totality as opposed to a series of discrete relationships. This might seem to be a trivial difference, but its impact is far-reaching because of the number of thorny questions that no longer need to be answered.

Although it is a physicalist theory, the spread mind is also radically externalist. "Consciousness is physical, and it is outside one's body. Our mind is physical and yet, ironically perhaps, is neither our body nor our brain (or any property of them)."[17] Again, we see the familiar externalist concept of the mind *being-in* the world – extracranial – but Manzotti takes this concept to an extreme and in so doing avoids the necessity of a subject/object relationship. In the following excerpt Manzotti presents a rigidly empirical argument against relationships reminiscent of Hume's observations on causality, completed by noting yet another troublesome problem in philosophy of mind that spread mind can conveniently dismiss; the nefarious bridging principle. (Italics are Manzotti's.)

If experience and physical objects are the same, the proposed solution can address another thorny notion – namely the relation between mind and world. In nature, one cannot observe any relation. No picture of relations has ever been shot. No relation has ever been measured. Relations – such as intentionality, semantics, and representations – have never been observed experimentally. They have been postulated to fit conceptual gaps between cherished theories and everyday life, but they are not found in the world as it happens, say, to stars, trees, and electrons. In this regard, the spread mind suggests a radical move. There are no relations of any kind in the world, there are only objects and everything is just identical with itself. If one's experience of the world is the world one experiences, no dubious relation is needed. In the physical world, *only one kind of relation is needed, and indeed available – namely, identity*. Once we relocate ourselves in the world, we no longer need any bridging relation. We are already there, so to speak.[18]

Of the three theories I have encapsulated thus far, the spread mind and Portalism perhaps have the least in common. An obvious difference would be that the bridging principle of Portalism is the portal itself, while spread mind requires no such mechanism at all. In spread mind theory, the subjective realm I postulate in Portalism is rejected along with all things non-physical. Manzotti must do this in order to maintain adherence to physicalism and empirical science. Manzotti's reasoning is analytic, empirical, and deductive, seeking to establish proof while my reasoning is continental, *a priori*, and inductive seeking only to establish plausibility. In addition, in my embrace of an alternative form of dualism, I am free to reason and speculate with no regard to the restrictions of empirical physicalism.

That said, there are also some similarities. The philosophical underpinnings of both our theories revolve around the importance of the world and hold that consciousness is not only in the world but actually *is* the world, although the relational concepts involved, or the lacks thereof, remain at variance. Both Portalism and spread mind require that the reader make a conceptual leap of faith before the details of the theories can be considered, but this can be said of nearly every metaphysical proposition.

Summary of Phenomenal Externalism

Of the three formal theories I have discussed in this section, it is left to ask how each addresses Chalmers' hard problem of consciousness, that being the problem of explaining how and why physical processes give rise to consciousness. If we accept this definition of the hard problem, we need to note the assumption that physical processes do in fact give 'rise' to consciousness. It would seem that we are presupposing that consciousness 'arises' from something physical, as it is held to do in emergentism, epiphenomenalism, or supervenience physicalism. To recount what I described in my defense of Portalism in the last chapter, Consciousness does not rise from anything, it being a fundamental force of nature that always already is. In Honderich's theory of Actualism, there is a subjective physical world per each perceiver. This collapses the concept of subject and object in to a perceived totality that simply is, and that is the unique reality of a given perceiver. Again, nothing is 'rising' from any physical preexistence. In Rockwell's mind-body-world nexus, he takes a Heideggerian slant in that 'we are the world', assuming the 'we' as a self to be a part of a necessary system in which the ontology of consciousness lies in the world, not the brain. Here again, nothing is 'rising' from anything, at least in the sense of emergentism. Finally in Manzotti's spread mind, the mind can't 'rise' from the physical because the mind *is physical*, and if such is the case, then the premise of the hard problem does not apply. Metaphysics is definitely not the place to be speaking in absolutes, if indeed any place is, so I will claim that in most (not all?) phenomenal externalist theories, the premise of the hard problem is not applicable due to its assumption that something physical within the cranium must give rise to consciousness, when in fact it is the world that gives rise to the unembodied, extracranial mind. But this does not release externalist theories from having to account for the *something-like-there-is-to-be* feeling of experience, which must still be explained regardless of where the locus of consciousness may reside.

In summarizing the ideas and theories of the philosophers I have presented in this section, it is of primary importance to note that although what each offers is fundamentally different from Portalism, there remain threads of similarity consistent in the thinking of all phenomenal externalists. The first is that, being metaphysical in nature, none of their theories can logically be proved wrong, which is a quality attributable to one the greatest metaphysicians that ever philosophized – Bishop Berkeley. Another is the concept of the world and the critical role it plays in the nature of reality. Strongly intertwined with this world concept is the rejection of cranialism, placing the locus of consciousness outside of the head, the precise character of its subsequent relationship-with or identity-to the world to be determined by the theorist. As noted previously, all externalist theories require the reader to apply a leap of faith, as all theories of consciousness come with assumptions that must be accepted in order to proceed. Finally, externalist thinkers tend to embrace some degree of phenomenological epoché in order to think beyond dogmatic boundaries, open their minds to radically unintuitive ideas, and question the impossible, if indeed the impossible even exists.

Most of these authors tread lightly in the presentation of their alternatives to mind-body identity taking great care to insure that their ideas are not taken as or confused with forms of dualism, positing different perspectives as to how there can be a non-cranial locus of consciousness without abandoning physicalism. If they make this case successfully, as I believe they have, they are then able to argue that their ideas, although unorthodox, continue to lie within the empirical mandates of science and the analytic tradition. Portalism labors under no such limitations. I have no problem whatsoever with anyone categorizing my ideas as dualist, as long as they are willing to consider that the principles of Portalism do not correspond to strict Cartesianism or to definitions of property dualism within this traditional philosophical division. As I see it, when one holds that the locus of the mind is extracranial then one has effectively abandoned monism, as holding so implies at least some fashion of a realm or horizon of subjective experience in concert with, and codependent upon, an objective physical world, with Manzotti's approach being the possible exception. Granted these may not be 'substances' in the Cartesian sense, they are at least distinct in their ontologies, each being necessary for the perceiver to know, and for the knowable to be perceived.

Imagining a Subjective Science

Many discussions concerning the value of science in affecting the overall condition of the human race ultimately degenerate into unresolvable ethical questions. For every Salk vaccine there are opioids, for every gasoline combustion engine there is air pollution, and for every Wright flyer there is a nuclear armed B-52 holding at failsafe. But these examples are not so much criticisms of science as they are judgements on how science and the possibilities of technology are employed by those they are meant to serve. In short, they represent the unintended consequences of scientific discovery, but they are the price of progress where the alternative is to do nothing but sit in the mud and pray. No matter which side of an ethical fence one finds themselves on, all serious and rational people should agree that it is science that is responsible for lifting us out of a millennium of mysticism and superstition. For example, it is unlikely that many people would welcome a return to the simpler days of 9th century Europe if it were their lot to be a peasant farmer scratching out a living working five days for the Baron and one for the Church, or where a simple procedure like pulling a tooth could easily result in infection, sepsis, and death (such a procedure nearly killed Elizabeth I). Sadly, there are millions on this planet that still struggle under similarly harsh conditions where they have no reasonable guarantee that they and their families will even survive the night. But is this the fault of science? It is because of science that we have the knowledge to change these things for the better, but it is here that the role of science ends and the role of humanity must begin.

The conclusion is inescapable; science, when practiced faithfully with no preconceptions as 'good' science should be, cannot help but go where the evidence of its research leads it, while the ultimate 'goodness' or 'badness' of the results of technology are merely labels that we assign. A classic example would be the Internet that has radically changed our world in an incredibly short period of time. Because of the Internet and the collateral technologies that accompany it, thousands of people have either lost jobs or been forced to undergo significant retraining, while millions of new opportunities have been unleashed as the commercial and corporate landscapes undergo an upheaval unseen since the industrial revolution. Granted, just because a technology can be developed does not assume that it is a *beneficial* technology, and a strong argument could be made that a few technologies and products may have been developed for no reason other than that scientists simply *could*, but it must be remembered that science is only a method, a process for determining facts and making predictions upon those facts. Science can create an Internet, predict the scalability of its bandwidths and solve the problems of its deployable infrastructure, but to predict its overall impact on the welfare of the society is beyond its mandate – that's not what science does. Morality does not drive science – logic drives science.

I believe it is high time for neuroscience to seriously consider the possibility that the locus of consciousness lies within a non-physical realm of existence – a subjective reality – which is exactly what consciousness is. After all, "Nothing about a brain, when surveyed as a physical system, suggests that it is a locus of experience."[19] Both science and metaphysics need to redirect a significant amount of resources to fresh thinking and cease working in directions where the evidence is not leading them. This is not to say that neuroscience is not valuable, it certainly is and it should definitely continue, but its ultimate goal needs to be rethought. For science and philosophy to persist on the assumption that neurotechnology will someday give us the keys to mental illness, or prove that love, hate, and grief are biological, or that the brain and nervous system are capable of creating Titian's *Portrait of a Young Man*, borders on the irrational.

Current science and the scientific method have full license to operate in the physical realm. As the composition and behavior of objects are determined by physics, scientific models can be made, hypotheses tested, theories proposed, and predictions made. Such are the benefits of working in the finite realm of the empirical, where nothing unreal or supernatural exists. As such, science has excelled at providing mankind with factual descriptions of the processes and mechanisms that make the world work, advancing the human condition and improving our overall quality of life. But what if, as Rockwell holds, there is more to the story? That consciousness exists is self-evident, because if I were not conscious I could not have made that claim, much less have written it down. If consciousness is not in the brain, then it must be somewhere else, and as Chalmers tells us, since consciousness cannot be defined in physical terms, then it cannot be physical. If it is non-physical, and it exists, then its locus cannot be in the objective realm. Consciousness is therefore subjective, and as such must reside in a *subjective* realm – a *metaphysical* realm – a realm 'beyond' physics.

Science, as it exists today, has no license to operate within the realm of the subjective, because it does not yet possess the necessary tools. For example, the objective scientific method requires experimentation so that hypotheses can be evaluated. Consider the case I described in an earlier chapter wherein experiments were conducted to ascertain the biology of mental illness, yet the results were not consistent nor were they reproducible. This is likely because mental illness is not physical and thus has no biology to experiment upon. Falsifiability is another tool that science uses to ensure the empiricism of its results, but non-physical phenomena cannot be falsified, yet they exist. Regrettably, attempts to apply these tried and true scientific methods metaphysically often result in some vulgar form of scientism, where nothing is brought forth, and no progress is made.

But just because science does not yet have the correct tools for explaining the nature of reality, it does not follow that science does not 'belong' in the subjective realm – it's not a question of belonging, it's a question of being useful and effective. There is certainly a place for science in the subjective realm – a vital place in fact – but not for science as it currently exists, unable or unwilling to explore a non-physical reality. In order for science to become useful in the metaphysical realm, it will need to develop new tools and methodologies. Science is resting on the laurels of the worthy contributions and amazing progress it has achieved in defining and characterizing the objective universe, but now science needs to *expand its horizons*. David Chalmers has made the appeal for a subjective science, and toward this goal science should seriously consider extending itself.

When science decides to admit at least the plausibility of

a subjective realm, the first goal might be the development of a *subjective scientific method* that could provide a heuristic operational framework for research involving the characterization of subjective experience. But how can this be achieved in an intellectual atmosphere where empiricism is the mandate and rationalism is dismissed? Epistemologically, analytic philosophy holds that knowledge is sensory and only those things that are observable and can be experienced are truly knowable, thus all knowledge can be traced to direct observation. Rationalists take a different view in that knowledge is not sensory but intellectual and deductive, and that reason, not experience, is the only true source of knowledge. These definitions are frequently drawn in an adversarial perspective, wherein reason versus experience and philosophy versus science. Indeed, when both epistemic positions adopt definitional absolutes like 'only' and 'truly knowable', the relationship between them can 'only' be one of opposition. I will submit that this intellectual conflict amounts to no more than a false dichotomy and, as others have pointed out, the two positions are not necessarily mutually exclusive. It is possible for the philosopher and the scientist to be both an empiricist as well as a rationalist. I am not proposing that philosophers and scientists embrace both Rationalism and Empiricism – I am proposing that philosophers and scientists stop thinking in these terms entirely.

When considered without competitive and absolutist definitional language, empiricism holds that the scientific method, the process of hypothesis, experimentation, and prediction made against observations is the way to obtain knowledge *a posteriori* of the natural world, while rationalists hold that it is also possible to obtain knowledge *a priori* through reason and logic, for example that three is greater than two, when both three and two are abstract concepts as opposed to observable things in the world. Which one is correct? The answer is *yes*. As stated above, the scientific method is the best tool to use in the characterization of *the natural world*. Yet its impracticality is all too evident when attempting its application to subjective experience. This is due to the inherently empirical premise of its basic operational framework. Before science can successfully apply itself to the investigation of a subjective reality, it must first accept that *a priori* reasoning is a source of knowledge, and further, that synthetic *a priori* propositions exist. In making this assumption, science will embrace that single element of Rationalism necessary to progress it toward the formulation of a subjective methodological parallel to the objective scientific method.

Extracting and embracing only the admission that *a priori* reasoning is a source of knowledge, there is no further need for a subjective science to have to reconcile itself to any of the remaining three traditional claims of Rationalism, those being the Intuition/Deductive, the Innate Knowledge, and the Innate Concept theses,[20] for these claims focus on the application of *a priori* reasoning as it pertains to the acquisition of knowledge in *the natural world*, and as we are no longer making any claims that it does, this allows us to happily relegate the acquisition of knowledge about all things objective to the realm of empiricism, and rightly so. We are able to do this because once having accepted that *a priori* reasoning can be a true source of knowledge, it then becomes a tool in our subjective science toolbox, and the precise epistemological mechanics of its application in the external physical world become uninteresting.

At this point I will remind the mind-brain identity theorists, who might object to this admission of limited Rationalism into a subjective science, that their own Principle of Identity is in itself a universal rationalist construct dating back to Plato, a fact that would seem to prove that such a reconciliation of the two positions as I have proposed is certainly not new.[21] It is important to keep focused upon the goal of determining the logical structure of reality, which materialists refer to as the physical, idealists refer to as the subjective, and dualists refer to as both, while none of them are able to produce a comprehensive solution. But if the world is reality and the mind is the world, as phenomenal externalism holds, then by definition the mind must reflect the logical structure of reality.

Although this identity would appear to explain a lot from the epistemic perspective, it still does not account for the *something-like-there-is-to-be-like* phenomena of subjective experience, the ontology of which must still be ascertained. One of the best tools to accomplish this is Husserlian phenomenology. As Käufer and Chemero explain in *Phenomenology: An Introduction* (2015), there are several flavors of phenomenological methodology in philosophy and psychology, so in an effort to eliminate confusion I am specifically referring to Edmund Husserl's 'transcendental' phenomenology because it centers upon experience, as opposed to Merleau-Ponty and James J. Gibson's focus on perception, or Martin Heidegger and Jean-Paul Sartre's focus on the phenomenological ontology of being. "Husserl's phenomenology is a systematic study of the essential content of our experiences. By 'essential' Husserl means the content that makes experiences into experiences of a certain kind."[22]

Husserl's phenomenology employs a system of transcendental reductionism designed to strip away all preconceptions we might have about a given experience. For example, what happens when I see an orange on a table? Because I have seen many oranges in my life, my mind is flooded with information pulled from episodic memory, disclosed from brain to mind through the portal connection in milliseconds. I believe that if I pick it up it will feel rough, probably weigh less than a lunchbox but more than a marshmallow, and smell – like an orange. All of the secondary properties of orangeness are made available to me through the memories of past experiences of 'orange'. Should any of them not turn out to be the case, I will be surprised, but that's about all that can happen. Yet none of what I have described has anything to do with the 'experience' itself – none of it can account for the *something-like-there-is-to-be-experiencing* an orange, but before I can truly comprehend this *experience*, I must first strip away everything that I think I already know about 'orange'.

Husserl calls this epoché: the process of removing mental preconceptions about a perception, but is more familiarly known as *bracketing*. "Phenomenology is a science of consciousness. It does not concern itself with physical objects, but with our conscious experiences of physical and other objects."[23] For example, I am typing this sentence and so I am conscious of the sentence I am typing, of my fingers hitting the keys, these being ready-to-hand actions within unreflective consciousness and will remain so until something causes the process to become unready-to-hand, like a word misspelled or my cat stepping on my keyboard. I am phenomenally conscious of what I am typing, but phenomenologically I am reflexively conscious of the *experience* of the act of typing.

So how is Husserlian phenomenology valuable in terms of becoming a tool for a subjective science? Reference the quote above where Stephen Käufer and Anthony Chemero rightly define phenomenology as a 'science' of consciousness. Physical experimentation is a necessary element of the scientific method, but in the subjective realm there is nothing physical to experiment upon. Does this mean that experimentation is thereby precluded from becoming a methodological tool within a subjective science? Perhaps we should rephrase the question, asking instead if phenomenology could benefit a subjective science functionally similar to the way that experimentation benefits physical science. But why experiment at all? How does the experimentation process benefit our knowledge base? One answer is that experimentation can reveal the essential structures of that which is being experimented upon, for example the separation of polysaccharides into their component elements. If we accept this answer, then could not the essential structures of mental acts be determined phenomenologically within a subjective science? I believe they could. As Käufer and Chemero correctly observe: "Since all content of our mental acts is available to self-conscious reflection, phenomenology spells out the essential structures of acts by reflecting."[24]

Phenomenology is a method traditionally associated with continental philosophy, but recent events would seem to demonstrate that at least the operational differences between the two traditions are beginning to dissolve. This is another example of 'good' science, wherein the obeisance to dogma is rejected in favor of the adoption of tools and methods showing promise for broadening the knowledge base. In the last chapter of their book Käufer and Chemero describe the embrace of phenomenology in the exciting and intriguing work of several prominent and respected psychologists, philosophers, and neurophilosophers. "As we can see from the previous chapter, phenomenology has had fruitful influences in many directions. ... we will now turn to the work of scientists, – psychologists, neuroscientists, cognitive scientists – who have followed the phenomenologists in taking on the nature of experience and the relationship between experience and ontology as their subject matter."[25] Granted, the accounts they relate focus primarily on the employment of phenomenology in cognitive and perceptual frameworks including robotics, artificial intelligence, and expanded minds, but if the metaphysical goal is the formulation of a subjective science that subsumes a viable subjective scientific method, one could argue based on the research described by these authors that such an effort has already begun, and is in fact well along the way.

Before closing I would offer a word on the division of philosophy between the analytic and continental traditions. I previously claimed that the dichotomy between the rationalists and the empiricists was a false one, as it is possible for one to be both. Here I will state that although the dichotomy between the analytic and the continental traditions of philosophy may indeed be false, it is unquestionably unproductive. Analytic philosophy embraces science and the scientific method and attempts to move philosophy into the realm of science, its perspective tending to rely upon reductionism in breaking down phenomenal structures into discrete problems so that they can be analyzed apart from their origins. The continental approach is more holistic, focusing on phenomenological experience and its relationship to time, space, culture, and history. Considering the two perspectives, there is no question of wrong or right, as both their methodologies can be valid and applicable depending upon the subject. Indeed, there are several philosophers that claim to be in both camps, demonstrating that there is no reason that the two traditions should be considered to be mutually exclusive or otherwise at odds. If it is assumed that mind-brain identity is the case, then neural correlates of mental states with brain activity would appear to require reductionism in order to identify the discrete structure of each mental correlate. This scientific methodology, that of analyzing the particular, has produced remarkable results in the characterization of the physical realm, but has yet to duplicate that success when applied to the question of consciousness. If phenomenal externalism is true and the mind is in the world, then as all things in the world are in some way related, phenomenal experience cannot be reduced to discrete particulars and must be comprehended holistically. Should a subjective science evolve to where the structures of consciousness can be revealed, then refined analytic methodologies might become valuable tools in that particular field of research. My point being that in the scientific exploration of consciousness, the philosophical methodologies of both traditions are likely to be required, thus collapsing the two and moving philosophy beyond this unproductive schism.

To summarize this section on the possibility of a subjective science, we should now examine the contents of our toolbox. In it we find several important items, the first being the acceptance that *a priori* reasoning is indeed a source of knowledge and that synthetic *a priori* propositions exist. This collapses the rational and the empirical into a single epistemological tool consisting of two acceptable methods by which knowledge can be obtained. The second is phenomenology; a tool for ascertaining the structures of consciousness and a heuristic component of a subjective scientific method. Finally we have the dissolution of traditional intellectual barriers between analytic and continental perspectives and philosophical methodologies in favor of what works best, based upon what the evidence indicates combined with what we think we know.

This is a good start, but it is nowhere near enough. More tools must be conceptualized, evaluated, and added to our box, if we are ever to be able to accurately define the character of consciousness, and ultimately the nature of reality.

A Future of Science or Scientism

In order for philosophy to stay relevant it must continue to incorporate science, but if consciousness is to be explained then that science must expand its ontology beyond the physical universe to include the realm of subjective experience. Both disciplines are required if the totality of reality is ever to be properly understood. It appears that this is already happening, as evidence of this symbiotic collaboration was described in the section where neuroscientists and neurophilosophers have been phenomenologically bracketing off dogmatic presuppositions and have begun looking for the locus of consciousness in a different place. These actions are indicative of good science, and I am optimistic that a subjective science will open new paths within the philosophy of mind. The analytic and continental traditions both have valuable contributions to make in this effort, as neither holds the entire answer. As Chalmers correctly observes: "One can recognize the distinctive problems that consciousness poses and still do science."[26] As the philosophy of mind represents the current state of analytic philosophy, while Postmodernism characterizes that of the continental, then instead of ideologically digging in further it will be more beneficial to both perspectives if we just stop thinking in those terms altogether, as those adhering to logic and the scientific method must understand that without meaning and existence the entire story of the nature of reality can never be told.[27]

Still, analytic philosophy is by far the dominant tradition taught in universities throughout the world. This is in no way a bad thing, particularly in view of the emphasis upon epistemology and logic arising from the Vienna Circle and from brilliant thinkers like Russell and Wittgenstein in the last century. Still, there are those within the analytic tradition that seem unable or unwilling to look beyond materialism and its assumption that only the physical exists. If this assumption is correct, then the mind must be the brain, in some form or fashion, or else what we believe to be the mind is merely the result of some confusion or misunderstanding of what must be a purely physical phenomenon. But this would seem to be a contradiction, as evidenced by materialists going back to Auguste Comte professing a binding trust in logic and science, while continuing to hold onto mind-brain identity theories in spite of the lack of any empirical supporting evidence. Given the decades spent pursuing this unsupported theory, one may think that science might be open to a fresh approach. "Actually, that is the purpose of science: given a new and unexpected phenomenon, to look always for its cause."[28] The obvious conclusion, analytically framed, would be that materialist dogma is simply bad science.

The unreasonable faith in a dogmatic assumption that the mental 'substance' cannot exist because science is unable to characterize its structures amounts to Scientism, and no rational thinker, analytic or continental, should ever want to go there. The first and foremost reason for rejecting Scientism is that it is self-refuting, as the neuroscientist Gerard Verschuuren observes: "Scientism steps outside of scientific territory to claim that there is nothing outside scientific territory."[29] Recalling the days of the Pre-Socratics when all sciences were philosophy, Scientism brings us full circle in that all philosophies will become scientific. If science can't define and characterize it, if it can't be observed, calculated or predicted, then it has no meaning and doesn't exist. Some are actually very comfortable with this idea, yet consciousness continues to defy definition, and the mind cannot be observed, calculated, or predicted, as those actions can only occur – in mind. Be warned, philosophy dies the day the gates of Scientism close upon it.

I for one do not believe that it ends this way – there are just too many really innovative thinkers out there for humanity to trade centuries of religious dogma for centuries of scientific dogma. Dogmatism is destructive in any context because it places limits on thought. Oddly enough, where I warn of scientism, Ted Honderich flips the mirror and warns of 'philosophism' – framing both as 'silly mistakes'.[30] I can't comment on the silliness of it, but I agree that they are certainly mistakes to be avoided, particularly in the quest for understanding the totality of subjective experience.

A Fond Farewell

Assuming that the reader has made it this far, I have a final task to present. Put down this book, turn off your phone, and go outside into the world. Of course you are always in the world when you are conscious, but by being outdoors you experience the wider field of perception, where hopefully some of the concepts you have been reading about will begin to make sense. Feel the breeze, hear the sounds, and inhale the smells. What you are experiencing is not an ideal copy of the world inside your brain, it *is the world*. As mind, you are *being-in* the world, and it is through this conscious connection that you are able to feel the *something-like-there-is-to-be* you. Rejoice, and dance while the music is still playing.

Notes and Citations

Introduction

1. Noë p. xxi (paraphrased)
2. Barrett p. 7
3. Chalmers COC p. 4

Chapter 1 – Overview of the Substance Debate

1. Harris p. 54
2. Descartes p. 33
3. Davidson p. 208
4. Bakewell p. 235
5. Kastrup p. 80
6. Kastrup p. 81
7. Coleman p. 87
8. Noë p. 24
9. Tallis p. 54
10. Berkeley p. 41
11. Chalmers COC p. 137
12. Thompson p. 13
13. Thompson p. 165
14. Honderich p. 161
15. Rockwell p. xii
16. Manzotti p. 92

Chapter 2 – Whither Consciousness?

1. Rockwell p. 31
2. McGinn (taken as quote from an article in *Mind Magazine*, Issue 98, 1989) URL – http://mindmagazine.net [Accessed 2021].
3. Noë p. 24
4. Chalmers COC p. 307
5. Kastrup p. 80

6. Kastrup p. 176
7. Rockwell – this derogatory term is coined by Dr. Rockwell and used periodically throughout his book.
8. Kastrup p. 137

Chapter 3 – The Concept of Portalism

1. Chalmers COC p. 127
2. Chalmers COC p. 19
3. Chalmers COC p. 33
4. Goff p. 42
5. Leibniz p. 47
6. Leibniz p. 48
7. Tallis AP p. 34
8. Leibniz p. 52
9. Tallis AP p. 35 (italics are his)

Chapter 4 – The World

1. Merleau-Ponty p. xvii
2. Noë p. 69
3. Harris p. 101
4. Harris p. 9
5. Noë p. 94
6. Searle p. 49
7. Merleau-Ponty p. 82
8. Merleau-Ponty p. 234
9. Honderich p. 114
10. Manzotti p. 23 (italics are his)
11. Manzotti p. xi
12. Rockwell p. 101
13. Heidegger p. 67 – the content of these paragraphs is taken largely from Heidegger's ideas as they are expressed in chapters 2 and 3 of *Being and Time*.
14. Heidegger p. 62
15. Heidegger p. 57

16. Manzotti p. 9
17. Palmer p. 145
18. Noted from Bertrand Russell's *Principles of Mathematics* (1903).
19. Searle p. 122

Chapter 5 – The Portal

1. Sartre BAN p. 15
2. Merleau-Ponty p. 351
3. Chalmers COC p. 27
4. These three paragraphs all contain references to a TED Talk by Dr. Stefano Mancuso (2015) entitled *Are Plants Conscious?*
5. This paragraph references a TED Talk by Dr. Ariel Novoplansky entitled *Learning Plant Learning* (2012).
6. Trewavas p. 413
7. Wohlleben p. 10
8. Excerpt taken from an article in *Quanta Magazine* by Dr. John Rennie – reference https://www.quantamagazine.org/the-beautiful-intelligence-of-bacteria-and-other-microbes-20171113/
9. Noë p. 8
10. Noë p. 181
11. Chalmers COC p. 295
12. Sartre BAN p. 121

Chapter 6 – The Brain

1. Noë p. 64
2. Rockwell p. 15
3. Tallis *Philosophy Now*, Issue 137, p. 54
4. Verschuuren p. 13
5. Noë p. 23
6. Harrington p. 82
7. Harrington p. 31
8. Harrington p. 14

9. Ibid
10. Foucault p. x
11. Foucault p. 252
12. Rettew – reference article: Is Autism a Mental Illness? The strange battle over what's psychiatric versus neurological. *Psychology Today* – https://www.psychologytoday.com/us/blog/abcs-child-psychiatry/201510/is-autism-mental-illness
13. Ibid
14. Harvard Medical School – reference article: Mental Illness and Violence. Harvard Health Publishing, Cambridge, MA, 2011 – http://www.biblioteca.cij.gob.mx/Archivos/Materiales_de_consulta/Drogas_de_Abuso/Articulos/55984270.pdf
15. Piore – reference article: The Genius Within. *Popular Science*, March 2013
16. MacMillan 2014 – Phineas Gage
17. MacMillan 2000 – An Odd Kind of Fame
18. Benderly – taken from an article in GradPSYCH – Benderly, Beryl Lieff: Psychology's tall tales. GradPSYCH: 20, *American Psychological Association*, September 2012. Accessed 2021.
19. Quotes and accounts in these paragraphs reference a *60 Minutes* interview with Anderson Cooper – reference: https://www.cbsnews.com/news/psychedelic-drugs-lsd-active-agent-in-magic-mushrooms-to-treat-addiction-depression-anxiety-60-minutes-2020-08-16/ [Accessed 2021].
20. This information in these paragraphs is taken from research articles appearing on the website for the Beckley/Imperial Psychedelic Research Programme and can be found at The World's First Images of the Brain on LSD – https://www.beckleyfoundation.org/the-brain-on-lsd-revealed-first-scans-show-how-the-drug-affects-the-brain/ [April 2016].
21. Ibid
22. Ibid

23. Ibid
24. Rockwell p. 104

Chapter 7 – The Mind

1. Honderich p. 27
2. Chalmers COC p. 503
3. Searle p. 47
4. Godfrey-Smith p. 138
5. Harris p. 91
6. Sartre TOTE p. 38
7. Weiss explains Hegel's concept of self-consciousness as reflexive self-awareness as opposed to the more modern definition of embarrassment, etc.
8. Weiss p. 65
9. Sartre TOTE p. 48
10. Kant p. 386
11. Heidegger p. 57
12. Chalmers COC p. 63
13. Chalmers COC p. 339
14. Searle p. 21 (italics are his)
15. Searle p. 164
16. Psychiatrist Dr. Humphry Osmond quoted in Harrington p. 149
17. Honderich p. 106
18. Hume p. 104
19. Reid p. 175
20. Dr. Richard Wahrer of the Kentucky State Department for Natural Resources (retired) – taken from a personal conversation.
21. Kastrup p. 40
22. Merleau-Ponty p. 412
23. Searle p. 49
24. Hyman – excerpts taken from a description pp. 597-607
25. Schopenhauer quoted in Hacyan p. 1

26. Davidson p. 137 (parens and italics are his)
27. Davidson p. 138 (parens are his)
28. Dr. Hamish Johnston – taken from his 2018 article in *Physics World* magazine. URL – https://physicsworld.com/a/quantum-mechanics-defies-causal-order-experiment-confirms
29. Paraphrased from a quote attributed to Alfred North Whitehead.
30. Merleau-Ponty p. 145
31. St. Augustine – *Confessions* – p. 243
32. St. Augustine – *Confessions* – p. 230
33. St. Augustine – *Confessions* – p. 231
34. Kant p. 69 §6
35. Kant p. 70 §6
36. Stagoll p. 24
37. Heidegger p. 314
38. Merleau-Ponty p. 415
39. Sartre p. 169
40. Leibniz p. 61 §83-§84
41. Roinila p. 10
42. Searle pp. 155-169 – paraphrased extracts taken from Searle's discussion of the brain in a vat problem.
43. Kant p. 45 – paraphrased from his General Observations on the Transcendental Aesthetic.

Chapter 8 – In Defense of Portalism

1. Chalmers COC p. 9
2. Chalmers COC p. 126
3. Chalmers COC p. 130
4. Chalmers COC p. 105
5. Chalmers COC p. 18
6. Chalmers COC p. 19 (italics are mine)
7. Chalmers PCEG – extracted from Dr. Chalmers' essay on Phenomenal Concepts and the Explanatory Gap.

8. Attributed to Johann Gottlieb Fichte as quoted from Bowie in *German Philosophy: A Very Short Introduction* – p. 39.
9. Merleau-Ponty p. 37
10. Heidegger p. 65
11. Manzotti p. 233
12. Manzotti p. 9 (italics are his)
13. Attributed to Dr. Benjamin Libet – this description of the experimental research of Libet, Wright, and Gleason (1983) is paraphrased from the account given by Dr. Gerard Verschuuren in *What Makes You Tick?* pp. 11-12.
14. Verschuuren p. 13
15. Ibid
16. Trevena pp. 447-456
17. Honderich p. 63
18. Dr. Georges Rey p. 1 (paraphrased from The Analytic/Synthetic Distinction in The Stanford Encyclopedia of Philosophy, 2010. URL – https://plato.stanford.edu/entries/analytic-synthetic). Italics are mine.
19. Quote is attributed to the pragmatist Dr. Charles Sanders Peirce. Ideas in this paragraph are paraphrased from A Neglected Argument for the Reality of God, pp. 90-112.
20. Rockwell p. 15
21. Dretske – quote is attributed to: Phenomenal externalism, or if meanings ain't in the head, where are qualia? *Philosophical Issues*, 7, 1996.
22. Berkeley p. 31
23. Dretske (italics are mine)
24. Rockwell p. 18
25. Honderich p. 21
26. Merleau-Ponty p. 28

Chapter 9 – Phenomenal Externalism and the Future of Philosophy
1. Noë pp. 23-24

2. Noë p. xii
3. Noë p. 94
4. Honderich p. 114
5. Ibid
6. Honderich p. 119
7. Rockwell p. xii
8. Rockwell p. 4
9. Rockwell p. 13
10. Rockwell p. 19
11. Rockwell p. 17
12. Rockwell p. 103
13. Rockwell p. 19
14. Rockwell p. 146
15. Manzotti p. 4 – much of this paragraph is borrowed from Dr. Manzotti's introduction.
16. Manzotti p. viii
17. Ibid – parens are his
18. Manzotti p. ix
19. Harris p. 56
20. Pete Markie – excerpts from his 2017 article in the SEP Rationalism vs. Empiricism. URL – https://plato.stanford.edu/entries/rationalism-empiricism/
21. Palmer p. 93
22. Käufer p. 25
23. Käufer p. 34
24. Käufer p. 33
25. Käufer p. 145
26. Chalmers COC p. 52
27. Paraphrased from Analytic vs. Continental Philosophy, an article by Kile Jones appearing in *Philosophy Now*, Issue 74, London, UK, 2009.
28. Hacyan p. 2
29. Verschuuren p. xiv
30. Honderich p. 170

Bibliography

60 Minutes – Cooper, Anderson. *Psilocybin Sessions: Psychedelics Could Help People with Addiction and Anxiety.* CBS News, August 16, 2020. URL: https://www.cbsnews.com/news/psychedelic-drugs-lsd-active-agent-in-magic-mushrooms-to-treat-addiction-depression-anxiety-60-minutes-2020-08-16/ [Accessed 2021].

Augustine. *Confessions.* New York: Oxford University Press, Inc. Translation 1991.

Bakewell, Sarah. *At The Existentialist Café: Freedom, Being, and Apricot Cocktails.* New York: Other Press, LLC, 2016.

Barrett, William. *Irrational Man.* New York: Anchor Book Editions, 1962, 1990.

Benderly, Beryl Lieff. Psychology's tall tales. GradPSYCH: 20, *American Psychological Association,* September 2012.

Berkeley, George. *A Treatise Concerning the Principles of Human Knowledge.* Pantianos Classics, 1710.

Berkeley, George. *Three Dialogues Between Hylas and Philonous.* Indianapolis, IN: Hackett Publishing Company, 1979.

Block, Ned. On a confusion about a function of consciousness. In N. Block, O. Flanagan, G. Guzeldere (eds.), *The Nature of Consciousness: Philosophical Debates.* MIT Press, 1998.

Bowie, Andrew. *German Philosophy: A Very Short Introduction.* Oxford, UK: Oxford University Press, 2010.

Carhart-Harris RL, Muthukumaraswamy S., Roseman L., Kaelen M., Droog W., Murphy K., Tagliazucchi E., Schenberg EE, Nest T., Orban C., Leech R., Williams LT, Williams TM, Bolstridge M., Sessa B., McGonigle J., Sereno MI, Nichols D., Hellyer PJ, Hobden P., Evans J., Singh KD, Wise RG, Curran HV, Feilding A., Nutt DJ. The World's First Images of the Brain on LSD. URL: https://www.beckleyfoundation.org/the-brain-on-lsd-revealed-first-scans-show-how-the-drug-affects-the-brain/ April 2016 [Accessed 2021].

Chalmers, David. *How Do You Explain Consciousness?* TED Talk, 2014. URL: https://www.ted.com/talks/david_chalmers_how_do_you_explain_consciousness?language=zh#t-141960 [Accessed 2020-2021].

Chalmers, David. *The Character of Consciousness*. New York: Oxford University Press, Inc., 2010. Cited as COC.

Chalmers, David. Phenomenal Concepts and the Explanatory Gap, in *Phenomenal Concepts and Phenomenal Knowledge: New Essays on Consciousness and Physicalism*. Oxford University Press, 2006. Cited as PCEG.

Churchland, Patricia Smith. On the Alleged Backwards Referral of Experiences and Its Relevance to the Mind-Body Problem. *Philosophy of Science*, Volume 48 (2) 1983 (165-181).

Churchland, Patricia Smith. *Neurophilosophy: Toward a Unified Science of the Mind/Brain*. Cambridge, MA: MIT Press, 1986.

Coleman, Sam. Neutral Monism: A Saner Solution to the Mind/Body Problem. *Philosophy Now – The Ultimate Guide, Philosophy of Mind*, Issue 3, London, UK, 2020.

Crane, Tim and Farkas, Katalin. *Metaphysics: A Guide and Anthology*. Oxford University Press, Inc., 2004.

Davidson, Donald. *Essays on Actions and Events*. Oxford, UK: Clarendon Press, 1980.

Dennett, Daniel. *Brainstorms: Philosophical Essays on Mind and Psychology*. Cambridge, MA: MIT Press, 1981.

Descartes, Rene. *Discourse on Method and Meditations on First Philosophy*. Indianapolis, IN: Hackett Publishing Co., 1998.

Dretske, Fred. Phenomenal externalism, or if meanings ain't in the head, where are qualia? *Philosophical Issues*, 7, 1996.

Encyclopedia Britannica. URL: https://www.britannica.com/science/information-theory/Physiology, 2020 [Accessed 2021].

Epicurus. *The Art of Happiness*. New York: Penguin Books, 2012.

ffytche, DH. *Hallucinations and the Cheating Brain*. World Science

Festival, 2012.

Foucault, Michel. *Madness and Civilization: A History of Insanity in the Age of Reason*. New York: Random House Inc., 1965.

Godfrey-Smith, Peter. *Other Minds: The Octopus, The Sea, and The Deep Origins of Consciousness*. New York: Farrar, Straus and Giroux, 2016.

Goff, Philip. The Case for Panpsychism. *Philosophy Now – The Ultimate Guide, Philosophy of Mind*, Issue 3, London, UK, 2020.

Guzeldere, Guven. Consciousness Resurrected. *Philosophy Now – The Ultimate Guide, Philosophy of Mind*, Issue 3, London, UK, 2002.

Hacyan, Shahen. Schopenhauer on Space, Time, Causality and Matter: A Physical Re-examination. *Volunta: Revista Internacional de Filosofia*, Santa Maria, Brazil, 2019.

Harrington, Anne. *Mind Fixers: Psychiatry's Troubled Search for the Biology of Mental Illness*. New York: W.W. Norton & Co., 2019.

Harris, Sam. *Waking Up*. New York: Simon and Schuster, 2014.

Harvard Medical School. Harvard Mental Health Letter, Volume 27 Number 7. *Mental Illness and Violence*. Harvard Health Publishing, Cambridge, MA, 2011. URL: http://www.biblioteca.cij.gob.mx/Archivos/Materiales_de_consulta/Drogas_de_Abuso/Articulos/55984270.pdf [Accessed 2021].

Heidegger, Martin. *Being and Time*. Albany, NY: State University of New York Press, 1953.

Honderich, Ted. *Mind: Your Consciousness is What and Where?* London, UK: Reaktion Books Ltd., 2017.

Hume, David. *An Enquiry concerning Human Understanding* (Second Edition). IN: Hackett Publishing, 1993.

Hyman, Ira E.; Boss, S. Matthew; Wise, Breanne M.; McKenzie, Kira E.; Caggiano, Jenna M. Did you see the unicycling clown? Inattentional blindness while walking and talking on a cell phone. *Applied Cognitive Psychology*, 24 (5) 2009: 597-

607.

Johnston, Hamish. Quantum Mechanics Defies Causal Order, Experiment Confirms. *Physics World*, IOP Publishing, 2018. URL: https://physicsworld.com/a/quantum-mechanics-defie s-causal-order-experiment-confirms/ [Accessed 2021].

Jones, Kile. Analytic vs. Continental Philosophy. *Philosophy Now*, Issue 74, London, UK, 2009.

Kant, Immanuel. *The Critique of Pure Reason*. Strand, London, UK: Penguin Classics, 2007.

Kastrup, Bernardo. *Why Materialism Is Baloney*. UK: iff Books, 2014.

Käufer, Stephen and Chemero, Anthony. *Phenomenology: An Introduction*. Cambridge, UK: Polity Press, 2015.

Leibniz, GW. *Discourse on Metaphysics and The Monadology*. LaSalle, IL: Open Court Publishing Co., 2005.

Levine, Joseph. Materialism and qualia: the explanatory gap. *Pacific Philosophical Quarterly*, 64, 1983.

Libet, Benjamin; Wright, EW; and Gleason, CA. Readiness-potentials preceding unrestricted 'spontaneous' vs. pre-planned voluntary acts. *Electroencephalographic and Clinical Neuropsychology*, Volume 54, 1983.

Macmillan, Malcolm B. *An Odd Kind of Fame: Stories of Phineas Gage*. MA: MIT Press, 2000.

Macmillan, Malcolm B. Phineas Gage, in *Encyclopedia of the Neurological Sciences*. Academic Press, 2014.

Mancuso, Stefano. *Are Plants Conscious?* TED Talk, 2015. URL: https://www.youtube.com/watch?v=gBGt5OeAQFk&lis t=LLjW-Zct4xbYYbJBa1i_CYjw&index=131 [Accessed 2020-2021].

Manzotti, Riccardo. *The Spread Mind: Why Consciousness and the World Are One*. London, UK: OR Books, 2017.

Markie, Pete. Rationalism vs. Empiricism. The Stanford Encyclopedia of Philosophy (Fall 2017 Edition), Edward N. Zalta (ed.). URL: https://plato.stanford.edu/entries/

rationalism-empiricism/ [Accessed 2016].

McGinn, Colin. Can We Solve the Mind-Body Problem? *Mind*, 98, 1989.

Merleau-Ponty, Maurice. *Phenomenology of Perception*. London, UK: Forgotten Books and Co., Ltd., 2015.

Noë, Alva. *Out of Our Heads*. New York: Hill and Wang, 2010.

Palmer, Donald D. *Structuralism and Poststructuralism*. Writers and Readers Corp., 1997.

Papineau, David and Selina, Howard. *Introducing Consciousness: A Graphic Guide*. London, UK: Icon Books Ltd., 2013.

Peirce, Charles Sanders. A Neglected Argument for the Reality of God. *Hibbert Journal*, Volume 7, 1908 (90-112).

Piore, Adam. The Genius Within. *Popular Science*, March 2013.

Ramsey, W. Where Does the Self-Refutation Objection Take Us? *Inquiry*, 1991.

Reid, Thomas. *Inquiry and Essays*. IN: Hackett Publishing, 1983.

Rennie, John. Seeing The Beautiful Intelligence of Microbes. *Quanta Magazine*, 2017.

Rettew, David. Is Autism a Mental Illness? The strange battle over what's psychiatric versus neurological. *Psychology Today*, 2015. URL: https://www.psychologytoday.com/us/blog/abcs-child-psychiatry/201510/is-autism-mental-illness [Accessed 2021].

Rey, Georges. The Analytic/Synthetic Distinction. The Stanford Encyclopedia of Philosophy, 2010. URL: https://plato.stanford.edu/entries/analytic-synthetic/ [Accessed April 2021].

Robinson, Dave and Garratt, Chris. *Descartes: A Graphic Guide*. London, UK: Icon Books Ltd., 1999.

Rockwell, W. Teed. *Neither Brain Nor Ghost*. Cambridge, MA: MIT Press, 2005.

Roinila, Markku. The "Death" of Monads: G.W. Leibniz and on Death and Anti-Death, in *Death and Anti-Death, Volume 14: Four Decades after Michael Polanyi, Three Centuries after G.W.*

Leibniz. Ria University Press, 2016.

Russell, Bertrand. *The Problems of Philosophy.* Eternal Sun Books, 2016.

Ryle, Gilbert. *The Concept of Mind.* University of Chicago Press, 1949, reprinted 2002.

Sartre, Jean-Paul. *The Transcendence of the Ego: An Existentialist Theory of Consciousness.* New York: Hill and Wang, 1991. Cited as TOTE.

Sartre, Jean-Paul. *Being and Nothingness.* New York: Simon and Schuster, 1984. Cited as BAN.

Schopenhauer, Arthur. *Essays and Aphorisms.* New York: Penguin Group, Inc., 1970.

Schopenhauer, Arthur. *The World as Will and Representation* (W I and II). Translation EFJ Payne. Dover, 1966.

Searle, John R. *Seeing Things as They Are.* UK: Oxford University Press, 2015.

Solomon, Robert C. *Continental Philosophy Since 1750: The Rise and Fall of the Self (A History of Western Philosophy Vol. 7).* New York: Oxford University Press, Inc., 1988.

Stagoll, Cliff. Killing Time. *Philosophy Now – the Ultimate Guide, Metaphysics,* Issue 2, London, UK, 2019.

Tallis, Raymond. Against Neural Philosophy of Mind. *Philosophy Now,* Issue 137, London, UK, 2020.

Tallis, Raymond. Against Panpsychism. *Philosophy Now – The Ultimate Guide, Philosophy of Mind,* Issue 3, London, UK, 2020. Cited as AP.

Thompson, Evan. *Mind in Life.* Harvard University Press, 2007.

Trevena, Judy A. and Miller, Jeff. Brain preparation before a voluntary action: Evidence against unconscious movement initiation. *Consciousness and Cognition,* Volume 19, Academic Press, 2010 (447-456).

Trewavas, Anthony. Green plants as intelligent organisms. *Trends in Plant Science,* Cell Press, 10 (9): 413-419.

Verschuuren, Gerard. *What Makes You Tick? A New Paradigm for*

Neuroscience. Antioch, CA: SOLAS Press, 2012.

Watts, Alan. *Become What You Are.* Boston, MA: Shambhala Publications, 1995.

Weiss, Frederick G. *Hegel: The Essential Writings.* New York: Harper and Row, 1974.

Wohlleben, Peter. *The Hidden Life of Trees.* Vancouver, Canada: Greystone Books, Ltd., 2016.

IFF
BOOKS

ACADEMIC AND SPECIALIST

Iff Books publishes non-fiction. It aims to work with authors and
titles that augment our understanding of the human condition,
society and civilisation, and the world or universe in which
we live.
If you have enjoyed this book, why not tell other readers by
posting a review on your preferred book site.

The Vagabond Spirit of Poetry
Edward Clarke
Spend time with the wisest poets of the modern age and of the
past, and let Edward Clarke remind you of the importance of
poetry in our industrialized world.
Paperback: 978-1-78279-370-0 ebook: 978-1-78279-369-4

Readers of ebooks can buy or view any of these bestsellers by
clicking on the live link in the title. Most titles are published in
paperback and as an ebook. Paperbacks are available in traditional
bookshops. Both print and ebook formats are available online.
Find more titles and sign up to our readers' newsletter at
http://www.johnhuntpublishing.com/non-fiction
Follow us on Facebook at
https://www.facebook.com/JHPNonFiction
and Twitter at https://twitter.com/JHPNonFiction